SECRETS OF THE SANCTUM.

AN

INSIDE VIEW OF AN EDITOR'S LIFE.

BY

A. F. HILL,

AUTHOR OF "OUR BOYS," "THE WHITE ROCKS," "JOHN SMITH'S FUNNY ADVENTURES ON A CRUTCH," ETC., ETC., ETC.

PHILADELPHIA:
CLAXTON, REMSEN & HAFFELFINGER,
624, 626 & 628 MARKET STREET.
1875.

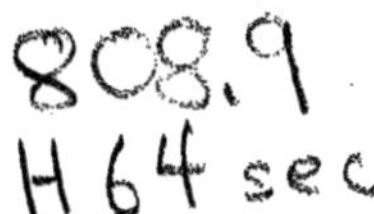

J. FAGAN & SON,
STEREOTYPE FOUNDERS,
PHILADELPHIA.

Dedication.

TO THE FRATERNITY:

To the Editor;

To the Reporter;

To the Correspondent;

To the Contributor;

To the Proof-Reader;

To the Copy-Holder;

To the Pressman;

To the Foreman;

To the Compositor; in a word,

To the Devil,

The Author most Affectionately dedicates his

"*SECRETS OF THE SANCTUM.*"

CONTENTS.

CHAPTER XXXI.

CHAPTER XXXII.

CHAPTER XXXIII.

SECRETS OF THE SANCTUM.

CHAPTER I.

EDITORS' QUALIFICATIONS.

EDITORS of newspapers, together with poets, novelists, historians, and other literary men, are looked upon by a numerous class of persons, who seldom or never come in contact with them, as very superior beings. The merchant, the banker, the mechanic and clerk in the city—and even the plowboy in the country—unconsciously learn to associate in their minds a mysterious dignity with the unseen being whose brain conceives what appears "in print," to be read by thousands and hundreds of thousands. They realize that, while their own sphere is very narrow, that of the writer, whose thoughts are placed in type and repeated to thousands, is in a manner illimitable. So they naturally grow to regard the invisible writer with feelings akin to veneration. It is not entirely unreasonable. If there is anything that ought to raise one man above another, *as* a man, it would seem to be intellectual power, rather than wealth, a proud ancestry, physical strength, or a fine personal appearance.

Those not familiar with the literary man are perhaps a little too prone almost to apotheosize him—picturing him as tall, dignified, commanding, and exceptionally "fine-looking." In this they err. As a rule, editors and authors are not strikingly handsome, and, moving unknown in a miscellaneous crowd, few of them would be picked out as probable men of mark. One of the homeliest men I ever saw, although not disfigured, was an editor, and an unusually brilliant one, as well as a rare poet, wit and satirist. It was years ago that I last saw him, and he is now at rest; but when I recall him I do not think of his unsymmetrical features, his commonplace form, his tangled and neglected hair, his fading eyesight, his careless dress: I remember only the brilliant mind and noble soul that grew deeper into nature than the ephemeral body. I refer to George D. Prentice, of the Louisville *Journal*, whose keen wit and stirring humor made millions laugh, whose trenchant satire made many a political opponent "writhe." He had some bitter enemies while living, but in his grave he is remembered by all as a warm-hearted, pure and upright man.

Among the first in the catalogue of men who will always be rated as famous American journalists, the name of Horace Greeley naturally finds a place. Indeed, he was foremost among the founders of enterprising journalism in America under the new order of things, in the epoch of steam-power presses, and other wonderful machinery of late years introduced in printing-offices. He was the son of a common New Hampshire farmer, and was a green, awkward country boy when he left his home to seek employment in a large city. If at that time he had told his simple neighbors that he proposed to become an editor, he would of course have been laughed at, and that very immoderately.

This brings me to one of the subjects first to be considered in this volume—the aspirations of young persons to be writers. It would scarcely be an exaggeration to say that twelve of every dozen young people who find themselves capable of writing a few acceptable verses, or a correctly-worded communication to a newspaper, begin to entertain notions of writing regularly for the press. The truth is, every one, no matter what his occupation may be, *ought* to be able to write a sensible and grammatic letter, either to a newspaper or to a friend.

It does not therefore follow that every one who can write well enough to "appear in print" creditably is qualified to be an editor, or to make writing for the press his regular calling. Journalism is a business, as much as watch-making, blacksmithing, banking, farming, or navigation. It is generally conceded among all classes that a youth should be trained to follow the business for which he exhibits the greatest taste, and in the mysteries of which he at least shows signs of some tact. Now, the actual duties of a journalist are little comprehended by the general public; and when I treat of this subject at some length in another chapter, it will be understood that great misconceptions of them exist outside of the fraternity.

It is a remark often made, that "everybody thinks he could run a newspaper." It looks so easy — in fact, the newspaper seems to run itself, in a manner, if only let alone. Yet it happens that, of all vocations, professional or mechanical, journalism is one of the most difficult to master. The reasons for this are numerous. There are few rules — a very few general rules — by which to be guided; work that would answer in one community would not answer in another; work that would be satisfactory in one establishment would not be satisfactory in another, even though it might be in the same city or community; what would be all right at one time would be all wrong at another; and, in fact, in no office, in no city or community, and at no time, could the editor please everybody, even though he possessed the attribute of omniscience.

Thus, only long years of experience, and patient, unwearying application, backed by a natural fund of common sense and sound judgment, and a taste for the business, can ever make a proficient editor. When a writer has been five years a journalist, he has just gained one most essential point, namely, a proper sense of how little he knows and how much is yet to be learned. When he has spent an additional five years in various offices—daily and weekly—he discovers that there is still something new to be learned almost every day. This view may appear discouraging; but the man who intends to adopt journalism as his business, and is ambitious to deserve the title of editor, may as well make up his mind at the start that he has a stupendous task before him, and prepare to look upon his first three or four years of labor in that sphere as a rigorous apprenticeship, in which he must work hard and exercise an uncommon amount of patience.

Yes, almost any one can be an editor—after a fashion. A rich man may become an editor, or make one of his son or nephew, on the shortest notice. There is nothing to prevent his buying or renting a building adapted to his purpose, having the requisite materials put in, hiring the necessary labor, and "starting" a newspaper, with his name, or that of his *protégé*, on it as the editor. This he may do without possessing the slightest knowledge of the business, and he may continue to "edit" and publish his paper just as long as he chooses to sink certain sums of money in the enterprise; but he will surely never make it a success unless he intrust its management to experienced hands, the services of which his money may command. Then he is only the editor in name, but is no more an editor in fact, and has no more made himself one by this process, than a man who never handled a hatchet or saw in his life would make a carpenter of himself by buying a chest of tools and employing a real carpenter to use them.

In country districts, where journalism has not advanced nearly so far as it has in large cities, persons not infrequently become "editors" by buying and taking the control of weekly papers, or by setting up and conducting small newspaper establishments with a few hundred dollars. Many of these who pass for "editors" year after year in their own communities were merely born to blush unseen, and waste their talents on the rural air. They will never make their mark in journalism, for the good and sufficient reason that "it is not in them." Many a good mechanic, farmer, school-teacher, yea, and printer, has been spoiled in the process of making a poor editor.

There are a number of qualifications that are indispensable to success as a newspaper editor. Among them are a thorough knowledge of grammar in its various branches, notably syntax and orthography; a clear and active brain; a good memory; familiarity with ancient and modern history, and with the leading events of the day; an aptness for writing at once rapidly and correctly; and an unusual command of language.

Who has not sent "voluntary contributions" to newspapers, only to have them rejected? I remember that at a "tender age" I sent a "poem" to a country newspaper, (to which I had repeatedly, though at respectable intervals, sent contributions that were either "respectfully declined" or "treated with silent contempt,") and it was accepted and published—printed, strangely enough, without even one typographic error. I also remember that I experienced an amount of delight at first seeing one of my "effusions" "in print," to describe which just now I have no adequate words at hand; also, that I vainly (yes, vainly) thought I saw in myself the germ of a great poet. Probably it *was* "great poetry." Had I then been familiar with some of the really meritorious verses written by such poets as Dryden, Bryant, and Drake, at the age of from eight to ten years, I must have been impressed with such an awful sense of their superiority over my own boyish "poetry" as would effectually have cured me of poetic aspirations. I think I may venture the opinion that there are not many actual poets in the world.

To have a manuscript rejected, as of too little merit even for publication, after one has spent hours, and perhaps days, in elaborating and amplifying it, and after he has flattered himself—as, of course, he has—that it is an extraordinary production, has an extremely depressing effect upon the spirits of the ambitious writer, rivaling even that refined soul-torture one endures just after getting up from the gaming-table at which he has lost his last hundred dollars. Indeed, I know of no keener mental anguish—while it lasts; but the sharp edge of the agony soon wears off, and the chances are that scarcely a week elapses before the literary aspirant tries it again, once more braving the awful contingence of the receipt of a "respectfully declined" manuscript. When a certain editor had grown to be able to look back and smile at these little disappointments, he, a few years ago, through the columns of a Boston paper, addressed his respects to an unaccepted literary production after the following fashion:

TO A REJECTED MANUSCRIPT.

Thou thing! I pity thee. I hate thee, too;
For I have spent some labor on thee, now
Thou dost come back to me, without regard
To feelings—which are very sensitive.

Thou contribution—thou gratuitous
Piece for a paper; yea, thou article!
Thou lucubration, which I deemed should rend
The heavens and the earth—convulse mankind—

Make men of women, women of vile men—
Make mighty presidents, and unmake kings—
Uproot society and shake from its
Foundation ev'ry boasted work of man—
Thou—thou rejec—respectfully declined?
I do despise thee, fiend!

For thee I burned
The midnight oil; for thee I racked my brain
To frame each sentence with a with'ring power—
Searched Noah Webster through and through to get
The proper word; for thee consulted all
The latest rules in rhetoric; for thee
Sat all alone at midnight's ghastly hour,
When ev'ry eye within the domicile
Was sealed, except mine own!

Thou graceless thing!
I feel that I could clutch thee up and rend—
Tear—burn—destroy thee—let the hissing flames
Enwrap themselves about thy hateful form
And feed on thee with grim voracity!

But I'll be calm, and nothing do in haste.
In fact, now that I think, I'll lock thee up
For thy offence; and when I bring thee forth
Into the light again, thou wayward thing,
Re—vise thee!

CHAPTER II.

THE REPORTERS.

THERE are but few thorough editors who have not, at one time or other, been reporters; and there are many excellent newspaper men who do both editing and reporting with equal facility—alternating "inside" and "outside" work. In fact, it is next to indispensable that a finished editor, particularly one who is called upon to assume the editorial management or the city editorship of a daily newspaper, shall have acquired a clear knowledge of the duties of a reporter. He often has to give specific instructions to the reporter; and how shall he do it, unless he has had experience in that line himself? There are many, however, who are distinctively reporters, and who so remain all their lives, without ever once taking a place in the sanctum, to do "inside" work. This by no means indicates a lack of journalistic ability, but is often due to a mere preference for "outside" work, or to the force of circumstances. Many a reporter prefers to be a reporter. The editor must sit in his chair all day, or nearly all night, as the case may be, while the reporter is "in and out," rarely being confined to the not-very-cheerful rooms of the newspaper for any considerable length of time.

A thorough reporter, competent to perform any task that may be assigned him, must be a phonographic or "short-hand" writer, for the most rapid penman, who is not a short-hand writer, cannot report in full a long speech, debate, trial in court, the proceedings of a meeting, or the deliberations of a legislative body. In all cases where every word is to be reported a phonographist is indispensable. Yet there are many reporters, regularly employed on large dailies, who are not short-hand writers, but who nevertheless perform their duties just as well as though they were. Such a reporter is frequently sent to meetings, courts, etc., when only a general outline or abstract report of speeches or trials is desired; he collects the items at the police-stations, making certain daily or nightly rounds for that purpose; or he goes out to the suburbs to gather the particulars of any interesting event, such as a public disaster, or a crime, to make brief notes thereof, and to hurry back to the office and "write it up" from them in time for the next edition of the paper.

The reporter is a news-gatherer, and, if he is a good one, he will aim to collect *all* the facts possibly obtainable relative to any event he is detailed to write up, and to relate them in good, plain and simple language. The amount of space accorded to any one specific event must be determined by its importance, together with a consideration of the whole amount of available space. Sometimes an unimportant item may be "crowded out," or "left over," to make room for a full report of a very important affair. The city editor, through whose hands every local paragraph should pass, regulates this matter. On occasions he finds it necessary to "cut down" or amplify a paragraph, but this he does not often find necessary when the reporter is a competent and sagacious one.

Common defects in the style and idiom of many reporters might here be appropriately pointed out, with advantage, I trust, to at least a few who may read this volume. The subject is one which I almost hesitate to take up, not only because of its extensive proportions, but also because I shrink from what might seem an attitude of pedantry. Both these considerations, however, are overcome by the conviction that I should fail to do my whole duty should I neglect to refer to this subject; and when I do refer to it, I do so after the manner of the ghost in Hamlet, "more in sorrow than in anger."

But let me not be understood as imputing *all* the blunders that occur in the public press to ignorance on the part of the writers. Such blunders, as every newspaper-man knows, are often due to the hurry that is inseparable from the preparation of daily newspapers. I have seen some of the most ludicrous bulls and anachronisms perpetrated by the ablest editors in moments of hurry — a few examples of which will be found on another page.

Nevertheless, there are men engaged in the business of reporting who have no natural or acquired fitness for its duties, and who are cursed with a poverty of language, and an imperfect knowledge of its proper use, that ought to have strongly suggested to them the choosing of some other vocation — one in which "the less they would have had to say, the better," and especially one in which they would seldom have been called upon to put their thoughts in writing.

When a man or boy concludes to be a reporter, he ought to determine to be a good one; and I would suggest the following as the first bit of instruction that should be strongly impressed upon him:

> "Say what you have to say in plain and clear language; avoid all redundance, all high-sounding, far-fetched and foreign phrases; be as accurate, truthful and direct as though you were speaking from the witness-stand; as careful as though you were shooting at a target for a wager: let your object be first to see your mark distinctly, then to hit it exactly."

One of the "drunkest" men ever seen in the street stated that he and his brother were engaged in the advancement of the temperance cause, adding: "He lectures on the evils of drunkenness, while I set a frightful example." Probably *he* did the more effective work of the two. In any event, I shall proceed with my instructions to reporters by citing (not setting, I hope) a few frightful examples. I find the following paragraph in a leading New York daily:

FATAL ACCIDENT.—An old widow woman, eighty years of age, named Mrs. Mary Clark, residing at No. — East Thirtieth Street, was found, at a late hour last night, lying at the foot of the hall stairs in an unconscious and dying condition, and soon afterward expired. She had probably fallen down the stairs while ascending to her room. The coroner was notified.

Here, the reporter sets out by stating that the subject of his paragraph was "old," and almost immediately afterward gives her age as eighty years. If he intended to mention the age of the deceased, I cannot imagine why he should also say she was "old"—except that he feared the reader might think Mrs. Mary Clark was a *young* woman or a little girl "eighty years of age," although few people are considered very young at that age.

Next, he informs the reader that the widow was a "woman," thus discouraging the popular delusion that a widow may in some instances be a male instead of a female. It is to be wondered at that the fulsome writer of the paragraph neglected to inform the public that the widow's husband was dead. It seems to me that this reporter might well have saved himself the trouble of writing several superfluous words, and still have been as clearly understood by the reader of news, if he had begun the paragragh, after writing its head, thus:

Mrs. Mary Clark, a widow, aged eighty years, residing, etc.

I believe that the average reader would not have fallen into the error of thinking that Mary Clark was a man—and her name would have suggested that she was a female, without adding "woman" to "widow;" nor would she have been deemed a little boy or girl, or a very young woman, in the absence of the word "old," as "aged eighty years" cannot be construed into meaning extreme youth. If the reporter had written of a "colorless liquid without color," or an "imponderable substance without perceptible weight," he would have made himself scarcely more ridiculous. On a par with the defective paragraph above quoted, is one recently announcing the "death of a wealthy citizen of New York, worth a million dollars." The reader might have been allowed to judge whether the man "worth a million dollars" was wealthy or not. *I* think he was: Rothschild, Vanderbilt, Astor, or Stewart mightn't think so.

Again: I find, under the head of "Accidents," also in a first-class New York daily:

> Charlie Jones, a little boy of five years, fell into a cistern at, etc.

This is another "frightful example" of plethoric reporting. The reader is first told of the existence of a person named Charlie Jones, and is then informed that Charlie is a "little boy," not a little girl; then, having been told that he is a "little" boy, he is told that the "little" boy is five years old; just as though anybody ever saw a big boy or a grown-up man of the age of five years! "Charlie Jones, five years old," etc., would have been clear enough — would it not?

There are daily hundreds of instances in which this ludicrous redundance of expression occurs in the work of careless — or shall I say, ignorant? — reporters. Astounding defects are found in the local columns of many first-class daily newspapers. For example, you take up your morning paper and read that a man — a victim of accident or violence — was "covered over" with blood, and you may be pardoned for wondering why the word "over" was necessary, as "covered" expresses the whole meaning. You also read that something was done "*in the* meantime," whereas the word "meantime" alone would have expressed what was wished understood. You also read that John Smith was struck *over* the head. Now, if John received the blow *over* the head, he had a fortunate escape; for if the weapon or missile went *over* his head it went above it, and so missed him altogether. Probably he was struck *on* the head. A man may receive a blow or a wound *over* the eye or knee — not *over* the head.

There is no doubt *but* that the man will be arrested, as skillful detectives are on his track.

In this sentence the public is informed that there is but a single doubt in the case, that doubt being that the offender will be arrested; his being arrested is the only doubtful thing about it. What is meant is: "There is no doubt that the man will be arrested." That makes it right; put in the word "but" where it is not wanted, and the meaning is exactly reversed. I mention this execrable solecism, because it is one almost constantly perpetrated by careless writers for the public press.

Jacob Jones died Sunday.

If you heard some one read this, and so did not see the orthography of the word "died," you might ask, "What color did he dye it?" The word "on" should precede the name of the day, in this case, just as much as the word "in" should be used in its place in this sentence: "He did the work in his office." If you omit the word "on" in the sentence announcing the death of Mr. Jones, you may as well omit the preposition "at" in the sentence: "The train will go at eight o'clock." How would it sound to say: "The train will go eight o'clock." I could n't go it. This may appear like a trifling matter, and I have only been induced to allude to it at all by the fact that I have frequently seen this defect in the news paragraphs of some of the most carefully-conducted papers in the country. Besides, it is but proper to point out even the smallest of every-day errors, that they may eventually be corrected, for whatever is worth doing at all, is worth doing aright; and it is highly important that the language of newspapers — the educators of the masses — should be brought as nearly to perfection as possible, and as soon as possible. Let the reader ask himself whether this is not true, before he pronounces me hypercritical or pedantic.

As already hinted, errors of a novel and amusing character sometimes find their way into the manuscripts of the brightest journalists, owing, mainly, to the rush and hurry incident to their work. I cite the following sentence, from an article relating to a certain cemetery, which appeared (the article, not the cemetery itself,) in a Boston daily with which I was connected at the time, the bull being no less amusing because it was the work of The Editor himself:

> Owing to a disputed title, doubts arose as to the permanence of the cemetery, and therefore but few were ever interred there, many of whom have since been exhumed and recommitted to the earth in other cemeteries.

When you come to subtract *many* from *a few*, all your mathematical skill must be called into requisition to give even an approximate idea of how many are left.

A companion to this is the following paragraph, taken from an Associated Press dispatch from New Orleans, relating to the sinking of the steamer Empire:

> Several passengers left the boat upon her arrival, otherwise the loss of life would have been very large. As it is, eighteen passengers and many of the crew are believed to be drowned.

According to this, the fact that "several" (a few) passengers had left the boat, prevented a "large" loss of life. The second sentence, following the first, sounds very odd, too. "As it is" (any large loss of life having been averted by the escape of a few passengers), "*eighteen passengers and many of the crew* are believed to be drowned." If this was not a "large" loss of life, notwithstanding the escape of "several" passengers, what would be considered a large loss of life? In this bull, however, ridiculous as it looks, I see only evidence of the haste with which the man who sent the dispatch had to do his work. It was late at night, too, and I suppose that few news editors detected the singular defects of diction, or made any alterations in it.

The following paragraph is from a leading London paper:

> In a dilapidated house in a narrow by-way, at the back of the Refuge in Newport-market, lived a man named John Bishop, who had been living for some time past with a woman named Ford in the second floor back. Bishop had lately been in the receipt of decent wages, and at times was addicted to drink. On Saturday night he returned home with about 1*l.* 13*s.* 6*d.* It is said he left his money on the mantel-shelf, and returning a short time afterward, missed a sovereign. He complained of his loss to *deceased*, but she denied having seen it.

It will be perceived that down to where the word "deceased" occurs there is not the slightest allusion to a murder or a violent death of any kind, nor any hint as to which of the persons spoken of had so suddenly become "deceased." A person having read this much of the article might begin to wonder what the reporter was talking about. The account, however, goes on to state in detail that, after some quarreling, Bishop murdered the woman. The writer had the idea in his own head all straight enough, but allowed his thoughts to outrun his pen; hence, he unconsciously obliged the readers of the paper to take something for granted merely because he knew it himself, and the result was somewhat novel. I can readily see how it might occur, and how it occasionally does occur, even with practiced writers. Such a lack of clearness, though, is the exception rather than the rule in the writings of the most proficient journalists.

Here is another curious paragraph, also from a London daily paper:

> The Duke and Duchess of Edinburgh left Balmoral Castle on Monday morning, and traveled by special train to Aberdeen, where they arrived at 12 o'clock. After a brief stay, the Duke and Duchess left by the 12.23 mail train for London.

Here we are told that the Duke and Duchess arrived at Aberdeen at 12 o'clock, and that, "after a brief stay," they left just twenty-three minutes later. How could their stay have been otherwise than brief, if they arrived at 12 and departed at 12.23? It is difficult to conceive by what means their Royal Highnesses could have stayed a day or two, or even a few hours, in Aberdeen, within the space of twenty-three minutes—unless, indeed, they possessed the power which Milton ascribes to the Almighty to "crowd eternity into an hour, or stretch an hour into eternity."

Accuracy is important in reporting, if reporting itself is of any importance, but it is not always strictly observed by a certain class of careless reporters or compilers of news paragraphs. For example, almost every day something like this may be read in our daily newspapers:

> John Brown, a well-known citizen of Binghamton, was instantly killed, on Thursday, by being thrown from his horse.

Very good, so far as it goes; but *where* did the accident happen? It might have been in Hong Kong, in Melbourne, or Constantinople, or in Palestine, so far as the information goes; for although it is stated that Mr. Brown was a citizen of Binghamton, it does not follow that he was killed there. Probably, in such a case, the accident did happen in or near Binghamton, and it is left to be taken for granted; but as the Browns do not remain at home all their lives, and in fact are even proverbial for their rambling disposition, the writer should have said, "in that city," or "near that city," as the case may have been.

There is lying before me a most carefully-conducted Philadelphia paper, and, although I am certainly not on the look-out for something to carp at, one of the first of its local paragraphs to catch my eye is this:

SHOCKING ACCIDENT. — George Drake, aged 33 years, had his left arm torn off at the elbow by having it caught in a belt at McCallum's mill.

If this is news worth publishing at all — and I have no doubt it is — it should surely have been stated *when* and *where* the accident occurred. Both these essential points have been overlooked by the reporter, probably through the usual hurry; and the reader is left in the dark as to whether the accident occurred yesterday, last week, or last year; also as to the location of McCallum's mill. True, it may be inferred, from the fact that the paragraph is found in the local columns, that the mill is somewhere in or near Philadephia; but in what quarter? in what ward? near the junction of what two principal streets of that widely-extended city? All this the reporter allows to remain a mystery, and the reader — like a person who is told but half a secret — feels that he would rather have known nothing whatever of the story, if he cannot know the whole.

I should make this chapter too long if I should refer at length to all the blunders and solecisms, of various grades of enormity, that are daily noticeable in the public press. As I am desirous, then, that my labors shall result in "the greatest good to the greatest number," (including number one,) I will, as succinctly as possible, give some advice to the green or careless reporter.

Young man, never say "*a* Mr. John Smith," or "*one* John Smith," as no one will make the mistake of supposing that John is more than one person. Plurality will not be even suspected when the name is so singular.

Never say "lower down" or "higher up," because an object could not be very low up or high down.

Never say "a few moments," when you mean a few minutes, because a moment is an indefinite amount of time, however small. You might as well say "a mass of coal, about the size of five lumps of chalk." Our language is rich in clear words and expressions, and a fair idea of a small amount of time may always be conveyed by some such term as "a second," "a few seconds," "half a minute," or "a few minutes," as facts may warrant.

Never say "full complement." The latter word alone means "full quantity," and the tautology in the former expression would be just about evenly matched with that in such a term as "a white white house" or "a red red head." A man who would say "full complement," deserves no compliment at all.

Never commence a report of a homicide in the suburbs by saying: "The quiet village of Cabbageville was startled and thrown into an intense state of feverish excitement by one of the most diabolical," etc. It's too horrible. Keep cool, and don't get your nerves worked up to any such a pitch. Be calm, and relate the mournful tale in fewer and milder words. Yet there are reporters who do begin an account of a murder in just such words as the above.

Never say "insane asylum," because, whatever may be the

mental condition of the inmates, the building itself is usually in its right mind, and has seldom been known to commit even an error of judgment. Say "lunatic asylum," or "asylum for the insane."

Don't say that a man was "executed," when he was merely hanged (for some such little hereditary eccentricity as murdering his father, for instance). The sheriff did *execute* the sentence of death, but he only *hanged* the culprit. He did not *execute* him. You might as well say, when he takes a convict to the State Prison, that he "executes" him into the hands of the warden. In both cases it is merely the sentence that is executed. Nevertheless, I am bound to say that "usage," that loose and careless teacher of language, has recognized this application of the term "execute" in cases of hanging (or beheading). Webster himself gives it a mild sanction; while we also find in Shakespeare (Richard III., Act V., Scene 3):

> —— Lest being seen,
> Thy brother, tender George, be *executed.*

Richard Grant White, the eminent philologist, however, deprecates the use of the word "execute" in this connection.

Use plain language. Don't affect Latin or French, or words and phrases from any foreign or dead language.

Don't go out of your way to hunt up rare words. Make rare words rarer still by using only words often used and well understood by all who read.

If you speak of a dog, call it "a dog;" do not say a "mammal of the *genus canis.*" To reiterate an old precept, "call a spade a spade," not "a metallic agricultural implement for displacing and rearranging the soil."

Be not too positive in making your statements, especially when, by possible inaccuracy, they may unjustly work to the prejudice of any person, society, or institution. When there is the slightest room for doubt that a certain person did a certain discreditable thing, of which it becomes necessary to make any report at all, do not say he did it; say it is "reported," "alleged," "charged," or something of that noncommittal nature. This careful course would be dictated by a simple sense of justice, even if there were no laws against libel, because many persons are suspected and charged with offences, arrested, and afterward found to be entirely innocent. I have a paper before me which gives a man's name, and says he "was arrested yesterday *for* stealing a blanket." This is saying, in effect, that he *did* steal it — an assertion that no paper has a right to make before a man has been tried and convicted of the alleged offence. The reporter should have said that the man was arrested "on a charge of," or "charged with," stealing a blanket.

Don't always be on the alert to be witty or droll, and don't constantly drag in far-fetched puns or outlandish and unusual expressions. A reporter is not employed as a humorist; certainly he is not in every case born one; and as certainly he can never make himself one. There is such a thing as a good pun, and there is such a thing as real wit; but both must be spontaneous. No straining. A donkey might as well try to make his bray sound like the roar of a lion by straining his voice.

I think I heard a legitimate pun once, on board of a steamer running between San Francisco and Panama, and I am sure it was spontaneous. Several passengers were discussing the probable nationality of a very tall and slim foreign lady who "put on" unusual "airs," and who, it was said, represented herself as belonging to a titled family. "I think she is a Swede," said one. "A Russian, more likely," ventured another. "*I* should say," remarked a waggish fellow of the group, "that she looks more like a *Pole*."

Young man, don't use the editorial "we." No reporter on a first-class daily thinks of doing so; nor would it be allowed, if he did. The reporter is a news-gatherer, not an editor, and must give no opinions, although his position, if he fills it creditably, is a very honorable one. He must not say: "We learn that," etc. He will find ample scope of expression in such phrases as, "It is reported," "it is understood," "it is said," "it is rumored," "it is thought," etc., according to the strength which the statement may be allowed to assume.

I have thus referred briefly to the shortcomings of many careless or inefficient reporters; and while I urge accuracy and directness of language, I should regret to be understood as being captious or exacting; nor do I claim that I myself should ever be so rigorous in the matter of accuracy as a certain "country editor," who thus quoted two lines of a hymn sung at a funeral he reported:

Ten thousand thousand (10,000,000) are their tongues,
But all their joys are one (1).

CHAPTER III.

THE CITY EDITOR.

NEWSPAPER men know well enough what reporters have to do, and how they do it; but few persons outside the fraternity have any very clear idea of the inside workings of this or any other branch of journalism. As thousands of the readers of books and newspapers have never been inside of a newspaper office, a brief description of the rooms of the City Editor of a first-class daily newspaper in a large city will here be entirely in place. With this view, I cannot do better than to quote from a sketch that appeared in *Packard's Monthly* a few years ago — Mr. S. S. Packard, the publisher, at present conducting Packard's Business College, in New York, having kindly given me permission to do so. The sketch from which I quote was one of a series written for *Packard's Monthly* by Mr. Amos J. Cummings, a member of the New York *Tribune's* editorial staff, and in which he gives very graphic descriptions of the whole machinery of the *Tribune*, which may well be taken as a pattern of American daily newspapers. The following is Mr. Cummings's description of the City Editor's room, in which the reporters receive their assignments to duty and daily return the results of their labors:

The walls are covered with maps. A perpendicular viaduct, for communication between the counting-, editorial-, and composing-rooms, with speaking-pipes, copy-boxes, and bells, runs from the low ceiling through the center of the room, like the succulent branch of a banyan tree. A small library of books relating to city affairs leans against the viaduct. A water-pail and a tin jar of ice-water occupy one corner of the room. Paste-pots and inkstands are scattered over the desks in lazy confusion. Bits of blotting-paper and scores of rusty-looking steel pens are strewn about the tables. A dozen reporters are seated at a dozen small green desks. Some are writing, a few are reading, and two are smoking briarwood pipes. The City Editor arrives at the office at 10 A. M., and immediately overhauls the morning papers, reading the advertisements with special care. Every announcement of a political meeting, lecture, horse-race, excursion, real estate sale, execution, hotel-opening, steamboat-launch, etc., is clipped out and pasted in a blank book. At noon the reporters enter, and copy their assignments from the book, drawing a line under each of their names, to assure the City Editor that they are aware of their detail and will attend to it. Look at the book, and you will find such entries as these:

John Allen's Prayer-Meeting, Water Street, 12 M. — *White*.

American Geographical Society, Historical Society Rooms, Second Avenue and Eleventh Street, 8 P. M. — *Meeker*.

Grant and Colfax Meeting, Broadway and Twenty-Second Street, 8 P. M. — *Armant*.

Dog-fight at Kit Burns's, Water Street, 9 P. M. — *Mix.*
Special service. —*Gilbert.*
See Longstreet, and have an interview with him at New York Hotel; make a column. —*Gedney.*
Police headquarters. —*Morey.*
Jefferson Market Police Court. —*Mix.*
A two-column article on Local Nominations. —*McGrew.*

Such is a brief extract from a description of the City Editor's rooms in the office of the New York *Tribune*. They are nearly the same in every large daily newspaper establishment in this country.

CHAPTER IV.

CERTAIN REPORTERIAL WORK.

THE reporter's life is not an easy one. There could be no greater misconception of it than a belief that its duties are light. The Reporter has much hard and irksome labor to do; he must often work beyond the time at which he sadly needs rest or refreshment; he must do mental work requiring careful attention in noisy assemblages, often through the long hours of the night; and is nearly always so hurried, so pressed for every minute of his time, that it is not strange if the brain is thrown into a state of confusion that wastes it too rapidly away. There is very little work done on a daily newspaper that is not done hurriedly — very little that could be delayed for a mere matter of ten or fifteen minutes. The editors, reporters, proof-readers, compositors, pressmen, folders and mailers all have to work pretty close to time. A delay of five minutes is often a serious matter. This may readily be believed when it is stated that a large morning paper, such as the New York *Herald*, contains as much matter as a volume the size of this work, and each issue of the paper must spring up into existence in a night.

Most of the reporters on a morning paper work at night, straining their eyes in dimly-lighted places and vexing the brain with labor during unnatural hours. They must sit in crowded halls, and, while they write with the rapidity of lightning, listen intently to catch each word of a wheezy-voiced orator, sometimes at noisy and tumultuous political meetings, sometimes amid the uproar and confusion incident to a "stormy" session of a "deliberative" body.

I cannot make this work what I think it should be without frequently referring to my own experience in journalism, and I trust that the generous critic and the generous public will exempt me from the imputation of deliberate egotism. Most experienced editors will bear me out in the assertion that if any young journalist is disposed to "think more highly of himself than he ought to think," a few years of thorough training will teach him better. I know of no vocation in the pursuit of which a man so soon finds out how unimportant he is in the wide world. Indeed, I believe that few persons ever reach proficiency in the profession until they have "had the conceit taken out of them."

To proceed: It once became my province to report the proceedings of "the most numerous branch" of a certain State Legislature, in which, while it embraced a number of able men, the rural element was largely represented. The Speaker himself, selected on account of his influence, was a leading politician in a small city, and, I believe, a courteous gentleman, as regarded his private life; but he was not a finished parliamentarian, unaccustomed to positions of mark, and failed to preside over the deliberations of "the House" with the calm demeanor, the stately ease and grace I have seen exhibited by the presiding officers of some legislative bodies. There are men who seem to have been born to preside over assemblages; but this Mr. Speaker was not one of them. He was not calm; he was not serene; he was not self-possessed; and he made many — I have to say it — blunders which, however amusing in a general way, were very annoying to "us reporters," whose duty it was faithfully to record the proceedings. For example:

A gentleman arises to address "the Chair;" he is Mr. Miller, the member from Bedford; he says:

"Mr. Speaker: —"

It is now the duty of the Speaker to "recognize" him in this form:

"The gentleman from Bedford, Mr. Miller."

Let him do this correctly and distinctly, and the reporter will proceed to write:

"Mr. Miller, of Bedford, said that —"

But our Speaker, owing to his inexperience, bashfulness and general unfitness for his position, finds it difficult to articulate the words, either plainly or connectedly. He sputters out:

"The gentleman from Miller, Mr. Bedford."

The reporter does not know Mr. Miller, and, following the confused and erring Speaker, proceeds to put him down as "Mr. Bedford," which is merely the name of the town he lives in — without the "Mr."

A slight smile floats over a portion of the body at the Speaker's mistake, and he, becoming more confused and frightfully red in the face, stammers:

"The — the — Mr. — the gentleman from Bedler, Mr. Milford."

The smile extends like contagion; the reporter does not know what to write, or whether to write anything at all or not, and the Speaker, whose confusion and mortification now amount to torture, tries it again, with this result:

"The gentleman from Midford, Mr. Beller."

The smile of the amused members who see the Speaker's blunder, and of others who did not at first notice it, merges into an "audible grin;" and the Speaker, earnestly wishing that the earth would open and swallow him up, makes one more desperate essay to announce the name of the waiting member, and in trembling and barely intelligible tones stammers:

"The — ah — I would say, the gentleman from Melford — the bentleman from Jilford —the Mr. from Biddleford — the Middleford — the bentle — the Beddle — the middle — the meddle — the — "

By this time the House is in an uproar, and bursts of laughter, with no further attempt to restrain them, roll out like they do in the audience of a minstrel show when the comic part is at its height; the Clerk gets up and whispers to the Speaker, who finally manages to "recognize" the member from Bedford; but the reporter must have remained very attentive during the confusion, if he has succeeded in correctly understanding and recording the name of "Mr. Miller, of Bedford." If he has failed, he has no time now to ask the Clerk near whom he sits, (but will try to think of it before sending his manuscript to the office), for he must proceed, as the confusion subsides, to take down every word uttered by "the gentleman from Bedford, Mr. Miller."

Another scene in the same deliberative body, same session, two days later than the foregoing:

But let me preface it with a brief explanation. At the beginning of the session, and immediately after a permanent organization, each member has assigned to him a seat which he shall occupy every day during the whole session, which contributes toward making things smooth and orderly. That perfect fairness may characterize the distribution of the seats, which are all numbered, they are drawn after the manner of a lottery. There are in the House, embracing three hundred members, about twenty experienced legislators, who will be supposed to do nearly all the talking, and, in a manner, "run the whole machine" themselves, while the green members sit quietly in their seats, listen attentively, vote at the proper times, and in what their leaders teach them is the proper manner, but rarely have the audacity to get up and speak. It is not to be supposed that mere chance would give the twenty "smart" members front seats, near the Speaker's desk, where, of course, they earnestly desire to be. Some happen to get back seats, but they don't keep them long. They go and speak pleasantly to a corresponding number of green ones who have had the luck to draw front seats, and, by representing that their hearing is imperfect, that their eyesight is bad, and that they each have fifteen or twenty bills to introduce and advocate in long speeches, contrive to "swap" with the lucky green ones, who "take back seats," where, after all, they can vote just as vigorously as they could near the Speaker's stand. So, on the second day, you see all the "old stagers" ranged along on the front row of seats, a few perhaps as far back as the second row — then all is well.

The obscure members, as before intimated, do not often address the Chair, but sometimes they do. On such occasions the Speaker is more than usually confused, and so is the reporter. The green member, when he becomes so daring as to attempt to offer some remarks, arises from his seat away back at the farther side of the Hall of Representatives, a hundred and fifty feet distant, and, "unaccustomed as he is to public speaking," (I can't help it!) says, "Mr. Speaker," in a faint voice, compared with which an ordinary whisper would sound like a clap of thunder. Indeed, so puny is the voice that we involuntarily get the notion that he is about to utter his dying words. The Speaker is confused — in the first place, not so much by getting the country member's name intermingled with his residence, as by the fact that he does n't know him at all — does n't remember that he ever saw him in his life, or ever heard of him, and certainly has not the remotest idea as to where he lives. Nevertheless, while an awful presentiment of evil overshadows his soul, he bravely begins:

"The gentleman from —"

Then he looks appealingly at several well-posted members — those old stagers — in the front seats. There is a general turning of heads and a concerted staring at the country member, who, appalled at suddenly and unexpectedly finding himself "the observed of all observers," stands pale as a ghost, waiting to be "recognized." None of the members near the Speaker's stand happen to know him, and they, together with the whole House, only keep on staring at him.

Things are becoming painful. There is a moment of awful silence. Presently there is a slight movement among the other country members in the vicinity of the distant country member who has dared to arise for the purpose of "making a few remarks;" a gentle murmur, like the faint sound of the breakers on the distant sea-shore; heads turn to and fro, and shake and nod fantastically; and the name and residence of the member, obtained from his own lips, begin to pass from mouth to mouth in the direction of the Speaker's desk, slowly, painfully, over the heads of numerous members, till at last they reach the Chair. The country member is Mr. Brown, of Cobbville; but, of course, by the time his name and residence reach the Speaker they become "Mr. Cowan, of Bobbington," and the Speaker, after the usual agony, succeeds in announcing him as "the gentleman from Carrington, Mr. Bobbins." Thereupon the statesman from Cobbville proceeds with his remarks in low, tremulous tones, and here is what the reporter hears:

"I do no oo ah foo ow noo ore bore air o no to jo ih bo eh so high ugh for no go."

The Speaker also listens attentively, but of course understands about as much of what Mr. Brown says as the reporter does. The speech is not lengthy, and the reporter does the best he can for Mr. Brown, and for his paper, and for the Commonwealth, by writing:

Mr. Bobbins, of Carrington, made some remarks with reference to the amendment in question, in the course of which he suggested that careful attention should be given to the subject before definite action be taken.

Now comes some fun. When Mr. Brown, of Cobbville (erroneously announced as "the gentleman from Carrington, Mr. Bobbins"), has finished, a waggish member, a very able lawyer, arises with a merry twinkle barely visible in his eye, and says:

"Mr. Speaker: —"

Much to the reporter's astonishment, the Speaker succeeds, in the first attempt, in properly recognizing him as "the gentleman from Hampden, Mr. Edington."

The reporter, somewhat reassured, writes:

"Mr. Edington, of Hampden, said: —"

[That gentleman proceeds, in the most penetrating tones:]

"I can—not reconcile my views with those so ably expressed by the gentleman from Carrington." [Of course, like the Speaker and reporter, he has not heard one word of Mr. Brown's remarks.] "I could never question the purity of his motives, for I believe him to be one of the best and most patriotic members of this body. Coming from the beautiful town of Carrington," [there is no such town in the State, and Mr. Edington knows it,] "a town in whose sweet mountain air I have breathed many a delightful summer breath, he brings with him to this hall the very fragrance of sincerity and truth. Yet, Mr. Speaker, I cannot — however hard I may try — succeed in bringing my mind to the same view he takes of this important matter; and I do believe, Mr. Speaker, that, after maturer thought on the subject, after a more deep and careful penetration of its many intricacies, his candor will induce him to admit that, if the course he at present advocates should prevail, it would in the end prove prejudicial to the truest interests of the Commonwealth."

Mr. Brown, of Cobbville, is of course very much delighted at the marked attention he has received at the hand of the eminent Hampden lawyer, and subsides into a dreamy silence, from which he will probably no more issue during the session.

The Speaker of a "House" has it in his power to worry the reporter very much, and often does so — of course, without intending to — by the manner in which he rushes through his routine work, such as reading notices of bills, reports of committees, etc. Some Speakers, with glib tongues, fly over these forms with a rapidity that sets the reporter's brain in a whirl, and often defies the skill of the most skillful. Notices of bills, for example, are sometimes read off so rapidly that the Speaker appears to commence each word before he has finished pronouncing its predecessor; and here is about what the reporter hears:

"Meer Smis Sissfeel giz notes zat he ill 'n t'mars um foosh day int'oose bill tiled nack t'mend nack mentery secon leven chaper th' nine shen'l statutes rel'v vation game."

Here is what he ought to hear:

"Mr. Smith, of Smithfield, gives notice that he will, on to-morrow, or some future day, introduce a bill, entitled, An Act to Amend an Act Amendatory of Section Eleven, Chapter Thirty-nine, of the General Statutes, relative to the Preservation of Game."

Reporters are only mortal; and, although they plod along patiently through their many tedious hours of exhausting work, they are occasionally guilty of shortcomings that evoke stirring anathemas, or, at the very least, diabolical scowls from the City Editor or the Managing Editor, as the case may be. I once knew a generally prompt and faithful reporter, who was sent to bring back an account of a very important matter, and who became irritated in his pursuit of information and came back to the office without a line, when a column and a half of matter was expected. He told the City Editor how it was, and added:

"I suppose you'll give me notice to quit; but I don't care a d—n. I'm disgusted with the business!"

But the City Editor knew that he only had a fit of the blues, which would probably disappear by the next morning, not to return again for a year, if ever, and could not have been induced to part with him.

One summer morning — let us say about twenty years ago — I was sent to report an "open-air" celebration at a place about twenty miles from the little New England city of S——, in which I was employed as a reporter on the *Journal*, one of the two daily evening papers published there. The other daily — the *Press* — employed a reporter formerly of New York, a very genial fellow, Mr. M——. The Managing Editor, Mr. D——, told me he desired a very full report, and I promised, and certainly intended, to give it.

Arriving at the ground by excursion train, we found, in front of the only house in that vicinity, a rude platform to accommodate the orators and others connected with the ceremonies of the occasion, and near it an ordinary table, for the use of reporters, with some improvised board benches around it. The table stood on the greensward, and, unluckily, right in the broiling sun of June, while a tree but imperfectly shaded the orators' platform.

The deficient accommodations for reporters greatly discouraged M—— and myself, both because the glare of the sun on white or yellow paper is exceedingly trying to the eyes, and because it is considered perilous to sit still with the hot rays of that orb beating down upon the top of the head. This danger is much greater in the case of a person accustomed to being much indoors, and unfamiliar with such hardening work as haying or gathering in the sheaves of grain. We remembered, with much concern, that there was such a thing as a plain sunstroke; and both of us had, perhaps, written up more than one "fatal case" of that kind. The subject was "nearest the hearts of both," or at least in our heads, for I was about to offer a remark relative to it, when M—— said:

"Well, I declare! Is this where we are to sit?" And he looked anxiously around, hoping against hope that there might be, on the other side of the platform, a table for reporters in the cool, sequestered shade. But the shade was not so sequestered as it used to be; for all the space protected from the sun by the spreading branches of the "gnarled oak" — that 's the kind of tree it was — was occupied by dense masses of country people who had flocked to the celebration.

"It seems so," I replied, to M——'s remark. "Right in the sun, too."

"In the sun, but not *right* in it," he rejoined.

We sat down by the table, and I observed that he looked very grave, particularly during the prayer with which the ceremonies were soon afterward opened. When it was concluded, some brief formalities took place; then an "eminent orator" was introduced, and work began in earnest. There were at the table several reporters from Boston, of course representing dailies of that city; and, having reverently sharpened their pencils during the prayer, and got their note-books in trim, they went vigorously at their task, taking down everything "full." M—— and I wrote a few seconds in a hesitating kind of way; then I stopped altogether, and whispered:

"M——, I can't stand this."

"Neither can I," he replied, also ceasing to write. "What do you say to quit?"

"I agree," I replied, while the orator thundered away like the paddle-wheels of a very large steamer going at full speed. "I feel that it would really endanger my life to sit here at this work for two or three hours."

"And I, too. I was overcome with the heat once, while noting a Fourth-of-July procession in New York, and fainted. The doctor said it was a light case of sunstroke, and that I must be careful."

"I was similarly affected one hot day in Philadelphia," I returned, growing more and more alarmed.

"Come, then, let us go," he said.

"All right."

We put our note-books and pencils in our pockets, arose and elbowed our way out of the crowd. We saw no space in the shade where we might even have stood and endeavored to write, holding the note-book in the left hand; so, we gave it up altogether and walked away and sat down among the fragrant clover under a tree about a hundred yards distant from the orators' stand, and began to swallow some refreshments which we had not neglected to bring with us, properly packed, from S——.

"I would n't kill myself in the hot sun for any paper," I remarked.

"Nor I," he replied. "Besides, now that I come to think of it, why should the *Journal* and *Press* want it reported at all? It will all be in the Boston papers, and they will reach us in good time to-morrow morning. We can then clip it bodily."

"Sure enough. We'd be a couple of fools (here, take a little more of this) to sit there sweltering like those Boston fellows. They're doing the work for us, in a manner. I really pity them."

"So do I."

Sitting in the blessed shade of that giant oak, with the summer breeze gently fanning us, and with discreditably frequent resorts to those "refreshments," we allowed the beautiful summer day to wear away in sweet forgetfulness, while we steadily grew more and more indifferent as to whether there was either a celebration or a newspaper in the world or not.

By and by we rambled awhile in adjacent groves, and the voices of the orators died away in the distance. Time went by unnoticed — and so did the three o'clock train, by which we ought to have returned to S—— with our reports. This we discovered when it was only half an hour too late. We could now do nothing but wait with helpless patience for the seven o'clock train, which we safely boarded, and which landed us in S—— at eight. M—— and I then parted, and, with some unaccountable misgivings, I went to the *Journal* office. The Managing Editor had long since been home to dinner, and returned to the office, where he impatiently awaited my arrival.

"Good evening," I said, cheerfully.

"Ah, good evening," he replied, with less animation than I had exhibited. "I — I fully expected you down by the three o'clock train."

"Missed it," said I.

He was perceptibly vexed, but he smothered his disappointment, and said :

"Well, I 'm glad you 're here, anyhow. Better late than never. Let me have your manuscript, please, as I want to arrange it to be set up very early in the morning. Three of the compositors are to come round at six o'clock for that purpose, as to-morrow will be a busy day, and we must get the celebration up and out of the way as soon as possible. What kind of an affair was it? Pretty grand?" And he held out his hand for my manuscript.

"Why, Mr. D——," said I, "the fact is — the fact is, I have n't any report."

"No report?"

"No. You see, the table for reporters was in the sun, and I could n't write there. I never told you — did I?— about being sun-struck in Philadelphia a few years ago? Besides, I thought it would all be in the Boston papers in the morning, and we might clip it from them. There were eight or nine Boston reporters there."

Mr. D—— gazed at me in a strange, weird way, like one in a dream, then deliberately put on his hat and left the editorial room, muttering a horrible oath as he passed through the doorway, leaving me standing there suffering such pangs of remorse that I fancied a moderately-easy death would have been quite welcome.

As ill-luck would have it, the Boston papers — Boston was sixty or seventy miles distant — were an hour later than usual the next morning, and when they did finally come, after things had been working backward and crosswise all the morning, I was chagrined to discover that they all contained only the most condensed account of the celebration. So, we were obliged to patch up a miserable and meager account, of four or five stickfuls, when, being so near the scene of the celebration, we ought to have had two-and-a-half columns. I felt mean for a month afterward, during which time I found it one of the hard things of this life to look Mr. D—— squarely in the face, although he had probably pardoned my delinquency in his heart within twenty-four hours after it occurred. He had himself been a reporter in earlier life, and there is reason to believe that he was personally aware of the manner of such things. He died about a year afterward, and when I was called upon to take his place as Managing Editor, I could not help shuddering at the thought that his suppressed anger at not getting that report might have hastened his death.

I cannot follow the reporter through every phase of his duties, but before leaving the subject I will say that long and tedious criminal and civil trials in the courts are among the leading things that severely tax his brain. I have more than once sat in the court-room for four hours at a time, during some important trial, carefully recording every word uttered by judge, counsel and witnesses — the words often pronounced with great rapidity, or in a low and almost inaudible voice, or in poor English, and I have thought that there was nothing more irksome or exhausting in journalistic life.

There are sometimes episodes of an exciting or amusing nature that relieve the tedium, and the reporter usually feels a little more cheerful after them. Of course, they are of short duration. There must "be silence in court," even if the sheriff or tipstaff has to scream out the words every ten seconds. In cases no less serious than murder trials there is an occasional lively tilt between lawyers, or between a cross-examining lawyer and a cross-examined witness, in which sharp sallies and keen retorts are followed by more than audible laughter — which, however, is promptly checked.

I once reported a notable murder trial in a large city on the Atlantic side of the country, in which an eccentric female witness created much merriment by her droll responses to the interrogatories of a sharp lawyer. Several times the "audience" was fairly convulsed with laughter; and even the murderer himself, forgetting his little troubles for the moment, was once or twice highly amused.

The woman had heard certain suspicious sounds, on the night of the murder, in a building adjacent to her residence, where the crime was supposed to have been committed; and the counsel for the defense wished to shake her testimony, and make it apparent that at the time in question she was in a state of health — being a married woman — that might have rendered defective her faculty of receiving impressions correctly, and her memory of events inaccurate and untrustworthy.

He put a question to her on this point, and she proved herself to be the very reverse of imbecile, by retorting in a way that nearly extinguished the eminent legal gentleman — for he was a man of wonderful forensic powers. The usual hearty laugh followed, and the two grave judges who sat on the bench themselves joined in it most undisguisedly. What followed this amused me more than the woman's witty reply. The sheriff was present, and had already once or twice reproved the spectators for exhibiting mirth in the court-room; and he now calmly waited till "their Honors" had got done laughing and subsided into their usual gravity, then arose with a severe frown — of course, he was not supposed to know that the judges had so much as smiled — turned toward the spectators, and with much sternness said:

"Now, look here! Just — as — sure — as this laughing is repeated, but barely once more, or if I even see so much as a grin, or hear so much as a whisper among the spectators, I shall clear the court-room! Mark that! You ought to be ashamed of yourselves! I would like to see any one here dare to repeat such conduct!"

He resumed his seat, and there was no more laughing in the court-room that day — no, not even by "the Court" itself.

CHAPTER V.

SLANG.

THE use of "slang" words and phrases has become so extensive in the public prints, and the fact is so much to be deplored, that I cannot refrain from devoting a chapter to the subject. I never was more in earnest than I am when I urge that slang ought to be kept out of the newspapers. Distinctive circles of society may indulge in it without great general harm, but its continual use in the public press, from which the masses in a great degree shape their style and morals, ought to meet with the most emphatic disapproval. If only a few journals, of limited influence and unlimited obscurity, tolerated slang in their columns, I should not deem it my province so explicitly to deprecate it. But I am sorry to say that slang is too often to be found in the columns (notably the "local" columns) of some of the most widely-circulated and influential newspapers in the country. I could mention one or two leading New York dailies (but will not do so, lest the others should be jealous) whose reporters are apparently allowed to use slang "at discretion," and in whose columns are continually to be found such expressions as "went for" (for assaulted), "boozy" (for intoxicated), "lip" (for offensive language), etc. This is not creditable to any reporter, and, so far from being witty, is on a par with the outrageous pun that is produced by severe straining. Reporting is a business, should be reduced to a business, and the language of a reporter should be generally as direct and pointed as the writing and figures in a book-keeper's entry in his day-book or ledger. Imagine a book-keeper slightly changing the name of a customer, or altering the sum of a column of figures, in order to make a joke of it. This world is not, as some reporters seem to imagine, one stupendous joke; certainly it has not been such to me.

Everything can be said against the use of slang, and nothing in favor of it. It introduces unnecessary words, and confuses our language so that the pupil of the next generation may not be able to distinguish the pure English words from the spurious stuff called "slang." It gives new and ridiculous meanings (if any meanings at all) to old words, true, tried and familiar to every tongue. The use of slang takes the place of real wit and humor, and seems to threaten to drive them off the field. Legitimate fun is discouraged when we arrive at a point where only a few coarse slang words will create a horse-laugh, and where refined and courteous humor is not even understood. This slang business becomes a serious matter, when even our standard dictionaries take dozens of its words from coarse and foul mouths, and give them as part of our vocabulary — although marked, *colloquial and low*.

About twenty years ago, I think, the prize-ring began to be one of the recognized "institutions" of this country, coming from old countries whose vices we seem to display a wonderful aptness for imitating. Those were the days of Hyer, Sullivan, Morrissey, Heenan, Sayers. If the newspapers gave voluminous reports of "battles" for the championship between leading pugilists, they only supplied a demand; for I believe I do not exaggerate, when I say that a majority of the whole people of the country began to take a more or less animated interest in the prize-ring, and certainly read with avidity the long accounts of physical contests between strong men. Of prize-fighting and its effects, if any, on the morals of the people, it is not my purpose nor my province here to speak; and I even doubt whether the morals of those who engage in or witness it are seriously affected. I refer to the subject only to say that to prize-fighting, so fulsomely reported in the public press, we probably owe more for the amount of slang in circulation than to any other specific cause.

The reporters, in looking upon a prize-fight and writing it up, naturally caught the "technical" expressions of the fraternity, and their accounts as naturally bristled with such words and phrases as, "caught him on the mug," "lit out with his left," "got him in chancery," "sent him to Coventry," "made him kiss his mother," "handed him one on the jaw," or on the "meat-trap," the left "peeper," etc.

These, and whole scores of kindred terms, were made familiar as household words, and passed from the mouths of reading people back into the mouths of "young and rising" reporters; and many of the latter, deeming it a very good and easy way to be "witty," or "spicy," lost no opportunity of introducing the idiom of the prize-ring into their reports of everything, in season and out of season. So did the language of many a newspaper, and again of its young readers, become tainted.

If an encounter between two men occurred on the street, the reporter, on the strain to be witty, did not think of so ridiculous a thing as telling all about it in language at once simple and respectable; but of course described how the aggressor "went for" the object of his wrath; how he "handed him one on the bugle;" how the other, in turn, "put up his props;" how he "squared away" at his assailant and "pasted him on the nose," or "whacked him on the snoot," or "put a head on him," or "fitted him with a tin ear," or "sent him to grass;" and how the aggressor, having been worsted in the fight,—although the reporter carefully avoids saying so,—"throwed up the sponge" and eventually "walked off on his ear," unless, indeed, "taken in" by a "cop."

Every institution, profession and trade has its peculiar nomenclature, to be used only within each respective fraternity; but what confusion it would create to attempt to introduce all, in a kind of figurative, allegorical, or semi-literal way, into an every-day language! No such wholesale attempt to Babelize our language has yet been made; but it does seem that the whole jargon of the prize-ring, about the rudest of all distinctive nomenclature, has been chosen by reporters to enrich (?) our diction and polish the tongues of the people.

But why not go into other spheres where "slang" of a more refined nature may be obtained? The realms of science, for example, are rich in expressions that would aid the reporter in making his language as obscure and unintelligible to the masses as possible, which seems to be the object aimed at by some reporters. For example, he gives an account of a man committing suicide, one who had been low-spirited for some days before his death; why not say that "the mercury in his glass had been depressed to the unusually low figure of 27.05?" or that "the humidity of his soul had advanced to 99.999?" Or, dropping meteorology and going into astronomy, if the man suffered temporary aberration of mind common to his ancestors, it might be said that he had recently "moved in an elliptic orbit," and (if a love affair was the immediate cause of the trouble) that "the eccentricity of the said orbit was due to the periodical proximity of a certain planet." This might mean a *star* actress with whom the poor fellow had fallen in love, to the extent of deranging his mind, but no one would ever guess it, and thus the reporter would succeed in his prime object — that of not being understood. All these things will be found highly advantageous — that is, if the desired end is to make language as unintelligible and as nearly useless as possible.

The idiom of sailors is sometimes affected by such young writers as seem to think that language is most valuable when it is most occult. There are reporters who, in a happy vein — but it must be spontaneous, and not studied — occasionally produce very amusing caricatures by some such means. For example, I some years ago sent a reporter — one who seldom attempted to "make a joke" — to see what was going on in a certain municipal court. He reported one case pretty fully, in which a sailor was the defendant; and as he assured me that "Jack" really did use many nautical terms in the course of his "statement" of the case, I consented to publish the following exaggerated account of the trial, the more readily because it carried its meaning with it:

ASSAULT AND BATTERY. — William Myrtle, a sailor, was before Judge L——, this afternoon, on a charge of assault and battery.

Charles Welde, a clerk in the dry-goods house of F. F. Brown & Co., testified that while walking along Pine Street yesterday afternoon, the sidewalk being somewhat crowded, he accidentally ran against Myrtle; that he tried to step aside to allow defendant to pass; that defendant was unreasonably angry, and used very offensive language; and that when he (witness) remonstrated with him, the defendant struck him a blow with his fist, knocking him down. The face of the prisoner showed some marks of violence, especially in the vicinity of the left cheek-bone.

The judge asked Myrtle if he had counsel—explaining that counsel meant a lawyer to defend him — and he responded that he had not. His Honor then asked him what he had to say concerning the breach of the peace charged against him, when the following remarkable scene ensued, Myrtle beginning:

"I'll tell you, sir —"

"Call him 'Your Honor,'" whispered an officer, who stood at the elbow of the prisoner.

"Your Honor," the prisoner proceeded, "I'll tell you, sir, how it was, sir. I was standin' on my course, runnin' before the wind, and, as I happened to be keepin' a look-out off the port bow —"

"What is that you say," asked his Honor, interrupting the prisoner; "I don't quite understand you."

"Keep trim, sir; keep trim," responded the prisoner, "or you may shift your cargo and lay on your beam-ends. Only don't get a list, and you may batten down my main hatches if I don't —"

"Tut! Such nonsense!" interrupted the judge.

Here an officer stepped up to his Honor, and pointing to the prisoner with a significant gesture, said something in a low tone; whereupon Judge L—— said aloud:

"O — ah, yes; I see. Well, send for the interpreter."

An attendant left the court-room, the prisoner remaining standing and staring about him as though apprehensive that some one had been sent for to come and hang him. But the attendant soon returned, bringing with him a mild-looking man who did not look much like an executioner, but who was no other than Mr. Edmoine, the sworn interpreter of the Court of Common Pleas. When he had taken his position, the judge told the prisoner to go on.

Myrtle brightened up when he perceived that he was not to be immediately hanged, for he seemed to take in the situation, and proceeded:

"Well, sir, seein' I've an old shipmate alongside, I'll tell you. As I was sayin', not keepin' a look-out dead ahead, but havin' an eye out for a sail on the port bow, fear o' bein run down —"

"What is that?" asked his Honor.

"Guarding against a collision with some one approaching on his left, your Honor," explained the interpreter.

"Well?" said the judge, to intimate that the prisoner might proceed.

"You see, sir," resumed the prisoner, "all at once this old craft" — pointing to Mr. Welde — "rounded to and struck me amidships, and —"

"What? He struck you first?" interrupted his Honor, looking inquiringly at the prisoner, then at the interpreter.

"He means," explained the interpreter, "ran against him, the prisoner receiving the accidental shock somewhere about the pit of the stomach."

"Then says I," continued Myrtle, "says I, sir: 'Ship ahoy! Port your helm and run up your mains'l, or I can't clear your bows,' and —"

"Your Honor," put in the interpreter, perceiving that the judge looked puzzled, "he wished to convey the idea to the complainant in this case that he had better turn to the left, and so pass on the prisoner's right."

"But that mainsail?" said the judge, inquiringly.

"Meant," responded Mr. Edmoine, "that the complaining witness should exercise more alacrity in passing, just as a small craft will move faster by setting an additional sail."

"Ah, I see," said his Honor. "Well, Myrtle, proceed. What did he say?"

"Say, sir? Signaled as much as to order me to haul down my colors, and —"

"Gave him to understand," interrupted Mr. Edmoine, "that he must be less aggressive in his manner."

"And what did you say?" queried Judge L——.

"'Look out, there!' says I, 'or you'll get your fore-t'gallants'l carried away —'"

"A threat to knock his hat off, your Honor," put in the interpreter.

"Did he reply to you?" asked the judge.

"Yes, your Honor — wanted me to lower my topgallant yards; so —"

"Keep his hands down," explained Mr. Edmoine.

"An' says I: 'Take a reef in your upper fore-tops'l, or I —'"

"Meant, to keep his tongue more quiet."

"Well?"

"Then, sir, he rigged his spare spars and began to h'ist 'em —"

The judge looked bewildered.

"Evidently," said Mr. Edmoine, "he means that the man rolled up his sleeves slightly and raised his hands."

"So," resumed Myrtle, "says I, 'Look here, old craft, if you don't respond to signals, just look out for your starboard light —'"

"Mind his right eye," said the interpreter.

"Then I just run up my topgallant yards, set spanker, trysails, staysails, jib, flying-jib and jib-boom, and bore down on his starboard bow —"

"Seems that he rushed at him and struck him a blow about the right cheek-bone, I should say," remarked the interpreter.

"And stove a hole below his water-line, so that he filled instantly and went down by the stern, while runnin' up his ensign, union down."

"Knocked the man down, who, it seems, was so alarmed as to call for the police," said the interpreter.

"And," concluded the defendant, "just then a man-o'-war run up alongside, head on, threw out his hawser and made fast to my capstan, and towed me into dock."

"A policeman arrested him and took him to the station-house," explained the interpreter.

"Ah, exactly, I see," said his Honor. "Well, William Myrtle, you probably thought you had some provocation, although the collision between you and the complainant may have been, and probably was, purely accidental on his part. But it is, in any event, necessary that a rebuke should be promptly administered to any one who resorts to violence—any one who, except in self-defense, strikes or lays hands on another. In this view I am supported by a jurist no less eminent than Mr. Justice Blackstone, as well as by distinct statutes of this Commonwealth. In view of the fact, however, that the act appears to have been entirely unpremeditated, the Court will deal with you as leniently as section two of chapter sixty-one of the Revised Statutes will allow. The sentence of the Court is, that you be imprisoned in the county jail for a period of ten days."

"Ay, ay, sir!" responded the sailor, in a hearty voice.

The judge once more looked inquiringly at the interpreter, who said:

"He means he'll go, your Honor."

Thereupon, a "man-of-war" made fast to the "jolly craft," and towed him out into deep water.

Perhaps I cannot more appropriately conclude this chapter on "Slang" than by quoting these verses, written a year or two ago for *Saturday Night*.

OLD GRANDPA'S SOLILOQUY.

It was n't so when I was young—
We used plain language then;
We did n't speak of "them galloots,"
When meanin' boys or men.

5*

When speaking of the nice hand-write
  Of Joe, or Tom, or Bill,
We did it plain—we did n't say,
  "He slings a nasty quill."

An' when we seen a gal we liked,
  Who never failed to please,
We called her pretty, neat an' good,
  But not "about the cheese."

Well, when we met a good old friend,
  We had n't lately seen,
We greeted him, but did n't say,
  "Hello, you old sardine!"

The boys sometimes got mad an' fit;
  We spoke of kicks an' blows;
But now they "whack him on the snoot,"
  Or "paste him on the nose."

Once, when a youth was turned away
  By her he held most dear,
He walked upon his feet—but now
  He "walks off on his ear."

We used to dance, when I was young,
  An' used to call it so;
But now they don't—they only "sling
  The light, fantastic toe."

Of death we spoke in language plain,
  That no one did perplex;
But in these days one does n't die—
  He "passes in his checks."

We praised the man of common sense;
  "His judgment 's good," we said:
But now they say, "Well, that old plum
  Has got a level head!"

It 's rather sad the children now
 Are learnin' all sich talk;
They 've learnt to "chin" instead of chat,
 An' "waltz" instead of walk.

To little Harry, yesterday —
 My grandchild, aged two —
I said, "You love grandpa?" Said he,
 "You bet your boots I do!"

The children bowed to strangers once;
 It is no longer so —
The little girls, as well as boys,
 Now greet you with "Hello!"

Oh, give me back the good old days,
 When both the old and young
Conversed in plain, old-fashioned words,
 And slang was never "slung."

CHAPTER VI.

INTERVIEWING.

INTERVIEWING" is a phase of journalism which, I think, does not either necessarily or properly belong to it. It is of comparatively recent creation, and has already assumed disgusting proportions. I trust that, agreeably to the rule governing the decline of things of rapid growth, its decay will be commensurately rapid, and its end sudden and violent. As an adjunct to journalism, interviewing is out of place. It is little and undignified, placing both the interviewer and the interviewed in a very undesirable attitude before the public. Views which a prominent man may express, in season, on some question in which public attention is largely absorbed, may be published with perfect propriety; but it does seem, to me, little short of audacity on the part of a newspaper to send a reporter to "bore" any man, get him to "say something,"—it may be, without mature reflection,—take down his words in short-hand, as they fall from his lips, and publish them.

As a rule, when it is important that a man's views on any particular subject should be known, the propriety and good taste of sending a reporter to hunt him up, or hunt him down, in his office or parlor, and talk them out of him by inches, are not apparent to me. On the contrary, if the said public man is in a position in which his proposed policy may affect the public welfare, it seems to me that it would be in perfect keeping with his dignity voluntarily to give a statement of his views to the anxious public in "a card" in the newspapers (when no more regular channel is presented); and, in doing so, he would not only appear more dignified than in the attitude of being cross-examined by a reporter, but would thus gain the material advantage of being able to present his thoughts more clearly, by putting them in writing himself, when alone and unbored, and in moments of cool judgment.

But the fact is, many of the so-called "interviews" with public men (if I may be considerately pardoned for exposing the secret, or, rather, fraud on readers of newspapers) are "arranged." I mean that the interviewed party, in the awfulness of his dignity, does not wish to appear in the light of seeking to "put himself right" before the public; and so one of his "friends," for example—sometimes his modest self—arranges with the editor or proprietor of a newspaper to send a reporter "around" at a certain time and "interview" him; and it is a remarkable fact that the reporter always finds the "great man" in his private office, "on time." Then the interview proceeds after the following fashion, as afterward published:

Reporter.—The Hon. Peter Snuggs, I believe?

Hon. Peter Snuggs.—Yes, sir; I have the honor of being that person.

Rep. — I represent the daily *Pryer.*

Hon. P. S.— Ah? Be seated.

Rep. (thanking Hon. P. S., and being seated.)—If I am not intruding, Mr. Snuggs —

Hon. P. S.— Not at all.

Rep. — Then I would like to ask your opinion on a question of great public interest, provided, of course, that you have no objection to having your views published.

Hon. P. S. — What is the subject?

[NOTE (*not* by the reporter). Hon. P. S. knows well enough what the subject is, and has all his answers to the expected queries prepared, and committed to memory.]

Rep. — The subject is one of great delicacy. You are doubtless aware that public attention is just at this time directed to the great question of an increase of the duty on imported raw materials for ladies' chignons?

Hon. P. S. — I cannot be blind to the fact that this question is convulsing the popular mind.

Rep. —You have, no doubt, given the subject much attention?

Hon. P. S. —Well — yes; although I had not thought of giving publicity to my views just at this time. Might not such a course be considered a little premature?

Rep. — Not at all, Mr. Snuggs. The public are breathlessly waiting to hear what you have to say on this great question; and, as some of your political adversaries have undertaken to say what your views are, and so probably placed you in a false light, it is but justice to yourself and to the community that your views should be published, with the stamp of authority.

Hon. P. S. — If I thought so — (hesitating.)

Rep. — You can rely on it, I assure you, Mr. Snuggs.

Hon. P. S. — (After a moment's thought.) — Then the question would seem to be as to whether I should regard any increase in the duty on the materials referred to as deleterious?

Rep. — Exactly. Would it, in your opinion, be bad public policy to increase the duty on those materials thirty-three and one-third per cent., as proposed?

Hon. P. S. — (Emphatically.) — I have no doubt of it.

Rep. — Do you think, then, that the proposed increase of duty on the materials for this important — I might say, indispensable — article of female attire would place it beyond the reach of many excellent women, and that on that account their equanimity of temper would be disturbed, and so their usefulness impaired?

Hon. P. S. — I do. Nothing seems to me so inimical to the public welfare as any measure calculated to irritate the ladies, especially the married ladies, and so to involve the peace of homes. On the tranquillity of households and hearth-stones depends the future growth of our population, the numerical strength of posterity; yes, and the morals of the rising generation, who, if brought up in the midst of domestic broils — which could not fail to be largely augmented by the infamous proposition largely to increase the duty on raw materials for the manufacture of chignons — would lose their respect for women and their appreciation of the beauties of domestic peace, and arrive at manhood familiar with scenes of anger and violence. The proposed measure, sir, if adopted, would be little less than an enormity!

Rep. — Do you think it will prevail?

Hon. P. S. — (Thoughtfully.) — I can scarcely think it will. I know there is much political corruption in these days, and that a large moneyed influence will be brought to bear in favor of the measure; but I am not yet prepared to believe that the American people can have become so nearly lost to all sense of patriotism — can be capable of so ignoring that spirit that fired the hearts of 'Seventy-six — as quietly to submit to an increase of thirty-three and one-third per cent. in the duty on raw materials for chignons! No, sir, (excitedly.) — No, Sir-ee!

Rep. — Then I understand you to say that you have no doubt of the efficacy of a liberal supply of chignons — and everything else that the ladies desire — to preserve the peace of families?

Hon. P. S. — Emphatically.

Rep. — And that you still have an amount of faith in the patriotism and manly independence of the people that justifies you in offering the confident assurance that this iniquitous measure — the proposed large increase in the duty on raw materials for chignons — is not likely to prevail?

Hon. P. S. — Em—phatically.

Rep. — Thank you. I trust that in this intrusion —

Hon. P. S. — I beg that you will not think it an intrusion, and I assure you that I do not so regard it.

Rep. — Then I have not seriously disturbed you in the exercise of your arduous public duties?

Hon. P. S. — Not at all. (Very earnestly.) Not — at — all.

Rep. — Thank you.

Hon. P. S. — Not at all. If, in giving my views to the public at this time, through the excellent medium of the *Pryer*, I have benefited that public and given any material assurance of a probability of continued domestic peace, I shall only be too happy.

Rep. — (Rising.) — Thank you. Good-morning.

Hon. P. S. — Good-morning.

And so this "interview" is terminated, and so published, and so the views of the "great man" — who, by the way, "at the urgent solicitation of numerous friends," has consented to run for a re-nomination — become known to that breathlessly waiting public.

It would be unjust, however, to assert that *all* interviews are pre-arranged, as in the case of the eminent Snuggs. Reporters do sometimes call upon public men, unexpectedly to the latter, and entirely without any collusion with "friends." As an example of the improvised interview, I cite a case which occurred some time before the autumn of 1874. A New York reporter called on President Grant, and the following was the result:

Reporter. — Your Excellency, I have come to ask you, if the inquiry be deemed pertinent, what your views are on the third-term question. The press —

President Grant. — I have nothing to say on the subject.

Rep. — Well — I thought, as the subject occupies a large share of public attention —

P. G. — I have nothing to say on the subject.

Rep. — At least, I might be pardoned for asking you if, in case —

P. G. — I have nothing to say on the subject.

Rep. — I was merely going to say that in case you had good reasons for not wishing to commit —

P. G. — I have nothing to say on the subject.

Rep. — Of course, your Excellency, I had no notion of being importunate, but thought that —

P. G. — I have nothing to say on the subject.

Rep. — I trust, your Excellency, that this will not be deemed an intrusion?

P. G. — I have nothing to say on the subject.

Rep. — At least nothing could have been further —

P. G. — I have nothing to say on the subject.

Rep. — (Going.) — Your Excellency, I am, in any event, glad that I have had the pleasure of —

P. G. — I have nothing to say on the subject.

Rep. — (Pleasantly and politely.) — Good-morning.

P. G. — I have nothing to say on the subject.

CHAPTER VII.

JENKINS.

IF I have to condemn the practice of "interviewing," as unworthy of decent journalism, where shall I find language in which to express the detestation and loathing with which I look upon "Jenkinsism"? Of all the questionable work a reporter has ever been called upon to do, Jenkins reporting is the lowest and meanest. If a reporter is called upon by the managers of the paper he is connected with — proprietors who mistake the mission of a newspaper — to do such work, and if he has no relish for it, he is to be pitied; if he has a relish for it, he is to be despised. A writer with such tastes as would make it agreeable to him to expend his "talents" in describing the petticoat of a bride or the coat-tails of a bridegroom, or the watch-chain and whiskers of some corporation autocrat, no more deserves to be rated as a journalist than a painter and glazier deserves to be classed with the Rembrandt Peales, the Edwin Landseers, the Michael Angelos, and is not one-fortieth part so much to be respected!

I do not enjoy the privilege of knowing personally any so-called journalist of the Jenkins type, but I can readily fancy a picture of the Jenkins reporter, as he might appear on so important an occasion as the marriage of Miss Lucinda, daughter of the Hon. Mr. Buggles, the wealthy contractor (formerly a hod-carrier), to Mr. Ichabod Snubbs, son of the opulent and princely speculator in railroad stocks (who, by the way, began his useful business career as the sole proprietor of a peanut-stand). I can imagine Jenkins, as he stands in a thoughtful attitude in the full glare of the parlor chandelier. He is a man of small stature, and his hair is equitably and exquisitely parted in the middle. He has little reddish eyes, peculiarly adapted to views of domestic scenery as observable through key-holes; and a small, turned-up nose, whose sharpness is suggestive of its adaptability to prying into hidden things that concern neither him nor the public. Just beneath that penetrating nose a fragile mustache struggles for existence, like a meager tuft of weak and fading moss that is starving on the face of a barren rock; while his unplethoric cheek (which, however, is ample in a figurative sense) is fringed with a straggling whisker. His whole aspect is one of strangely-mingled self-importance and imbecility.

He is in his holiday attire, Jenkins is; and he struts about with an air of greatness that even the bride's father, the wealthy ex-hod-carrier, would scarcely dare to assume. His polished boots shine and glitter as they shuffle over the Brussels carpet of the parlor, and glisten under the gas-light of the halls and stairways, as he glides about, like a freshly-incarnated imp, peering into bed-chambers and poking his nose into closets. I can fancy him, in his tour of inspection, entering the bridal-chamber itself, noting the wall-paper, the ceiling, the floor, the gas-burners, and, above all, the interesting couch; closely scrutinizing the lace-ornamented pillow-cases, the soft blankets, the snowy coverlets and sheets; and even stooping reverently and looking under the bed, as though, like many a timid dame on the point of retiring, to see if "there 's a man under it."

Then I see him in the presence of the "happy pair," pencil and note-book in hand, turning about the lappel of the bridegroom's coat, counting the buttons, then gently lifting the tails to examine the silken linings. I see him gaze intently upon the snowy linen handkerchief of the bridegroom, as the latter gracefully draws it from his pocket at such seasons as its usefulness cannot be ignored, carefully examining the corners and noting the handsomely-worked initials. I can fancy his running his fingers daintily through the fragile textures of the bride's apparel, carefully examining her from head to foot, and making notes to be written up in some such shape as this:

The bride's dress was simply elegant. The front breadth and first gores were cut to fit the figure closely, and had no trimming on them, but at the sides seams were cut in battlements. and lapped over on to the back widths. These formed a very long train, which latter was finished on the bottom by a side-plaited flounce. The chatelaine corsage was cut high, with Marie Antoinette sleeves, trimmed with satin plaitings and lace flounces. These flouncings were made to match the over-dress, as was also the lace garniture of the corsage, and formed a part of it. The dress itself was not the ordinary point which is really intended to do service as a shawl, but a full-trained skirt, falling to the hem of the satin dress, and gracefully looped with orange-blossoms and stephanotis. The same flowers formed a half-wreath on the corsage, and completed the ornamentation of the sleeves. The vail of filmy tulle that finished this simply elegant costume, fell to the dress hem, and was fastened by an aigrette of white blossoms, from which a pendent wreath outlined the left side of the vail throughout its entire length. Her ornaments were diamonds presented by her brother-in-law, Mr. Street-Contractor Overbust, and in her hand she carried an elegant fan of natural flowers, tuberoses and stephanotis being the principal ones. The other side, upon which they were mounted, was of white satin, covered with Duchesse point. The hair was parted on the side, and rolled in a twist, *a la Grec.*

Then must follow a description of "the presents," *so* interesting to the news-reading public, after about the following style:

A diamond cross and ear-rings, from Mr. Peter Munderly. The solitaire ear-rings are very handsome, and the stones in the cross clear and of great size.

A flower-stand, in crystal and silver, from Gen. (of militia) Buglehorn.

A silver card-rack, designed like an open oyster, from Mr. and Mrs. Stumps.

Two bronze figures (mantel ornaments), from Major Wagontire.

A dozen silver butter-dishes and a dozen silver salt-cellars, from Mr. and Mrs. Blim.

A set of silver ice-cream spoons and ladle, from Hon. Snooks Jones.

A costly pearl necklace, from Mrs. Shimsham.

An enameled watch, chain and locket, from Col. Oldbumm.

A heavy gold chain and locket, from Capt. Fitz-Burns Snobbs.

A gold necklace, from Mr. J. Hardpan Smith.

A brooch and ear-rings, Roman mosaic, set in Etruscan gold, from Miss Blubberly.

An inlaid inkstand, from Gen. Snakes.

Silver inkstand, from Miss Susanicus Windowsash.

No one will accuse me of exaggeration in the above, when I append the following description of the wardrobe of a bride who, in 1874, married the son of a wealthy upstart, and which description, given by the giant-minded Jenkins, was published, I blush to say, in hundreds of newspapers in this country:

The white wear composed one dozen *robes de nuit* of fine linen, silk, Paris muslin, fine jaconet and Lonsdale cambric, and one dozen of the best and smoothest long cloth; one dozen linen and cambric and grass-cloth chemises, and one dozen ordinary fine Wamsutta; one dozen linen and lawn and muslin embroidery corset covers, and two dozen pairs of underwear of the same materials. There are three dozen white underskirts and four very elegant *robes de soir*. The bridal corset was made of a piece of the white satin of the bridal dress. It had one hundred bones in it, and was stitched with blue silk! A white silk corset was covered with a delicate tissue of Mechlin lace. A blue satin corset, stitched in white, and a pale lavender stitched in blue, were among the orders, and a lace coutil completed the list. Sachets of costly and delicate perfumes were stitched into each of the corsets, and lent a delicious odor. The three dozen skirts spoken of did not include a single trained or full dress jupon. Puffings and embroidery alternated with tucks and ruffles. It took a whole week to laundry them, and four women working every moment with fluting scissors and embroidery irons. The grand *robe de nuit* was a wonderful garment, made of Paris muslin, grass-cloth, and the finest Swiss embroidery, every stitch of the work in it being done by hand. The hosiery comprised morning, dinner, reception, carriage, promenade, and evening hose. There are silk stockings in Bayadere stripes, pearl color and pink, blue and white, gray and blue, and other mode tints, costing $12 per pair. Another lot of useful articles of apparel were of the Turkish pattern, buttoning just below the knee, and with ribbons to match.

In a country like this, a country of republican institutions, a country where born rulers and titled families are unknown, must we grovel so low as to worship not only a rich bride, but also the toes of her stockings? For shame! Let the respectable press of the country decry this hideous flunkeyism. Shades of our grandmothers! I never so thirsted to see the plain old-fashioned women of other days in their home-made flannel dresses, as when I read the smaller than puerile jargon I have just quoted! O Jenkins, Jenkins, Jenkins! Get thee to a cemetery.

CHAPTER VIII.

THE EDITORIAL ROOMS.

THE owner or "proprietor" of a newspaper is not always the editor, either in name or in fact. He may be the business manager, devoting his whole time to the counting-room; he may be his own foreman of the composing-room; he may be his own Managing Editor's assistant; he may be the very reverse of a literary man, or editor, with but a vague and imperfect notion of the mysteries of the paste-pot and scissors. Yet, by virtue of his ownership, he is The Editor, generally; and, more still, he dictates the abstract sentiments and general tone of his paper, as he certainly has a right to do. He of course employs a Managing Editor,—unless he acts as such himself,—who is the supreme authority in the editorial rooms; who says what shall go into the columns of the paper and what shall not; who says how this shall be done and how that shall not be done; who organizes and reorganizes his department; who engages his assistants, agreeing with them as to their salaries, and who also dissevers their connection with the paper whenever, in his judgment, their services are of insufficient value or their places may be filled by more efficient men.

On the other hand, the owner or one of the owners of a paper is often The Editor in fact, as well as by courtesy. He writes for, "works on," the paper; but, as he cannot give his attention to every detail, he, too, employs a Managing Editor, thus leaving his own mind more free for the preparation of elaborate editorials, which often require much research, involving careful examination of voluminous statistics, as well as much thought. The Editor himself usually writes the leaders, or some of them, when he can, but has a Managing Editor who can readily do it when he himself is absent, ill, or not in the mood for writing. Horace Greeley, for example, was The Editor of the New York *Tribune*, as well as one of its proprietors; so was George D. Prentice, of the Louisville *Journal;* so was Henry J. Raymond, of the New York *Times;* so is Charles A. Dana, of the New York *Sun;* Manton Marble, of the *World;* "Sam" Bowles, of the Springfield *Republican.*

Before treating of the details of editorial work, — which I ought to be able to give from my own experience, — I shall again quote briefly from Mr. Cummings's sketches of the inside workings of the New York *Tribune*, published a few years ago in *Packard's Monthly*.

Young (John Russell Young, at that time the Managing Editor of the *Tribune*) is a strict disciplinarian. He runs the editorial department like a machine. Every clog strikes its groove with punctual regularity. When he is absent, his duties fall on Mr. John R. G. Hassard. If Hassard is missing, Mr. Cummings takes the manager's chair; and so perfect does everything jibe, that if all the editors were absent, the oldest reporter, like the senior sergeant of a company destitute of commissioned officers, would take charge. An editorial council is held in the Managing Editor's room every day, between the hours of 1 and 2 P. M. Mr. Young presides. When all are seated, Mr. Young nervously dances around his desk for forty seconds, and then dumps on the table a basket piled with manuscripts, memoranda and newspaper clippings. While these are being assorted a running fire of gossip springs up, and jokes fly about the table. The pile being assorted, business begins. Mr. Young picks up a newspaper slip, looks at it a second, taps it with a scurvy pair of scissors, and says:

"Now, this Associated Press dispatch is evidently a lie."

Here the slip is crumpled up, rolled briskly into a little ball between the palms of his hands, and then tossed into the waste-basket. A copy of the *World* goes spinning across the table to Cummings, with the remark:

"I think the *World* beat you in its account of that murder this morning."

"That's very probable; but we beat them on the fire and a murder in Weehawken," Cummings replies.

Young here seizes a pile of manuscript and hands it over to Hassard, without a word. On the back of the pile is written:

"Mr. H., please read, and report. J. R. Y."

Another glance at a memorandum, and McEwen is told to telegraph Smalley, in London, to send a man to Roumania immediately, to watch the insurrection there. "And ask * * * *, in Constantinople, if there is any truth in the report from Washington that the Turks are about to withdraw from Crete. Use the cipher."

Both orders are directly filled, a bell-cord is jerked, and in one minute a *Tribune* boy is trotting to the telegraph office with despatches for London and Constantinople in his pocket. A pile of foreign letters, ranging from Chili to Japan, *via* Europe, is tossed to Schem, accompanied with the words:

"Oh, Schem, I want an editorial from you to-night on Louis Napoleon's suppression of *La Lanterne!*"

Each editor is then asked for his report of the previous day's labor, after which suggestions from every one present are in order. The meeting is then dismissed. The editors pass out the door, through the city apartment into the main editorial room, and drift to their desks. In ten minutes a half dozen pens are vigorously scratching out ideas for the next day's issue. The child is in embryo, and will be born in the morning. Everything will move with the regularity of clock-work. The editorial room resembles a lurking-place for owls; the ceiling is low, the floor is dirty; a dozen rickety cane-bottomed arm-chairs, with high backs, three cases filled with books of reference, ten old desks, spattered with ink, two cabinets, a chained copy of the *Tribune* Almanac, complete, and a dozen old pictures, give an idea of a rushing business, with an occasional dash at the fine arts."

Having thus quoted from Mr. Cummings's description of the editorial rooms of a representative daily paper, I may next devote a chapter to the routine work of an editor.

CHAPTER IX.

EDITORS' WORK.

COME with "us" and see "a day's work" on an afternoon or evening paper. We are going right now to our office. We don't saunter along like aristocratic people who never think of breakfasting before ten or eleven o'clock. We work. We must have our breakfast by seven, and if the big church-bell near the office strikes eight while our feet are on the third flight of stairs, we feel that we are not a moment too early. Our usual time is eight, and we have exactly as much work to do as we can do between that hour and ten, at which time the "outside" goes to press. If we are five minutes late, we feel the extra "hurry" all day.

We enter the sanctum, take off our coat and hat and hang them in a gloomy closet, whence we take a lighter coat, of dilapidated appearance, and put it on. This is done in five seconds, after which we drop into our chair, at a long, flat writing-table in the center of the room, on which are numerous exchanges, all neatly spread out from their two or three final folds and laid in a pile. This has been done by the Boy, who also removed the wrappers; and he now stands at one end of the table, waiting for the day's active business to begin.

Now, sit down, spectator, and watch us; but don't say a word to interrupt us. We can't bear a bore.

"Where 'n the devil 's my scissors?" we sing out, with no time for correct verbal syntax.

Before us are some copy-paper; three inkstands, one with no ink in it; a paste-pot, freshly filled by that Boy; three red pen-holders, only one of which has a pen in it; a whole pencil and a piece of one only one inch long; a clean blotter, one less clean, one nearly used up, and one hideously defaced; a paper-cutter; some paper-weights; but — no scissors. Who could edit a paper ten minutes without scissors!

"Here!"

It is the Boy who speaks, and who, starting as if from a dream, dashes our scissors upon the table before us. He has been abstractedly clipping his finger-nails with that sacred instrument!

We scowl at him, then — go to work.

Not at writing. An editor is not always writing. True, we take from our drawer an editorial headed, "The Rapid Development of Science," and send it up to the composing-room by the Boy; but that was written last night, when we dropped in, long after the last edition of our paper went to press. Our first work this morning is paste-pot-and-scissors work; it is to compile a column headed:

ACCIDENT AND CRIME.

A portion of it has already been prepared, from late exchanges of yesterday, and we must now add the freshest items to the department, and so complete it for our outside. We first run our scissors through a paragraph relating to an accident of which we yesterday prepared a condensed account. We see by it that the victim has since died of his injuries.

"Sonny!" we sing out, and the Boy starts.

"Run up to the foreman and ask him to send down a proof of the 'Accident and Crime' I gave him last night."

The Boy flies away on his errand. When the proof comes down we shall simply place a caret (∧) at the end of the paragraph in question, and write on the white margin something like this: "The unfortunate man died a few hours after the accident."

We have an exchange in our hand, which we perceive to be the Reading (Pa.) *Eagle*, and in it we find this paragraph :

RAILROAD ACCIDENT.

AN AGED COUPLE INSTANTLY KILLED ON THE EAST PENNSYLVANIA RAILROAD.

This morning, about fifteen minutes past 7 o'clock, a very sad accident occurred at "Bernhart's Crossing," near Engel's Hotel, Muhlenberg township, on the line of the East Pennsylvania Railroad. Henry Leitheiser and Susan, his wife, both aged about sixty years, who resided about a mile this side of "Blind Hartman's tavern," were on their way to Reading with a load of potatoes, and they reached the railroad just as the mail train No. 2 came along, the engine of which collided with their vehicle. The engine struck the forepart of the wagon, completely demolishing it, and threw the aged couple upon the railroad and instantly killed them. Their clothing was caught by the car-boxes, which whirled them around and dragged them ten or fifteen feet, during which the aged lady had an arm taken off by the wheels passing over it, and her husband had his leg run over at the ankle. The scalp of Mrs. Leitheiser was also removed during the accident. The engineer immediately stopped the train and backed to the scene of the accident, when Mr. and Mrs. Leitheiser were both found dead, and the horse which had been attached to the vehicle was lying beside the road, with life also extinct. Within half an hour after the accident an undertaker conveyed the bodies back to the former home of the deceased. It is stated that not the slightest blame is attached, on account of the accident, to either engineer or conductor, as the usual signal was given upon approaching the crossing. A man by the name of Paul, and Henry Leitheiser, a son of the deceased, were within a quarter of a mile of the crossing, and they distinctly heard the whistle of the engine, but the aged couple were partially deaf, and evidently did not hear the signal.

This is an important "Accident" item, and we have not had it by telegraph. But then Reading is, for example, distant from us, and here the accident will not possess the same interest as in Reading, near which city it occurred. Besides, we glean scores of such items from our exchanges from all parts of the country, and all must be condensed. Having read the paragraph hastily, we do not attempt to clip and paste any part of it, because in this case we can say all about it that we have space to say more quickly by writing it. So we clutch our pen savagely, dip it in the ink, and, after writing "Accident, etc.," on the upper right-hand corner of the first sheet of copy-paper, and drawing a curved stroke around it, so as to fence it off from the actual "copy," we thus rapidly condense the paragraph:

Henry Leitheiser and wife, each sixty years old, were instantly killed yesterday morning, while crossing the track of the East Pennsylvania Railroad, in a market-wagon, in the vicinity of Reading, by being run over by a mail-train, and their bodies shockingly mangled. Both were partially deaf, and did not hear the engineer's signal.

We glance hurriedly over the paper, and seeing nothing more in it that we want for this department, throw it aside, and take up the Washington *Star*, of yesterday, in which we see an interesting paragraph of twenty lines, with a full head and sub-head. This is it:

TOO LIGHT A PUNISHMENT.

A MAN WHO SETS A BULL-DOG ON A CHILD.

Yesterday, between 4 and 5 o'clock P. M., quite an excitement was caused at the corner of Twelfth and D Streets, by the savage attack of a bull-dog upon a little girl. It seems this little girl, with a companion, were crossing Twelfth Street, when they were met by Bill Coleman, colored, who was leading the dog by means of a stout chain attached to his collar. In passing, Coleman set his dog upon the little girls to frighten them, at the same time giving out the slack in the chain, when the dog sprang upon this girl, and nearly tore her left ear off, and lacerated the back part of her head shockingly, at the same time, with its powerful paws, tearing off nearly all her clothing. Coleman was arraigned in the Police Court this morning, charged with assault and battery on Rachel Coleman, to which he pleaded guilty. After the hearing of several witnesses, the judge sentenced him to six months in jail.

This must also be boiled down for the department of "Accident and Crime," and we thus do it:

In Washington City, on Tuesday, a colored man named Coleman, in mere sport, set a bull-dog upon a little girl who was passing along the street, and the brute shockingly lacerated her head, tearing her left ear completely off. A Washington paper alludes to the case as one of unusual atrocity, and thinks Coleman received too light a punishment, as he was sentenced yesterday morning to only six months' imprisonment.

We next take up a Western paper, in which we find a column "local," with the following head-lines:

SAD ACCIDENT!

SUDDEN AND VIOLENT DEATH OF A WELL-KNOWN CITIZEN.

It begins thus:

It is with pain that the announcement is made of a sad bereavement that has befallen this community and one of its most esteemed families. Hon. William Martin —

We run over the whole article, which, by the way, embraces a brief sketch of the life of the deceased, and find we can thus succinctly dispose of it:

Hon. William Martin, a prominent citizen of Dayton, Ohio, and an ex-member of Congress, fell from the eastern abutment of the railroad bridge over the Miami River, a short distance west of that city, on Wednesday, and was instantly killed. He was nearly seventy years old.

Just now the door opens, and the Boy hurries in, saying:

"Mr. Craig" (the foreman) "says he'd like to have the rest of the 'Accidents' as soon as possible."

"In five minutes, tell him."

The Boy vanishes, and our scissors dive into the local columns of the New York *Sun*, and come out with a dozen-line nonpareil local, with a top head, which we thus dispose of, very coolly appropriating a few lines of the *Sun's* own language, a liberty we do not hesitate to take, because it is reciprocal, and that journal will get even with us inside of a week:

~~A POLICEMAN ON THE RAMPAGE.~~

according to ~~Several complaints of brutality are lodged against~~ ~~Roundsman~~ Roger O'Halloran, ~~of the Leonard~~ *a New York* *the Sun, he* "a ~~Street police.~~ ~~A~~ few nights ago, while crazy drunk, ~~he~~ ran along Greenwich Street, clubbing indiscriminately men, women and children. ~~On returning~~ *policeman, is* to the police-station with a respectable young man, *in trouble, for* whom he had beaten without provocation, he was suspended from duty by Captain Petty. Another *the reason* accusation against him is that he beat an elderly woman as she was quietly entering her house, *that,* knocking out several of her teeth."

Well, anything for the sake of peace.

In a few hours this item will appear as a compact paragraph, in five lines of brevier type, without a head, and looking as fresh and clear as though it had never been so shockingly defaced.

Next, we dispose of four stickfuls, thus:

Hon. J. Smith, ex-Mayor of Smithfield, R. I., was almost instantly killed near that city, on Monday, by being thrown from his carriage.

Next, we find in a Philadelphia paper a thirty-line paragraph, with the side head, "A PHYSICIAN SHOT." We have not room for the particulars, but discover that, owing to the proper construction of the paragraph, we can use several contiguous lines of the "reprint," and thus, by clipping them and pasting them on, — the work of four seconds, — save an amount of writing that would require perhaps half a minute. Then our paragraph is formed thus:

~~A PHYSICIAN SHOT.~~ — On Tuesday morning, Dr. Wevill, living at No. 1014 South Third Street, *Philadelphia,* *in the knee* was shot ∧ by Christian Hansen, residing at the north-west corner of Fourth and Canal Streets*, while attending upon the latter's wife Hansen professed to be jealous, but Dr.*

Wevill, whose leg has since been amputated, and who lies in a critical condition, declares it to be a case of attempted black-mailing, in which he alleges "both Hansen and his wife were concerned."

We find half-a-dozen additional paragraphs relating to crimes or accidents, in various exchanges coming to us from towns and cities scattered from the Atlantic to the Pacific, — paragraphs of from six to twenty lines each, — and of each we make a paragraph of from two to three lines; and so, in a minute or two more we have completed the department of "Accident and Crime," by adding in these tiny paragraphs the essence of what we find headed, "Attempted Murder;" "Shocking Affair;" "Church Robbed;" "Forgery;" "Danger from Gas — Eight Children Nearly Smothered;" "Horrible Casualty — a Man's Arm Wrenched Off;" "The Boston Bank Robbery;" and, "Suicide."

"Sonny!"

The Boy snatches up the copy, and flies up-stairs with it to the foreman, who could not well afford to wait sixty seconds longer for it.

We clutch another exchange and our scissors.

The terrible clatter of the Boy's feet is heard on the stairs, as he falls, rather than steps, down from the composing-room. Then he bursts into the room.

"Mr. Craig wants two more stickfuls of 'Frivolities!'"

That 's the funny column, outside. Thought we left enough last night. No matter: in the exchange before us we see a column headed, "This and That." We know what this (and that) means. We run over nearly the whole column — for two reasons: we want to get two stickfuls of the best in it; and we want to avoid clipping anything we have before published at any time during the last six or eight years. Of course, a bit of memory is necessary, but that is one of the requisite qualifications of a newspaper man. In one minute six or seven small funny paragraphs are hurriedly pasted on a bit of copy-paper, marked "Friv." in the right-hand upper corner, and the Boy seizes it and again "races" up to the composing-room.

That Boy! In our calm moments we could not find it in our heart to give him even a cross look. He works for three dollars a week; he is here at seven in the morning, to dust things, to build a fire in the stove, when necessary, and to open exchanges and see that paste-pots and ink-stands are filled, and that things generally are in readiness for the terrible Editor; he flies up and down those stairs one hundred and forty-six times a day; he runs out when he "must not be gone a minute," to buy us a cigar; and so his every day goes by. If we do occasionally hand him a matter of ten cents "for himself," we feel mean at the thought that, if we could afford it, it ought to be twenty-five.

We have, down to this time, read and "slashed" six columns of "print," and boiled it down into one; and the clicking types up-stairs are rushing it into a uniform shape.

Now, spectator, you have seen how we have "done" the department of "Accident and Crime." Next, for the "outside" we must get up a department of "State News." It is very true that we did some of it last night, but we must do three-quarters of a column yet. We rapidly select from our pile of exchanges all the papers published within the State in which we are at work, and, as in our "Accident-and-Crime" work, take their local departments and boil down from six to ten columns of "Youthful Burglars," "Immense Potatoes," "Fires," "Accidental Shootings," "Deaths from Injuries," "Escapes from the County Jails," "Mysterious Disappearances," "Meetings of the Grand Juries," and "Sad Occurrences." We make nearly a column of them, all in paragraphs of from three to seven lines; — and the boiling process has occupied fifteen or twenty minutes of our time.

Ah! . We promised to "notice" two new books to-day; and as we want the book-notices to go outside, that we may have the more space inside for editorials, telegraphic and other fresh news, we snatch up the first one and consult its title-page. It is "Topographic Views of the Lower Mississippi." It is published by Messrs. Sew & So, done in attractive form, and is a 12mo of over 400 pages. These facts we quickly note on a sheet of copy-paper, in a corner of which we have already written "Literary;" then we place a thumb on the edges of the leaves and make them "flutter" from beginning to end, our eye not catching a single word. Then, more calmly, we open it at the middle, and read the words:

"— most beautiful and fertile, with wide-extended —"

We close the book, and add to what we have already written:

The work gives a graphic picture of the Lower Mississippi, with its rich cotton-fields and tobacco and sugar plantations; its level plains; its beautiful tributaries and wonderful bayous, where the fat and sluggish alligator basks from day to day, half sleeping, half shaded from the almost tropic sun. The work is written in charming style, its descriptive pages being especially fine, while it contains many interesting statistics compiled from accurate surveys, and other trustworthy sources.

The second book is a new novel, by a distinguished author with whose style we are already familiar; and, having written its title, name of its publisher, and mentioned its size and mechanical appearance, we dispose of the body of the work as we did that of "Topographic Views of the Lower Mississippi."

The Boy suddenly appears at our elbow, like a very Mephistophiles.

"Mr. Craig wants to know if you can send him four stickfuls of 'Miscellaneous,' in two or three little pieces."

We always have in a drawer a few miscellaneous selections that will "keep," that are "good at any time," and we hand the Boy two—one headed, "New Use for Petroleum," and the other, "Scientific View of the Geysers." Together with these, we hand the Boy the copy of our book-notices, completed in five minutes.

It is now half-past nine; we have examined thirty-three newspapers; cut out of them thirteen columns and boiled them down to six times their strength and one-sixth of their former volume; and now all the matter for the outside is prepared and "in hand," and the foreman can "go to press" with the outside forms *at* ten o'clock. He would, by the way, die of a broken heart if any miserable circumstance should detain him as much as three minutes beyond that time.

But our day's work is scarcely begun.

In our paper we have a column of "Political Notes," giving the opinions of the press, with an occasional remark of our own. We must prepare that department next, and to that end we hastily select from the heap of exchanges, and lay them in a pile by themselves, the New York *Herald*, *World*, *Tribune*, *Times*, *Sun*, *Express*, *Evening Post*, and *Journal of Commerce*, the Boston *Post*, *Transcript*, *Advertiser*, *Journal*, *Herald*, *Traveller*, and *Times*, the Springfield *Republican*, the Brooklyn *Eagle*, the Portland *Argus* and *Press*, the Albany *Journal* and *Argus*, the Rochester *Democrat* and *Union*, the Missouri *Republican*, the St. Louis *Democrat*, the Louisville *Courier-Journal*, the Detroit *Free Press*, the Cincinnati *Commercial*, *Gazette* and *Enquirer*, the Philadelphia *Press*, *Age* and *Inquirer*, the

Chicago *Times* and *Tribune*, the Washington *Chronicle* and *Republican*, the San Francisco *Bulletin*, *Examiner* and *Alta California*, the Sacramento *Union* and *Record*, the Virginia City (Nev.) *Enterprise*, the Milwaukee *News*, the Cleveland *Plaindealer*, the Indianapolis *Herald*, the Buffalo *Express*, the Pittsburg *Commercial*, *Post* and *Gazette*, the Baltimore *American* and *Sun*, the Concord (N. H.) *Patriot*, the Worcester (Mass.) *Spy*, the Providence *Journal*, the Richmond *Inquirer*, the New Orleans *Picayune*, the Mobile *Register*, the Charleston *News-and-Courier*, the Memphis *Appeal* and *Avalanche*, the Harrisburg *Patriot*, *Harper's Weekly*, the *Graphic*, the *Ohio State Journal*, the Uniontown (Pa.) *Genius*, the Wheeling *Intelligencer*, the Toledo *Blade*, the Sandusky *Register*, and one or two other newspapers of marked ability that give much of their attention to political matters.

The New York *Herald* has a leader on "The Destiny of Cesarism." We run over it like lightning, dash our scissors into the middle of it, and cut out ten lines that within themselves contain a pointed opinion or sentiment. We paste it at the top of a sheet of copy-paper, fencing off the word "Political" in a corner, to guide the foreman; make a dash at the end of the extract and write immediately after it, New York *Herald*, drawing a line under the name of the paper so that it may be set up in *italic*.

Next, we seize the Springfield *Republican*, "Sam" Bowles's paper, and clip a four-line editorial remark. It also has half a column of political notes, original and selected, and from them we select three stickfuls in five paragraphs, giving proper credit in each case, as we did in the case of the New York *Herald*.

We dive into the heart of a column-article of the New York *Tribune*, on "Free Trade," and snatch out eight lines; dart into a leader in the *World*, on "The Condition of the Cotton

States," and pluck out a summary of about half a stickful; from the Missouri *Republican's* leader on "The Rise and Growth of Parties" we take a thoughtful paragraph of a dozen lines; and fifty burning words from the New York *Sun's* "Queer State of Things at the National Capital;" and thus we go through them all like an arrow flying from the bow-string.

In the midst of this, while we are fairly bending over our table beneath the weight of our heavy work, a coatless compositor, with shirt-sleeves rolled up to his elbows, a stick half full of type in his left hand, and a sheet of our manuscript, all blackened and smeared, in his right, touches our shoulder, and says:

"Mr. ——, I could n't make that word out, for the life of me." [He points to one of our words, which at first almost puzzles even us.] "It is n't 'constitution,' it is n't 'consolation,' it can't be 'consideration,' it——"

"'Constellation,'" we interrupt, as the light suddenly breaks upon us; and the printer rushes up-stairs, while we bow to our work again.

This is not all of the departments. We must have a third of a column of "Personals." We select and condense them, as we did the items for the other departments, — "only more so," — getting a two-line item from a column report of a speech by Hon. Zebulon Smith, and a three-line item from a half column account of the marriage of Gen. Baldhead, etc.; and in the midst of this work we are interrupted by the Boy, who hands us a revise of an editorial on "The Darien Ship-Canal Project," which "went over" from yesterday.

"Mr. Kenyon," he says, meaning the proof-reader, "says there's something wrong there," — pointing to a note of interrogation in the margin, — "thinks there's an 'out.'"

We study it attentively for two seconds, and wonder what we could have meant when we wrote such meaningless stuff.

"Bring down the copy,—or, wait. Never mind. I see it now."

We discover that two words, as important to the article as the character of "Hamlet" is to the play of "Hamlet," have been omitted,—probably in the manuscript itself,—and we write them in the margin, indicate where they belong, by means of the simple and useful caret, glance over the proof, and send it up.

What comes next? "Amusements." Last night we visited two of the principal theaters, and saw two "stars" at important stages of the plays. There are several other theaters in the city, but with nothing special "on the boards" just now. So, for them we merely rely on the morning papers, to see that nothing unusual happened, and that there was no change of programme, and under the head of "Amusements" we write a third of a column of notices. We write that at the A—— Theater, where one of the stars is playing nightly, the house was packed; that Miss X—— was greeted with the usual warm bursts of applause; that she did a fine piece of acting in the crying scene of the second act, but that we think she scarcely did herself justice in the moonlight scene of the third act, although she played her part well; and that she was handsomely supported by the regular company. In a similar manner, we dispose of the B—— Theater, where the celebrated Mr. Y—— is playing "Macbeth." Then, consulting the morning papers, we write that the C——, D——, F——, and G—— Theaters, mentioning each one in a separate paragraph, are nightly crowded, the audiences never tiring of "Humpty-Dumpty," "Our American Cousin," "Colleen Bawn," and "The Black Crook," played respectively at these theaters.

Then we make up a little department of "FIRES," with a small-cap side-head.

That is not all. We have a department of "Various Matters," culled from the morning papers—items of general interest, referring to divers subjects, local and foreign, some of which came by telegraph last night. *As* telegraphic news, they are of no use to us; so we boil them down, making the following paragraph of a long dispatch describing an extensive fire and the loss of two lives:

> The M—— Hotel, in High Street, Columbus, Ohio, was entirely burned last night, and two chamber-maids, who could not escape from their room on the upper floor, perished in the flames.

Other items follow in rapid succession. An extensive burglary, an atrocious murder, or singular case of mysterious disappearance, occupying a quarter of a column in the morning papers, is condensed to from eight to a dozen lines; and it requires rapid thought to do it.

It is nearly eleven o'clock. In a New York paper lying before us our eye touches this full head: "Is Pool-Selling Gambling?" We catch up the paper and our scissors and clip the whole article. We find it to be an official letter of the Mayor of New York, addressed to the District Attorney of that city (or county, more properly), respecting the practice of selling election-pools, and the District Attorney's reply thereto. The two communications would make a third of a column in our paper. We cannot think of devoting half that space to it, and we thus dispose of it, writing a few lines and pasting on a dozen:

An Official Inquiry.—Mayor Havemeyer, of New York, has addressed a note to District Attorney Phelps, calling his attention to the practice of selling election-pools in that city, and asking *advice as to what statutes against gambling are applicable to the case. Mr. Phelps's reply is to the effect that "whether*

~~Whether~~ or not what is called pool-selling would come within the provisions of the law prohibiting gambling has never been determined by the courts of this State. ~~The practice of selling pools has, I believe, grown up since the passage of the act of 1851.~~ It would seem that the law is broad enough in its terms to cover the selling of pools, if it could be shown that more than $25 was won or lost at any one time within twenty-four hours. ~~With~~ *" He says*

that " it ~~pains to state them.~~ ~~It~~ is to be regretted that there is not more full and complete legislation on the subject. ~~I am, sir, with great respect, very truly,~~ *"*

The door flies open and a boy, breathless from the rapid climbing of stairs, bursts in, with the air of one hastening to summon a physician to the bedside of a dying father. It is the Telegraph Boy, and he hurls upon our table three or four sheets of thin white paper — paper so thin that it takes several sheets of it put together to make a fair shadow. This is "manifold" paper, and upon it, hastily scrawled by the telegraph operator, are several dispatches.

Don't ask us what "manifold" is, but we'll tell you in a second. This is an Associated Press dispatch. Half-a-dozen papers in this city, whose proprietors equally share the expenses, must each have a copy of it, and simultaneously. But to write out that number of copies too much time would be absorbed and too many clerks would have to be employed. So, the telegraph man who "takes" the dispatch writes six copies at once, and in exactly the same length of time it would require him to write one copy. This sounds like setting the simple "rule of three" at defiance, but it is plausible enough when you once understand it. The telegraph man performs this wonderful feat in a "book" of manifold paper, and when he wants to make six copies he takes six sheets of black paper, as thick as blotting-paper, and fits them into the "book," alternating them with the first six leaves of the manifold paper. This black paper is so prepared with a coloring matter that the pressure of an ivory pencil, or anything with a smooth point, running over the upper sheet, transfers the lines of the black coloring matter from the thick sheets to the manifold, and the six sheets of the latter receive alike, and simultaneously, every letter, and dash, and dot formed by the ivory point. The six sheets of manifold are then torn out and distributed to the six newspapers entitled to the dispatch, by means of that lively boy.

It seems that the process described requires this thin paper, on which the letters are about as distinct on one side as on the other. It is therefore very trying to the eyes, especially at night, when — But we are not doing night-work just now.

We take up the first silken sheet in nervous hurry, for it is five minutes late, when the door opens and a cheery voice sings out:

"Hello! How goes it?"

Good heavens! It is that lounger and bore, Wilkins Muggins. To think that he should happen in at such a time! What crime have we committed to deserve this? Yet, we have a sufficient reason for not wishing actually to snub him; and we know, too, that he does not come in purposely to vex us. He does not understand the case — has no appreciation of the importance of every minute just at this time.

"How are you to-day? Sit down — look over the papers — little busy just now — be through by and by," we say, rapidly, bending to our work again.

The Boy rushes in. He has been up to the composing-room.

"Mr. Craig wants to know if any telegraph has come yet."

"Tell him, yes. Will send up three or four stickfuls in one minute."

"Anything new?" asks Wilkins, as he leisurely drops into a seat and takes up a New York paper.

"No — nothing particular — that is, you'll find in the *Herald* there the particulars of that big fire. It was a serious calamity." And while he — thank heaven! — becomes absorbed in the *Herald's* account of a very common and every-day occurrence, we rush upon our task like lightning.

We begin to decipher the first dispatch, for we must understand it all, punctuate it, and give it the proper display heads before sending it up. It begins:

NEW YORK, Nov. 11.—A dispatch from Scranton, Pa., says that a terrible accident occurred there this morning. A party of six men were descending a shaft in the B—— Coal Mines, when —

The dispatch goes on to state at length that the cable broke, and that the car fell three hundred feet, killing all the men instantly; and to describe the recovery of the bodies, their mutilation, the excitement, the grief of the wives and children of the unfortunate men, etc. Having run over it, punctuated it and "got the sense," our next duty is to prepare a head or heads for it, a work that ought to occupy about eight seconds. We are about to dash into it, when Mr. Wilkins Muggins arises and takes his departure, remarking as he goes out:

"I see you're rather busy. I'll drop in again in a day or two."

"Do," we reply, cordially; and plunging a pen savagely into the inkstand, we write on a scrap of copy-paper the following head-lines:

PENNSYLVANIA.

TERRIBLE MINING ACCIDENT!

SIX MEN PRECIPITATED INTO A SHAFT, AND INSTANTLY KILLED!

This we paste at the head of the dispatch and send it up by the waiting Boy. It occupied two-and-a-half sheets of the manifold, and at the middle of the third sheet, where it ended, we of course severed it with our scissors, marking the three separate pieces of copy "A 1," "A 2," and "A 3."

Then follows:

LONDON, Nov. 11.—There is great excitement here over the news to the effect that—

This dispatch proceeds to mention and explain a certain diplomatic complication, and concludes by quoting an opinion of the *Times* on the subject, in which quotation occur the following very bewildering words:

But that this well be the time nation entire into the most rebellious religion hypothenuse.*

Such bosh! Here is a problem, compared with which the Gordian knot was a straight bit of string. But we must unravel it before we send it up; if we don't, the chances are that the compositors won't. We 've tested that matter before. Let 's see—"rebellious, religion, hypothenuse—." Only half-a-minute or so to study on it. Confound the dispatch; we 'll cut out that part of it! No—we 've got it. We remember "The

* An actual "case," with which the writer once had to wrestle while telegraph editor of a daily paper.

8

Thunderer's" stately language, and—evidently this is what the *Times* said:

> But that this will be the termination, enters into the most nebulous region of hypothesis.

That is, hazy, doubtful, speculative.

Delighted at our solution of the problem, we write the proper words distinctly with a pencil, head the dispatch, and send it up.

'T wasn't so much of a puzzle, after all, now that we see through it—very clear, in fact, compared with some cases we've had, and which, by the way, we've had to "give up." In such cases, a wicked stroke of the pen or pencil, accompanied by a muttered oath, adjusts the matter.

We seize the next dispatch.

The door opens, and a man, with a hesitation in his manner that would make a very fair companion to an impediment in the speech, comes in, looks around slowly and allows the door to swing to. We see at a glance that he hails from the beautiful place where the yellow corn, the pumpkins and melons grow—we instinctively feel that he is nearer to Nature than we are, that he is better and happier than we—we almost reverence him, and, although very busy—very busy, indeed—we cannot find it in our heart to deal other than tenderly with him. We drop our pen to give ourself a partial holiday of fifteen seconds, and anticipate him by saying kindly:

"How do you do, sir? Were you looking for—for—"

We allow him to interrupt us, which he does in this manner:

"Is this the office of the *Times?*"

"This is one of the departments. What did you wish?"

"Well, you see, my subscription to the weekly ended last March, and I then began taking your daily instead. By some mistake—"

"Continued sending the weekly?"

"Yes, and daily, too."

"Ah? Well, sir, please step down to the counting-room, and the clerks will arrange that for you. Just explain it to them. It is —"

"The counting-room?"

"Yes; you passed it, and came higher than you need have done. I 'm sorry. [So are we.] The counting-room is on the first floor, right at your left as you go down the last flight of stairs."

"O — O — thank you. Good-day."

"Good-day."

Slowly he withdraws, and, as we resume our work, we hear his careful feet planted one after another, with awful deliberation, upon the stairs he descends.

Here is a dispatch from Cincinnati — a rather lengthy account of a street-encounter — to which we give the separate heads: "Cincinnati — Almost a Riot;" but as, according to the dispatch, no one was killed and no one seriously hurt, we do not deem it quite worth the space it would occupy in its present shape, and so "cut it down" to about one-half its length, and that without stripping it of a single essential feature.

The agents of the Associated Press usually exercise very good judgment in such matters, but occasionally they overstep the mark a trifle. Then the telegraph editor of each newspaper cuts down the dispatch at his own discretion.

We send up the last of this installment of "telegraph," and the Boy comes down and says that "Mr. Craig would like to know if there is likely to be any more telegraph for the one-o'clock edition. Says he has plenty o' copy."

"Tell him, no — noth'n' more."

We have a column of telegraph for the first edition, also a column of "locals," with which we are having nothing to do to-day, and it is twelve o'clock. Now we go to lunch, and we may remain away an hour if we wish, but don't often do it. If, however, we approach the office after an hour's absence, we see the one-o'clock edition on the street, fluttering and scattering, like the brown November leaves, among the readers of news and the patrons of loud-tongued news-boys; and when we ascend the stairs we feel them trembling beneath us, shaken by the throbbings of the cylinder-press in the basement, that is rattling off the edition as if the whole world's welfare depended upon its expedition.

At our work again by one. Pens, scissors, paste, manifold, a few locals, a few clippings lying around; and the three-o'clock edition is a repetition of the one o'clock. Its outside is just the same; and inside it has the same editorials, the same locals, with something added, and the same dispatches. In addition to the latter, however, there is a whole fresh column of dispatches, and at its head, in large characters, are the words: "Extra! 3 o'clock!"

This edition "up," and we are on the home-stretch. Dispatches pour in between three and four o'clock, and by the latter time the last one arrives. It is on time, but should not be much later, for now but one hour remains, and in that time a long dispatch or two must be read, headed, set up, the proof read, corrections made, and the forms locked up and conveyed to the press. We have the last dispatch. It is a lengthy one, on an exciting topic. There has been a terrible disaster,—an ocean steamer lost—four hundred people drowned! The door opens, and a man comes in, saying with a glib tongue:

"This advertisement of ours—Brown & Co.—you see that, this slight mistake"—producing a slip—"makes it—"

"Just call at the counting-room, please, and see one of the clerks," we interrupt.

"I did, and the clerk said he'd have it fixed all right; but it's very important, and to guard against its possibly being neglected, I thought I'd just step in here —"

"O, exactly," we say; "but this is the editorial department, and here we have nothing to do with the 'ads.' We never even see them. But if you feel anxious about the matter, you might just step up to the composing-room and ask for Mr. Rogers, the man who has charge of the 'ads.' Tell him about it, and he will see that the correction is not overlooked; although he has probably made it already, as the clerk has no doubt sent up instructions through the speaking-tube."

A minute wasted by the interruption, and we can poorly afford to lose it. We dive into our manifold, punctuate and correct it, then write half a dozen head-lines, such as, "London," — "Appalling Calamity!" — "Sinking of a Steamer!" — "Four Hundred Lives Lost!" — "Panic Among the Passengers!" — "Frightful Scenes!" In a corner of the sheet we write the word, "Display," to indicate that the heads are to be set up in large type, and spread out; and on a corner of the manifold we write, "double-lead," which means to place two leads between each two lines, so as to string out the whole dispatch, and give it additional prominence.* Then the Boy takes it and flies up to the composing-room.

* I would explain that important dispatches are not treated in this manner in every newspaper office, some Managing Editors thinking that the style borders on the sensational. But the work is so done in most daily offices, many of them very solid institutions, as witness the Philadelphia *Inquirer*, New York *Herald*, or Boston *Journal*.

Just here, let me also explain to the uninitiated what "leads" are. They are thin pieces of metal, with a length equal to the width of the column in which they are used, and a breadth not quite equal to the length of the types. One of them is placed between each two lines of type, when it is

Now we have reached our leisure, you say? Yes, the day's work is done, so to speak; the last bit of copy for the last edition has been sent up, the types are clicking as the compositors work in concert to throw the last column together; before the lapse of another hour it will be read in proof, corrected, and five minutes before five o'clock the forms will be laid upon the press in the basement, and at five we will feel its throbbing, even up here in the fourth story.

Leisure? Yes, we don't leave till the paper goes to press, and so we have an hour's leisure before us, and we proceed to enjoy it by writing an editorial or two for to-morrow, because some of those dispatches contain matter demanding editorial comment. This will not consume all the "leisure" hour, but the rest of it will be absorbed by such little pastimes as selecting from exchanges, that have just come, little items for our funny column, our "State News," our "Personals," our "Political Notes," and other departments, for to-morrow; and, yes, here are two or three papers from which we always get good miscellaneous matter. We must make a few selections for "outside" from them. Here's one headed, "Danger from Wet Coal;" it begins:

> People who prefer wetting the winter's store of coal to lay the dust on putting it in their cellars, do not, perhaps, generally know that they are laying up for themselves —

Yes, that will do, and we know we have never published it before. We lay it aside to be carefully read before leaving, or

---

desired that the matter shall be "leaded" — that is, that the lines shall appear further apart than usual. When no leads are inserted at all, the printed matter is called "solid." If two leads are placed between each two lines of type, the lines are thus thrust still further apart, and the matter is "double-leaded." The general text of this volume is "leaded;" this foot-note is solid.

perhaps to-night, if we come back to the office after dinner. Here is another, headed, "Dutch Beauties." We read:

A writer in the *Jewish Messenger*, speaking of Leeuwarden, a town in Holland, says: "The women of Leeuwarden deserve a paragraph to themselves. There is a primitive air about them which —"

Another "available," and it is laid aside with "Danger from Wet Coal." Here are several others: "The Grave of St. Patrick," which we find to be an interesting extract from a tourist's letter; "Is Saving Wealth?" "Silk as an Article of Dress," "The Matrimonial Market," "Strange Freak of an Insane Man." These all prove to be good miscellaneous selections, for we find "leisure" to read them, striking out a line or two now and then, before the paper goes to press, and pasting each on a slip of paper, on which we write a word or two to guide the foreman or compositor, we hand them to the Boy with —

"There 's some copy for to-morrow."

And yet you ask us if we are tired!

Frankly, though, what you have seen us do to-day, was not the work of one man. All this writing, and scissoring, and pasting have been done by half a dozen editors, each having his own special duties to do — and then they have been kept busy.* One man has been known to edit a small daily, entirely unassisted; but the smallest daily in existence ought to have at least two or three editors, or it will be as poor and meager in its matter as it is small in size.

---

* It may be as well to remark here that the round of duties on a large morning paper, such as the New York *Herald*, *World*, or *Tribune*, could not well be measured by the standard outlined in this chapter. Such papers are made up with far more original matter and far less of matter obtained by the mechanical aid of the scissors.

CHAPTER X.

BOOK-REVIEWING.

IN the preceding chapter I have casually alluded to — not Book-Reviewing, but merely book-*noticing*, as it is frequently done by editors who are surrounded with other and more pressing duties, and who can scarcely spare more time than enough to look at the title-page of a book. Indeed, Book-Reviewing is done, as it should be done, by but very few papers in this country. Most of them merely "notice" newly-published books, and that, alas! too often favorably only in proportion to the advertising patronage the paper receives from the book-publisher. Hence it is too often — though not always — the case that when you read in a newspaper, "This work is the finest, most useful and interesting that has yet been produced on this subject," the editor has not read the book — possibly, not even seen it.

On the other hand, I have known instances of *abusing* a book to make it sell — publishers generally agreeing that "cold praise will ruin any book," whereas, a book handsomely abused is nearly certain to sell well. Heap a liberal amount of invective upon a book; let all the papers in the country condemn it in terms of bitterness, or ridicule it with all the power of satire, and people will rush to buy it, just to see what kind of a monstrous thing it is, anyhow.

The following example came to my personal knowledge in a Western city some years ago: A certain firm of publishers and booksellers were "stuck." They had one thousand copies of a certain book on hand, and they were going off at the rate of about one a year. The senior member of the firm mentioned the matter to a newspaper friend as very vexing, the more so because he thought the work one of unusual merit.

"Why," said the editor, "I can give it a notice in our paper that will sell every copy in a week, and create such a demand that you will have to put the plates to press again."

"Impossible! We have advertised it liberally, and it will not take."

"Let me try it."

"Very well. I'll send you a copy inside of ten minutes. I shall thank you just as much for your kind efforts if they are unavailing — which I think they will be."

"Send it up, and we'll see."

A copy of the unlucky book was laid on the editor's table that afternoon, and the next issue of the paper contained a notice giving the title, names of the publishers and size of the book, then proceeding to condemn it in satirical terms, declaring the writer to be little short of an imbecile, and concluding by saying that Messrs. Brown & Green, the publishers, had done themselves great discredit by printing such a trashy work, and that they deserved to be taught a lesson in the shape of a lively indisposition on the part of the public to purchase the book.

"What have you done?" exclaimed Mr. Brown, when he met the editor a few hours after the issue of the paper. "That's outrageous, really."

"Merely gave the book a little blowing-up to make it sell," replied the editor, without losing any of his complacence.

"Why, who will buy it after such a notice as that?"

"Nearly everybody that reads the notice and can raise the dollar-seventy-five," replied the confident editor.

"I don't believe it will sell a copy."

"Wait and see."

He had not long to wait. There began to be an unaccountable demand for that book, and in two days the thousand copies had all been sold and the stereotype plates were on the press again.

"I believe you were right," said Mr. Brown, the next time he met the editor.

"I rather think I was," said the journalist.

Such cases as this, however, are not of frequent occurrence. There are papers in the country, of the class of the New York *Herald*, *World* and *Tribune*, the Philadelphia *Press*, the San Francisco *Bulletin*, the Boston *Advertiser*, or Springfield *Republican*, that employ regular literary editors to review books, and who "do it right," without fear or favor. These reviewers are supposed to read every important book that is published, and very soon after its publication, and to write impartial criticisms; but they do not read from beginning to end very many *un*important ones.

The story is told that a literary man and book-critic one day entered the sanctum of a magazine editor and found him reading a book preparatory to reviewing it, when the following conversation took place:

"What are you doing?"

"Reading ——'s 'History of England.'"

"What are you reading it for?"

"Why, in order to review it."

"What!"—in astonishment—"do you actuallv *read* books before writing reviews of them?"

"Yes,"—rather surprised at the question,—"certainly, I do."

"Why, I never do. It 's apt to prejudice one so!"

There is another thing that sometimes "prejudices one" whose province it becomes to notice or review a book; namely, a personal dislike of the author. That literary man must be more than mortal — but I never saw one that was — who can see unusual beauties in a book written by a man he hates, and who, seeing such beauties, can write a notice of that book for publication warmly praising the book and extolling the genius of its author! But while I have known a few instances of unfavorable criticism of books on account of personal ill-feeling toward their authors, such instances are only exceptions. Probably in nine hundred and ninety-nine cases of a thousand the author and critic have never met, and know nothing whatever, personally, of one another. Therefore, as a rule, men who are regularly employed by respectable journals actually to "review" books do so with fairness and impartiality. Indeed, I have known of book-reviewers speaking very unfavorably of the literary work of a personal friend, when the task of reviewing such work could not well be left out of their daily duties. I believe I was once in a position where I was compelled to do a thing like this myself, or write a lie, and I could not help choosing the former course. I know it gave me more pain than it did the author, who, however, ignoring the fact of the pain on my part, was never able to get himself up to such a standard of magnanimity as entirely to forgive me. I have fully concluded, long since, that there are times, in this world, when to be truthful does not pay, but I don't think it will ever cease to be right.

CHAPTER XI.

EDITORS' PERSONAL CHARACTERISTICS.

THERE are all grades of newspapers, as hinted in another chapter, and so there are all grades and all kinds of editors. As a rule, journalists do not lack a proper sense of the courtesies that are due from one man to another; nor are they, of all men, ignorant of the "conventionalities of society." If I have not seen very generally among editors of newspapers, and other literary men, what any sensible person would consider the true gentleman, — not in the sense in which the word is used in England, — I have never seen any at all. Like persons in other occupations, they are of various temperaments, and exhibit various degrees of cheerfulness. Many are dignified and sedate, their minds seeming always to dwell on their work and on the great questions of the day; and many, except when hard at work, are as "jolly" as Mark Tapley himself. All have their seasons or moments of relaxation; and I have seen the gravest of "night-editors," while "waiting for telegraph" at one A. M., give way to a spirit of playfulness, and for a few minutes engage in the highly intellectual recreation of "sky-larking," which, in such cases, usually assumes the form of throwing bundles of exchanges at one another. But this is no daily or nightly occurrence.

Are there some "editors" who are dolts? Oh, yes. Almost any one may call himself an editor. Any one who can write a few (almost) grammatic sentences, and who happens to have two or three thousand dollars, can "start" a weekly paper and be the "editor." It is as easy to "start" a weekly paper as to start a blacksmith-shop. To "run" it profitably, and make it respectable, are other considerations. A man's money may make him an "editor," and make "editors" of all the male (yes, and female) members of his family; but it will never make them brilliant, or talented, or even sensible. The truth is, there are here and there journalists unworthy of the name, who have worked their way into the profession by some irregular process or other, just the same as there are unworthy "doctors" and "lawyers," known respectively as "quacks" and "shysters." In each case they are simply impostors, disgracing an honorable profession. Journalism is not exempt from its "quacks" and "shysters."

It has almost passed into a proverb that editors are "drinking men." So are all men; but it cannot be ignored that what is meant by "drinking men" is, men who habitually drink stimulating liquids. Well, to speak the truth, and I don't think of speaking anything else in this volume, I never met an editor who would not, in season, "take a drink" of ale or whisky; but there are probably to be found as few drunkards, or even immoderate drinkers, in journalism as in any other profession — if not fewer. There are many brilliant writers — some brilliant men outside of journalism and literature — who at times "drink too much," who, to put it bluntly, have actually been seen "drunk;" but these are exceptional cases, and they attract the more attention, and are the more talked about, because of the prominence of the unfortunate gentlemen.

I once called on a famous journalist whom I had never before seen,— although we had often exchanged thoughts through our papers,— and found him in a condition of hilarity evidently induced by too much alcohol. I will not mention his name, for if I did it would almost make intemperance respectable. But this man was not an habitual drunkard. He occasionally "drank too much" and it "went to his head," and he did his work — a great work, — and his private habits were nobody's business — except, perhaps, the business of idle and prying fools.

Nearly all editors drink more or less; a few occasionally "drink too much," that is, more than is physically good for them; but that dissipation is a characteristic of editors is a silly exaggeration that I am almost ashamed to have noticed at all.

Why do nearly all writers drink? Every physiologist will bear me out in the statement that brain-work — particularly when rapid and excessive — exhausts the nervous principles of vitality faster than the most arduous and irksome physical labor. The brain is the head-quarters of the whole body, and when a constant draft is made on it, for even so much as an hour, the drainage of power must be incalculably greater than when only the right arm is exercised.

Without entering upon the subject scientifically, or giving anything like an analysis of the brain, — which embraces about six hundred different kinds of substances,—I will only proceed to say that in my own experience I have suffered from a few hours' hard work, both as editor and reporter, a feeling of "goneness," of exhaustion, from the head down; a sense of being on the brink of falling to pieces; a notion of a hollow place in the skull, into which the air was trying to drive its way by the pressure of its own weight, and kindred feelings, never approached in my own experience, by sensations produced by excessive physical exertion, even when — as in the army — associated with a want of food. When this feeling — a kind of shadowy sense of dissolution — comes on, after hours of close application to the hardest kind of mental work, there is nothing that so quickly and fully restores the nerves and brain to a normal feeling, and so effectually props them up, as alcohol.

Night-work, for example, is a poison, constant and sure, to

editors, reporters, proof-readers and compositors, who, when employed on morning papers, must work chiefly at night and do their sleeping in day-time. In common with other intellectual night-workers, the night editor suffers "with his eyes." When I was a boy I used to think that the toothache was, perhaps, the finest bit of torture that could be devised; but I at one time, a few years ago, suffered so acutely from a temporary affection of the eyes, caused by newspaper work at night, that I would have welcomed the toothache as a ray of sunshine.

The manifold spoken of in another chapter, as being very trying even in day-time, is doubly so at night, when the glaring gas-light makes it a flimsy shadow, and this is a fruitful source of discomfort to the eyes and brain. The brain does not merely tire during intense intellectual labor; it burns up; it crumbles away, like the clay and gravel of a bluff scattering before the streams of water in hydraulic mining. I have often walked forth — tottered, I might say — from a newspaper office at three or four o'clock in the morning, with such a feeling of vital exhaustion, such a sense of a considerable amount of brain substance having been used up, and such a general sensation of nervous prostration, as to make the impression irresistible that the system had been worn down to a point from which it was in vain to hope to rally. This feeling is quickly counteracted by stimulants, which, used in moderation at such times, are a blessing to the night editor. Without them, the brain having become irritated by vexatious work through the long hours of the night, he will find it difficult to get into a natural sleep when he goes home. At such times more than usually applicable are both Cassio's remark, "Every inordinate cup is unblessed, and the ingredient is a devil," and Iago's reply, "Come, come, good wine is a good familiar creature, *if it be well used.*"

I have frequently — so have all journalists — on extraordinary occasions, stayed up and worked all night and a portion of the ensuing forenoon, finally going home at ten or eleven o'clock in the day, after working twenty-six hours without even a stolen nap of five minutes, and then I have experienced the greatest difficulty in getting to sleep at all. A morbid wakefulness, accompanied with a very sensible feeling of nervous weakness, would take possession of me; and when I did succeed in wooing sleep, my rest would be broken and unnatural, and could rarely be made to last more than a couple of hours, when, by all rules of proportion, I needed six times that amount of rest, and a much better quality of the article, besides. This is a mere glance at the hardships of the newspaper editor.

The prodigality as well as the generosity of journalists is proverbial, and I need say little on the subject. Few editors get rich, or try to. None are misers. I never saw more than one mean journalist. He had worked many years, lived poorly, amassed almost a fortune, merely from his salary, and was very generally despised by his colleagues. As a rule, editors insist on living well, although they eat to live, rather than live to eat. They are not generally "big eaters;" yet I have seen some who took in nourishment like men accustomed to great physical exertion. As might be expected, from the nature of their occupation, their sedentary habits and their often enforced irregularity in eating, they are more than ordinarily exposed to attacks of indigestion; although I have known of but few cases of actual dyspepsia among journalists.

There is a silly impression among some classes of persons, who, it is scarcely necessary to state, know least about newspaper men, that they have not a proper appreciation of the enormity of falsehood — that, in a word, they would a little rather publish an untruth, if it would answer the purpose, almost as well as the truth. It seems almost too ridiculous to be worth alluding to at all, yet it has been made the subject of "chaff;" and in circles of society where one might have had reason to expect a higher degree of knowledge—to say nothing of those "conventionalities"—I have more than once heard such humorous (but not witty) remarks as this:

"Oh, you don't expect to get the truth out of *him*, do you? He 's an editor."

The fact is, aside from the moral aspect of the case, there is no set of men whose *business* it so strictly is *to tell the truth* as it is the business of journalists. They are always seeking for facts—only *facts*—and always guarding against the possibility of even accidentally deceiving their readers. Occasionally, a respectable journal is "sold" by a perfidious correspondent, or falls into the blunder of publishing spurious news furnished by a chance ignorant or too-credulous reporter; and in such cases it becomes a target for the satire of its more fortunate contemporaries. Nothing so mortifies the proprietors and editors of a paper as to learn that, even through accident or inadvertence, their readers have been furnished with untrue or inaccurate statements. There is, to be sure, a good deal of lying done in the world, and the editor ought to be allowed to do his share, although I don't believe he does it.

I should be derelict, if, while on the characteristics of editors, I should fail to allude to the peculiarities of their manuscripts. It is the general impression—a pretty correct one—that editors are not fine penmen. I cannot better dispose of this subject than by quoting an article which I find in an old copy of the Concord (N. H.) daily *Patriot*, which journal I had the pleasure of conducting for a year or two for the Messrs. Bailey, formerly proprietors of the Boston *Herald*, and the enterprising gentlemen who made the latter the stupendous financial success to which it attained during the war:

It is scarcely necessary to remark that, as a rule, editors do not write so plainly as bank-clerks or schoolmasters. The fact is probably everywhere known, and nowhere disputed. But why is it so ?—or, in the language of Artemus Ward, "why is this thus?" If any one imagines that editors write a bad hand solely to annoy the compositors, he is entirely mistaken. Editors naturally acquire a habit of writing very rapidly; if they did not, they would seldom get their day's work done before the middle of the next afternoon—and haste is not favorable to the development of calligraphy. But this is not the whole solution of the problem. The truth is, the editor's mind is never on his penmanship. While he writes he is thinking of the subject-matter, and his pen travels along mechanically over the page before him, tracing his thoughts in some sort of characters which he intends for certain letters of the English alphabet, and which should never be termed "crow-tracks," for the reason that they are not half so symmetrical. It is a mistake, too, to suppose that compositors are continually "cussing" over the almost illegible manuscript of the editor. They "get used to it." It becomes part of the printer's art to decipher all sorts of mysterious manuscripts; and when, in addition to this acquired sagacity, he becomes familiar with the handwriting of a certain editor, by being brought in daily, and even hourly, contact with it, he reads it almost as readily as "reprint," although it would probably be an exaggeration to say that he actually prefers it to the latter. He does occasionally get "stuck" on a word, when he either goes to the editor for enlightenment or "guesses at it," putting in some word which is at least about the same size as the mysterious one, and which might, possibly, happen to be the right one. In the latter case, he generally guesses incorrectly, and a proof goes to the editor with the word "disappointed" for the word "disaffected;" "sirloin" for "saline;" "horse" for "house;" "mad-dog" for "mid-day;" "anguish" for "English;" "obscene" for "obscure;" "onions" for "union;" etc., etc. The editor, who is very busy, frowns tenderly, scratches out the wrong words and writes the right ones in the margin,—in a worse hand than before,—and wonders how the compositors could have been so stupid!

This nearly covers the whole ground. I might add an illustration. Suppose it were your object to get from your first floor to your second floor as many times a day as possible. How would you go about it? Would you stop to study grace of motion? No. That would be no consideration. Your object would be to get up as quickly as possible, even should you scramble up like an ape. It is so with the editor. His object is to record his thoughts as rapidly as possible; his penmanship becomes merely his flight of stairs. And, in this view of the case, one who for the first time sees a fac-simile of Horace Greeley's hand-writing, for example, might well exclaim: "*Such* a getting up-stairs!"

Much has been said of Greeley's extraordinary chirography, and I have to confess that when I first saw a specimen of it I was bewildered. It is not to be wondered at that compositors not familiar with his manuscript at first became confused, and made many amusing blunders. Many stories are told on this head. A *Tribune* compositor once told me several, among which were these: Greeley once wrote an editorial on the progression of the Celtic race, and headed it, "Footsteps of the Celt." The compositor was so nearly accurate as to get it, "Footsteps of the Colt," which certainly has a literal air about it. Once he wrote an article headed "William H. Seward," and of course the compositor did not fail to make it "Richard the Third."

In the "Life and Times of Horace Greeley," I find the following well-authenticated anecdote:

The town of Sandwich, Illinois, is a place of great progressive spirit as well as the home of many intelligent people. It has a lecture association, of course. Mr. M. B. Castle, banker and lumber-merchant, as his letter-heads plainly indicated, and also the proper officer of the association, wrote to Mr. Greeley inviting him to lecture at Sandwich. His reply, as published by the newspapers, should have read as follows:

"DEAR SIR.—I am overworked and growing old. I shall be 60 next Feb. 3. On the whole, it seems I must decline to lecture henceforth, except in this immediate vicinity, if I do at all. I cannot promise to visit Illinois on that errand—certainly not now.

"Yours, HORACE GREELEY.

"M. B. Castle, Esq., Sandwich, Ill."

Mr. Castle, with the aid of Sandwich experts, deciphered Mr. Greeley's letter on the wrong rule, and replied as follows:

"SANDWICH, Ill., May 12.

"HORACE GREELEY: Dear Sir.—Your acceptance to lecture before our association next winter came to hand this morning. Your penmanship not being the plainest, it took some time to translate it; but we succeeded; and would say your time, '3d of February,' and terms, '$60,' are entirely satisfactory. As you suggest, we may be able to get you other engagements in this immediate vicinity; if so, we will advise you.

"Yours respectfully, M. B. CASTLE."

Mr. Greeley's rejoinder to this letter was discovered to be emphatic, but it still awaits a literal "translation."

The story is told that Mr. Greeley once became disgusted with the blunders of one of the *Tribune* compositors, and sent a note up to the foreman saying that the said compositor was inefficient, and requesting him to dismiss him at once, and never again to employ him on the *Tribune*. The foreman obeyed instructions, and the compositor put his coat on. Before leaving, however, he managed to get possession of Horace's note to the foreman, and immediately went to a rival office, and applied for work, showing the note as a recommendation. The foreman to whom he applied "read" the note, and said:

"O, I see—'good and efficient compositor'—'employed a long time on the *Tribune*'—'Horace Greeley,'"—and incidentally asked:

"What made you leave the *Tribune?*"

'I've been *away* for some time," [meaning ten minutes.]

This was understood, however, to imply that he had been absent from the city, probably for weeks or months, and, returning to find his place filled, of course, could not go to work at once on the *Tribune;* so, the blundering compositor was at once set to work in a rival office, on the strength of Horace's certification of his inefficiency, having been "out of a job" about fifteen minutes.

The bearing of editors toward each other, as well as toward their friends, is marked by the most delicate courtesy; and those in authority never "give orders" or instructions to their subordinates in an abrupt or offensive manner. The Managing Editor never says, "Do this," or, "Do that," as the "boss" speaks to one of a gang of street-laborers. "Mr. Brown, will you be kind enough to make a note of this in your 'Amusements?'" says the Managing Editor to the Theatrical Critic, handing him a slip of paper; or, to some other member of the staff—"By the way, Mr. Smith, won't you please have that article on 'Railroad Statistics' ready for to-morrow?"—and that is about the harshest language you ever hear in the editorial rooms.

Newspaper men, while so accustomed to giving much attention to political matters as almost inevitably to make them politicians, are liberal in their views, and it is quite common to find an editor who is a Democrat employed on the staff of a Republican paper, or a Republican editor employed on a Democratic paper. This would excite no more remark in journalistic circles than the employment by a Democratic builder of a Republican painter to paint his house. *The* Editor and the Managing Editor of a paper, however, must, of course, be men who entertain views in keeping with its pronounced sentiments. I happen to know of a certain daily paper, in a large city, which had been a Republican paper up to the year 1872, when, after a long conference between the Editor and the Managing Editor, it was decided to make it a Liberal Republican paper, opposing the re-election of President Grant. About the conclusion of the consultation, the former gentleman said:

"Of course, Mr. A——, as we have heretofore supported Grant, we must not come out against him too abruptly or harshly, but oppose him—for awhile, in any event,—in a courteous and argumentative way."

"Oh, to be sure," responded the Managing Editor; "I should n't think of calling him an ass before about the beginning of September."

This was in June; and it will be generally agreed that such a careful spirit of deliberation as would prompt an editor to call a former political friend an ass only after three months' gradual preparation, is to be highly admired.

Editors, with minds nearly always deeply absorbed in some subject or other, are sometimes unconsciously guilty of conduct which amounts almost to "snubbing" people. An associate of mine, noted for his absent ways at times, was one day writing intently, when a visitor, one of his own intimate friends, sitting near his elbow, innocently asked:

"Have you seen Booth yet?"

My colleague, with an impatient shake of the head, and a general snappishness of manner, responded:

"Good God! Be still a minute, won't you?"

Then, scratch—scratch—scratch—in the midst of a surrounding silence; for he did not stop writing, for even so much as a quarter of a second; and at the end of a minute, having finished his editorial, he straightened himself up for a brief rest, scraped a match on his table and relighted a cigar that had lain neglected for fifteen or twenty minutes, and, perfectly unconscious of having uttered any harsh language, said, cheerfully:

"Oh, by the way, what was it you said just now, Charlie? I was busy, and I believe I forgot to answer you."

Editors, as a rule, are good-tempered, but their work has an undoubted tendency to make them irritable at times—on which subject more will be said in another chapter. When the editor is right angry "thou hadst been better have been born a dog than answer (his) waked wrath." One of the most animated scenes I ever witnessed was a wordy row between a Managing Editor and Foreman, on account of something having "gone wrong." Both stood straight up, glared upon each other like angry lions, and for some few minutes fairly tried which could swear the hardest; and, humiliating as the confession is, I have to say that the Foreman was victorious, being at least half-a-dozen plain "damns" ahead when the contest terminated.

CHAPTER XII.

EFFECTS OF BRAIN-WORK.

WHEN a man — the blacksmith is the usual example — is accustomed to using his right arm continually, striking heavy blows and swinging ponderous implements about his head from morning till night, the muscles of that right arm are developed to an unusual degree, and the whole member grows very strong, so that it will do more, endure more, and be less seriously affected by injuries from external violence than an arm accustomed only to an ordinary amount of exercise.

"It is just so with the brain," you will say; but it is not. True, the brain is developed by its exercise, in the shape of mental labor, and a continual habit of thinking fits it for thinking clearly and rapidly; but here the analogy ceases. The brain is of so much more delicate structure than the muscular arm, which is only one of its servants, and its functions are of a nature so much more refined, that it is naturally much more susceptible of injury, either from internal strain or external violence. You may sustain a considerable bruise on your arm; you may strain or overwork its muscles so as to produce soreness for a week or two at a time; and it will be no serious matter. A corresponding amount of injury to the brain would result in inflammation of the membranes, brain-fever, possibly insanity or congestion, resulting in death.

How shall I illustrate the rapid wearing away of the brain, the steady exhaustion of vitality, in the case of the hard-working editor? The brain may fairly be likened to the steam-engine of a large mill. It is the engine of the body, and the nerves through which it directs all the movements of the body are its belts and shafts. When the steam-engine of the mill is doing its legitimate work, disseminating power through the great building, sending the belts flying on their endless rounds, and whirling the heavy shafts and wheels, its action is normal and healthy, and, if I may be allowed to compare it to a living thing, it feels rather better when night comes in consequence of its exercise.

But sever its connection with the ponderous works that ramify through the building; relieve it of the exertion necessary to move the hundred pieces of machinery; leave it alone, with only its fires, its boilers, its cylinders, its piston-rods and fly-wheel, and let it rush on. It is then working all within itself, while the great body of the establishment stands still; its fires roar as usual; the vanishing streams of water rapidly as ever change into pent-up steam, chafing like a caged lion to burst the iron bounds within which it is confined; the piston-rods dart back and forth like bolts of lightning; the heavy fly-wheel hums round, making the walls and the earth itself tremble and shake; then that engine is wearing itself away much faster than if it were running the vast machinery of the mill, and it is in danger of sudden wreck.

It is so with the working brain. It is accustomed to running the machinery of the whole body, and so dividing and doling out its steam-like powers in steady streams. It directs every movement; it says to the right hand, "Do this," and to the left, "Do that," and out through the nerves it sends that strange life-power that enables the limbs to obey. Now, when the editor sits down to his work, the whole body, with the exception of the right hand, is at rest, and the brain works alone, like the crashing engine that finds itself freed from the heavy machinery that kept its motion moderate and steady. Through the long day or weary night the brain rushes on, like the detached engine that whirls its dizzy fly-wheel; and it is not strange that the tenement of the brain trembles, like the walls of the building; that the brain itself collapses, as when the engine flies to pieces; and that the whole fabric crumbles and falls before its time. The power of the mill is the steam-engine, yet nothing about the mill requires such careful and delicate attention; the power of the man is the brain, and one little overstrain upon it may do more harm than the mangling of all the limbs. A man may live, be physically healthy and mentally brilliant after all his limbs have been cut off; but the final burden under which the brain breaks down brings apoplexy, then speedy death. Of that disease, which fortunately is no lingering one, probably all hard-working, certainly all over-worked journalists have felt those warning symptoms — vertigo, unnatural drowsiness, imaginary black specks floating before the eyes, a sense of pressure and confusion in the head, and a temporary numbness apparently of the brain — sometimes of a limb.

Undoubtedly, one of the effects of continuous brain-work is irritability of temper. I have seen the best-hearted of editors, on very trifling provocation, fly into a passion and exhibit an amount of rage almost appalling; and I have more than once, when working hard at daily editorial work, allowed myself to give way to fits of irritability on account of little vexations that under other circumstances I might have merely laughed at. This is a subject that needs careful studying by physicians; but that they would be able to devise a remedy, except the entire abandonment of mental work, seems to me improbable.

Just here it occurs to me that a number of eminent literary men — so great a number as to suggest something more than a mere coincidence — have not lived happily as heads of families. Shakespeare, Byron, Bulwer, Dickens, and a number of others I could mention, even went so far as to separate from their wives. In each case it was the voluntary act of the husband. Might it be that the wives of those and similar men, while perhaps as good as the average woman, failed properly to "understand" their husbands — failed to realize the great importance, to literary men, of perfect tranquillity in their homes, where their wearing and chafing work is done? This is a phase of the subject that might well be studied with profit — not by physicians, but by the wives of journalists and other literary men.

Byron said that he could not bear to be interrupted while writing, and that Lady Byron (although one might think that she must have known it) paid no attention to this "whim." If there is any man who ought not to be subjected to petty annoyances it is the literary man at work, or the journalist who comes home after many hours of severe mental labor. When an editor has sat in his chair seven or eight hours, straining his brain at his arduous work, and gets up almost staggering and goes home with a dizzy head, it may well be surmised that he has need of quiet and peaceful surroundings; nor will it seem strange if, on such occasions, he does not always feel in the mood for going forth and taking his wife to the opera, or accompanying her on a bit of a shopping expedition, to bend his great energies to the task of superintending the purchase of a spool of thread.

CHAPTER XIII.

MY "ASSISTANT."

IN journalism, more than in any other vocation, it is difficult to give rules clearly to guide those seeking for information. In the cases arising under any rule that might be given, the exceptions would generally constitute a majority. It would be a stupendous task, for example, to divide all the newspapers in this country into classes. It has been suggested that, in the "Darwinian Theory" of the "descent of man," a link is missing — a link, I believe, between the lowest type of "human beings," such as certain tribes of wild Australians, and the actual brute, the gorilla — that but for that missing link we might clearly trace animal life, by regular steps, from the most highly-developed race of men down to the jelly-fish. In the newspaper world there is no such missing link. You may go from the lowest to the highest, and from the highest to the lowest, without discovering a well-defined break at which to draw a line; so, as Darwin, the eminent naturalist, says of all living creatures, you find yourself obliged to say of the newspapers: "They have a common origin; they are all, so to speak, one family; they are one flesh and blood; one life; — only, they are surrounded by various circumstances, and are in various stages of development." There are daily newspapers with a hundred editors, reporters and miscellaneous writers; some with only ninety-nine; some that sink to ninety-eight; some, I am ashamed to say, with only ninety-seven; and so on, clear down to *one*. Yes, I know of more than one daily whose whole staff, including editors, reporters, correspondents and miscellaneous writers, consists of but one man. He is The

Editor; he is his own Managing Editor; he is his own City Editor; he is all his own assistants and reporters; aye, all his own contributors and correspondents.

In a city about the size of San José, California, and no incalculable distance therefrom, I some years ago occupied the position of Managing Editor of a small daily, an afternoon paper. Its owner was a wealthy politician, ambitious for honors; largely interested in such extensive industries as mining; a shrewd business man, possessing good judgment in matters of every-day interest. He was The Editor, and his paper — the *Watchman* — gave him influence; but it was scarcely oftener than once or twice a week that he lightened my labors by contributing a "leader."

I had one "Assistant" (of whom I shall speak *at length*) in the sanctum, and one regular reporter, with a couple of occasional assistants; and I thus did the duties at once of City Editor and Managing Editor. Nor had we any regular proof-reader, so that the proof all had to be read in the editorial room. We issued two editions of the *Watchman* every afternoon, and gave daily fourteen columns of fresh reading matter, including two or three columns of telegraph dispatches and various carefully-compiled "departments." With no City Editor, I had to keep a strict eye to the "locals." I had to see and examine everything that went into the paper, as well as much that did not, besides doing a vast amount of actual work myself.

The work in the office was certainly enough for from two to three robust editors, but it was my misfortune, during a year of the time I served as Managing Editor of the *Watchman*, to be cursed with an "Assistant," of whom merely to say that he was inefficient would be an insult to the English language — would be equivalent to calling it a pauper! Good heaven! It was years ago, but to this day a gloom steals over me whenever I think of those miserable days of toil and vexation!

His name was Job Stretcher.

He was a lank, attenuated, long-legged, gangling gawk, over six feet in length, whose age might have been anywhere from twenty-five to forty years; and a glance at him would have suggested that his proper place was in the bean-patch — except, perhaps, for the great probability of his being mistaken for one of the poles. He was "hatchet-faced" to the last degree, so that it would scarcely be an exaggeration to say that it was necessary to take a side-view of his face in order to see it at all. It was so thin as to become, to one looking straight at him from the front, almost invisible, like a sheet of paper with the edge directed toward the observer. He was at once ugly, presumptuous, awkward, officious, uncouth, meddling, lazy, delinquent, insubordinate, negligent, careless, ill-mannered, a bore and an ass; more in the way than useful; and, to crown all, with such an over-toppling sense of his own greatness that one might have dreaded — had Job Stretcher been a fighting man, which he was n't — to hint in his presence the possibility of the existence of a man of a still superior mind, anywhere in the country, or the world, or the universe, in any age, past, present, or to come.

"How then did he maintain his place as 'Assistant' a whole year," you will ask, "the Managing Editor having the power to employ his own assistants?"

It was this way: I found him there when I first took charge of the *Watchman;* he was a distant relative of the proprietor — but that consideration taken alone would not have made much difference; and it happened to be hard just at that time to find the proper man to take his place. So, day after day, week after week, and month after month, I silently bore with him, till life itself began to be a bore to me. I had good reasons for wishing to remain in my position for some time; and, besides, I did not wish to leave the proprietor in the lurch, as it was no fault of his; so, I endured it. I had only had charge of the *Watchman* a month when I spoke to the proprietor on the subject.

"Mr. Wellington," I said one evening, when he and I were alone in the office, "Mr. Stretcher, although a very good fellow, I trust, in some other sphere of life, is, I am sorry to say, not competent as a journalist, and very poorly fills the position of 'Assistant' on the *Watchman*. As he is related to you, I thought I would not like to put another man in his place without first mentioning it to you."

"Ah?" he replied. "Well—the relationship is nothing. As you are aware, I know very little of the details of your department, and expect you to run it according to your judgment, purely with reference to the interests of the *Watchman*. I would like Mr. Stretcher to stay if he were a good and faithful 'Assistant;' but if he is not, get some one in his place. I leave the matter entirely in your hands. Look around for a proper 'Assistant,' and when you have found one employ him in Mr. Stretcher's place, at about the same salary. Don't confine yourself to the figure, if you find you cannot get the right man without paying a few dollars more."

This was fair enough, and spoken like the sensible man Mr. Wellington was; and from that time forth I spent most of my leisure time looking around for Job Stretcher's successor. For various reasons, it was a year before I succeeded in securing the right man. I once went to San Francisco and tried to engage an "Assistant." I did engage one, but he did not come. Another, who would have taken the place, died; another I found, in the course of a brief interview, to be no more competent than Job Stretcher himself; another, who seemed competent, wanted a larger salary than I got myself; and so on. I even advertised in a San Francisco paper, and took a run up on the train half-a-dozen appointed evenings, where at the office of a friend, a lawyer, I received a few applicants, none of which proved acceptable. Among others who responded, an ignorant man came with his son, a stupid-looking fellow of sixteen years, and offered him for the position, saying that the boy had never had any experience in newspaper work, but he was sure I could soon "learn" him, and that in the course of a few years he would prove of great value to me. So time wore on, and so day after day, for a year, I struggled through the work of two editors, enduring an amount of annoyance from my "Assistant" that I think was harder to bear than the work itself.

One afternoon, when the work of the day was over, and when the last copy for the five-o'clock edition had been sent into the composing-room, I was occupying a leisure hour by making a few miscellaneous selections from exchanges, for the next day, and Job Stretcher, looking lanker than ever, was lolling back in an old wooden arm-chair, his tremendous heels laid up on one end of the large writing-table in the centre of the floor,—a habit of his which I detested,—and he smoking a horrible pipe, I received a call from a distinguished tragedian who had a brief engagement in our little city. I had expected him at some time in the course of the day, and was glad that he came at so happy a time, the hurry of the day being over, for I anticipated some minutes of agreeable conversation with him, relative to the stage.

The tragedian (whom I shall here style Mr. B——) was ushered into our sanctum by Mr. F——, an old personal friend, and the editor of a rival paper, and both, I need scarcely say, were polished gentlemen. As I had never met the gentleman of histrionic fame, Mr. F—— promptly introduced us.

Of course, the presence of Job Stretcher could not be ignored —but how I wished it could!—and seeing Mr. B—— glance half-curiously at him I introduced my "Assistant" both to him and Mr. F——, who also had never met him before. The tragedian, as well as Mr. F——, greeted him politely, to which he merely responded, "H' are ye?" He did not even rise, but I was glad that he at least took his ponderous feet off the table—or rather allowed them to fall off, and they came down upon the floor with a crash, amid which general confusion, and mortification on my part, I managed to seat my visitors.

Then an awkward pause followed, and I could see that they marveled at the extraordinary deportment of my "Assistant," while I know that they did not fail to notice my mortification, and, I trust, to feel for me. But the silence did not last long. It was broken by Job Stretcher. Not that he spoke, exactly; but, thrusting his feet far away beneath the table, and reclining a little lower in his chair, he stretched his long form nearly straight, like a fence-rail leaning upon a stump in a corn-field, and opening his immense mouth to the verge of decapitation, executed an infernal yawn, with a vocal accompaniment like the growl of a dog, then closed his jaws with a snap, like an alligator entrapping flies. After that, he articulated.

"By jingo!" he said, with a nasal twang about as musical as the sound caused by the extrusion of a cow's foot from a mud-hole, and with a coarse disregard of the presence of my visitors that must have been little less than offensive to them. "I 'm darned glad this day's work 's over!" [How I wished the day was, too!] "Did you ever," he said, addressing the tragedian with the rude familiarity he might have assumed toward a daily lounger, "did you ever work on a newspaper?"

"No — I —"

"Well, you need n't want to," said Job Stretcher, interrupting Mr. B—— quickly, as if afraid he was about to say something very distasteful, if allowed to proceed. "No, sir-ee, you need n't want to. It 's work — work — work, all the time. No end to it!"

The audacity of the fellow! this worthless shirker of duty, who, perhaps, did daily one-tenth of the work of which he should have done about one-half! who came to the office at ten or eleven o'clock, when I was there at eight; who talked, and meddled, and "blowed" more than he worked when he did come! I was still too much annoyed to speak, and Mr. F—— kindly put in a few observations about the fine weather we were having. This gave the tragedian — who was from the East — a chance to say that he was delighted with our climate, of which he had heard much before paying our State a visit. I began to recover the power of speech, and was about to say that we enjoyed delightful weather — probably fifteen days out of every twenty of the whole year — when Job Stretcher put in, with an almost excited air:

"Yes — but you just ought to be here in the rainy season!"

"Unpleasant, then, at times?" suggested the actor.

Job Stretcher did not reply in the English language, but shook his head solemnly, elevated his eyebrows, puckered his mouth and uttered a long —

"Wh—e—w!"

Mr. B—— almost started in alarm, and I feared that he might think the strange person — Job — not only of unsound mind, but actually dangerous. Mr. F—— also looked a little puzzled. The very extremity of the case gave me strength and calmness, an awful and smothered calmness, and I found myself able to say:

"On account of the porous nature of the soil in this locality, Mr. B——, we find it almost impossible to keep our streets and public roads in a very tidy condition during the rainy season. That is one slight drawback — but of a transient nature."

"No end of mud," said Job Stretcher, entirely ignoring what I had said, and the fact that I had spoken at all. "Mud, mud, mud!"

There was another awkward pause, Job Stretcher being the only person in the room who was perfectly at his ease. It was again his prerogative — or he considered it to be — to break the silence. This he did in the following manner:

He laid, or rather threw, his pipe, from which he had recently taken several faint whiffs, upon the table, scattering a train of gray ashes over an exchange, seized the arms of his chair with his bony hands, poised himself on his seat, and dragging his feet out from under the table, drew his whole reptile-like body up, as if suffering from acute cholera, into something like the form of a "W," gave vent to an extended yawn, followed by a vigorous expulsion of vocalized breath in the shape of the cabalistic word "Hoo-hoo!" then uncoiled himself and stood up. As his ungainly form assumed a vertical position, like a bean-pole, and his ill-shapen head, with its long, neglected and straggling sandy hair, went sailing up toward the ceiling, like a toy-balloon released by a playful urchin, the tragedian stared in dumb amazement, apparently puzzled to divine what strange animal it was he was thus unexpectedly allowed to look upon free of charge.

Job Stretcher again yawned and extended his arms in a right line, giving to his attenuated form the shape of a dagger (†). Then he bent over the writing-table, placed the palms of his hands thereon, poised himself upon them, like a circus performer, and "kicked up his heels," to the great peril of a picture that hung upon the wall just behind him. The feet — those feet! — once more came down upon the floor with an awful thump and clatter; and again standing erect, this human ape actually allowed the exuberance of his spirits — *so* glad to be through with another hard day's work! — to find vent in a regular war-whoop. Then he thrust his hands into the pockets of his trowsers — which garment, by the way, fitted him almost as neatly as a coffee-sack would fit a crooked stick — and walked over and gazed out of the window, brushing rudely against the arm and shoulder of Mr. B——, in passing where that astonished gentleman sat.

There was very little more conversation on that occasion — that occasion, which I have not here exaggerated in the minutest degree, and which I cannot to this day recall without a shudder and a blush.

But the worst was yet to come. Job Stretcher had one very rare peculiarity, to keep company with his other idiosyncrasies: he never attended places of amusement — probably concluding, in some rare moment of rational judgment, that he was sufficient of a curiosity himself. I sometimes offered him tickets, as a matter of courtesy, but was always promptly "snubbed" (by my "Assistant!") with some such remark as, "Oh, pshaw! *I* don't care for such things!" This, in a very contemptuous tone, as indicating his great superiority over the low and groveling nature that could derive pleasure from a histrionic, literary, or musical entertainment.

So, one scene more, and my interview with the famous tragedian — which I had dared to hope might at least afford myself some pleasure — closed. He and Mr. F—— arose to go, and, as he extended a hand to me, he said:

"Did Mr. L—— " (mentioning his agent) "leave you sufficient tickets for to-night?"

I thanked him, saying I thought he had. I had two myself, which were all I needed.

Then — and I wished that the earth might open and swallow me (or Job Stretcher) up — the tragedian turned politely to my "Assistant," and said:

"I have half-a-dozen in my pocket. Mr. Stretcher, perhaps you — "

"Oh," interrupted Job, with a clumsy and contemptuous toss of the head, "*I've* got no time to bother with such things!"

If a jet of steam had been turned upon my face it could scarcely have felt warmer than it did, as I felt the hot blood permeating it.

The tragedian shook my hand none the less warmly for the rude conduct of my "Assistant;" and as he and Mr. F—— moved out I followed them into the hall, (I could n't help it,) and whispered apologetically:

"My 'Assistant' — he — he 's merely a little singular in his ways."

"Oh, that 's nothing," replied Mr. B——, pleasantly, and in a tone denoting that he comprehended the situation; then, with another cordial word of parting, he and Mr. F—— took their leave; whereupon I went into an adjoining room, which I sometimes used in cases of private consultation with Mr. Wellington, locked the door and sat down and cried.

I need not recount the various occasions on which, and the many ways in which that curious being, my "Assistant," vexed me, nor describe at length his indolence, coarseness and officiousness; but suffice it to say that his conduct in the presence of the tragedian and Mr. F—— was more than usually polite, for him! That, however, mortified and annoyed me more than any other single act of his; but I rejoiced at the thought that it was near the termination of his career as my "Assistant," for when the end of the week came I coolly dismissed him. I afterward informed Mr. Wellington of the fact.

"Ah, you have found a man to take his place at last, have you?" he said.

"No — no prospect of any yet."

"What will you do then?" he asked, in surprise.

"Until I find some one to assist me, I shall do all the work myself. I would rather do so than have that person about me any longer."

"Can you get through with it?"

"Yes, by coming to the office an hour earlier each morning. An hour's work is not less than he has done each day for the last year."

"Well, well; all right," said Mr. Wellington, rather pleased with the dismissal of his distinguished relative than otherwise; "do your best for a few days; but it's too much work. I won't rest till I have found a good 'Assistant' for you, and you shall have one if I have to pay a hundred dollars a week for him."

For two weeks only, I did the whole work myself — and it *was* work — preparing and reading the proof of fourteen columns of fresh matter every day. Yet, after all, I was happier and got along better than when pestered by that creature, Job Stretcher. At the end of a fortnight I was lucky enough, after all my misery, to secure the services of a capable, industrious and courteous "Assistant," and he remained with me — everything running smoothly — till, two years afterward, want of rest obliged me to give up the position of Managing Editor of the *Watchman*, and, knowing him to be qualified, I was happy to turn it over to him.

CHAPTER XIV.

THE RELIGION OF EDITORS.

I HAVE certainly known some editors of newspapers who would consider the title of this chapter a misnomer, claiming that there are very many gentlemen of our profession who, as viewed by orthodox eyes, have no Religion at all. In the course of my connection with the press, I have frequently conversed with journalists on this subject, and have found them generally partaking of "liberal" views. Some I have found to be liberal Christians; some I have found to have gone so far from the generally-recognized doctrines of Churches as to have arrived even at Atheism. It seems almost impossible to write a work like this, in this country and this age, without more than once referring to Horace Greeley. I believe that, whatever errors of judgment he may have committed in common with the rest of us, no one has ever thought of accusing him of insincerity; and it therefore becomes interesting to know his views on religious subjects. He was a Universalist from boyhood, and did not acknowledge the divinity of Jesus Christ, although I believe that many Universalists do. In his "Recollections of a Busy Life," I find a chapter with the title of "My Faith," which, after a careful review of his meditations and reasonings on the subject of religion, and of the circumstances which led to his thinking deeply on the rigorous doctrines of his orthodox father, concludes as follows:

Perhaps I ought to add, that, with the great body of the Universalists of our day (who herein differ from the earlier pioneers in America of our faith), I believe that "our God is *one* Lord,"—that "though there be that are called gods, as there be gods many and lords many, to us there is but one

God, the Father, *of* whom are all things, one Lord Jesus Christ, *by* whom are all things;" and I find the relation between the Father and the Saviour of mankind most fully and clearly set forth in that majestic first chapter of Hebrews, which I cannot see how any Trinitarian can ever have intently read, without perceiving that its whole tenor and burden are directly at war with his conception of "three persons in one God." Nor can I see how Paul's express assertion, that "when all things shall be subdued unto him, then shall the Son himself also be subject to him that put all things under him, that God may be all in all," is to be reconciled with the more popular creed.

Those who have never given the subject much attention would be surprised at the various grades of "unbelief" found among persons not adhering to strictly orthodox views. The Universalists, for example, do not believe in a place of eternal punishment, generally styled "hell," and many of them ignore the doctrine of the Trinity. The Unitarians believe in but one God, repudiating the Holy Ghost and the Son (Jesus Christ) as two other persons of the Godhead. These are church-people, nevertheless, but with liberal and advanced views. Next, the "Skeptic" might be mentioned. He is simply a doubter, as the etymology of the word indicates, a person who accepts nothing on bare faith — not even the Holy Bible. He wants proof of everything before he believes it, and claims the right to pursue his inquiries even into the mazes of the question as to whether there is a God or not, and to require positive and substantial proof that there is before he accepts it as a settled fact. A Skeptic may believe in God, may believe in the immortality of the soul, may even believe in the divine origin of the Bible, but it will only be after he has investigated, inquired and reasoned for himself, and has found what in his judgment is satisfactory proof; otherwise he would not be a Skeptic at all. A Free-Thinker is about the same as a Skeptic. He claims and exercises the right to think and investigate for himself, and to be exempt from dictation in the matter by a clergyman, or any one else. If, as the result of his own investigations, he arrives at the conclusion that the orthodox faith is, after all, correct, he is no less a Free-Thinker; but a majority of persons so styled seem to entertain an opposite view of the question.

I could not cite a clearer example of a Skeptic, in the true sense of the term, than Thomas, one of Christ's disciples. He had seen his Master put to death on the cross, and his side pierced with a spear, and he refused to believe that Jesus had risen from the dead until he had "thrust his hand in his side," where the wound was made, and examined the laceration caused by the nails in the hands and feet. In fact, a writer of Scripture — St. Paul, I think — commands us all to be Skeptics when he says, *Prove all things.*

There, too, is the Deist. He believes there is a God — some supreme and intelligent Power controlling the universe — but does not believe in revealed religion. He regards the Bible as only of human origin and of only historical value. Such was Thomas Paine.

The Atheist, as the word implies, does not believe there is a God; certainly does not believe the Bible to be other than of human origin; and usually sees no positive evidence of the existence of an immortal soul, although he may remain in doubt on this point all his life. Such was John Stuart Mill. It is possible, of course, for a man to ignore the existence of a God, yet admit the existence of a subtile principle of life within us, the Soul, which may outlast our decaying bodies and retain its identity and individuality. Many of the strongest Spiritualists, whose whole creed is of course founded on the immortality of the soul, deny or doubt the existence of a God.

"Infidel" is a general term, meaning "unbeliever," as generally used, but it may be applied, in the same sense, to almost any one who does not believe in the creed of another. The Buddhist might style the Christian an "Infidel," because the latter is an unbeliever in his faith; and so, with equal propriety, might a person of one Christian sect term an adherent to the doctrines of another Christian sect.

Besides the classes of "unbelievers" in the Christian religion thus hastily alluded to, there are, even in this country, societies of "unbelievers" whose creeds partake of the form of religion, but are irreconcilable with the views of orthodox Christians. Such are the Jews, the Mormons, the Swedenborgians, and a number of other non-secular societies. In other countries there are many more, as, for example, the followers of Mohammed and of Buddha. In England, persons not adhering to the Established Church are looked upon as little more or less than "Infidels" by many persons who do adhere to that church.

Science has done much of late years, in what we are in the habit of styling civilized countries, to enhance Skepticism; for in astronomy, geology, natural history, and other studies, there have been made various developments of facts which many persons consider difficult to reconcile with the theories which have their foundation in Scripture. Now, editors of newspapers are thinking and reasoning men, if there is any set of men who are such as a class; ever seeking for truth and facts, in all phases of life, as well as in the remotest corners of inert matter; and hence they are Skeptics, in the strict sense of the term, before they know it. They are reading men as well as writers, men whose business it is to know what is new, and they keep pace with the developments of the sciences. They cannot all be finished astronomers, geologists and physicists, but when there is anything new in these departments of science, they must be the first to know it. Such developments, indeed, have been made in the science of geology, that even eminent divines agree that new meanings must be attached to the language of Genesis relating to the Creation of the World. So, when old forms of belief begin to crumble, it is not easy to set up new theories immediately that will be readily acquiesced in by everybody.

There, too, is the startling theory of Professor Darwin, that all animals, including man, have a common origin, — that man has reached his present comparatively high estate through many successive stages of development, — that his ancestors of merely a few million years ago were very much inferior, even in the matter of form, to the present races of men. This is another theory irreconcilable with a literal construction of the account of the Creation given in Genesis. But that a simple belief in the Darwinian Theory does not make an editor a very irreverent man, may be conceded when I state that I once heard a well-known lecturer on geology say on the rostrum that an "eminent divine" — whom it would now be just as well not to mention—confessed to him that he himself (the divine) believed in the Darwinian Theory, that he considered it the only plausible theory of the origin of man, and that he believed the language of Genesis should be accepted as having only a figurative meaning. The "eminent divine" still believed in the Bible, of course, as God's revealed will and work, and also believed that "God works by means," and that he had made the laws by which the great work of Development has been so far carried out — that is, the development of man from lower animals.

From the nature of their occupation, journalists are of course the first numerous class of persons to become acquainted with new doctrines, new theories; the first to give them thoughtful consideration, and the aptest to regard them with calm and impartial judgment. I think the latter assertion is entirely reasonable, because editors are so used to dealing daily with startling things that in their eyes new and eccentric theories are speedily shorn of their novelty, and ready to be considered in a spirit of coolness and fairness.

In the course of their daily duties, too, journalists see so much that is calculated to disgust them — not with religion itself, but with many of its prominent votaries. Defalcations, embezzlements, "immoralities," and other villanies perpetrated by men "hitherto regarded as Christian gentlemen," etc.; church-quarrels and church-ruptures; church-scandals, in the course of which Ministers of the Gospel are often found to be incredibly carnal-minded; all these subjects are daily handled by the reporter and editor; daily given account of, and daily commented on by the journalists; and so it is not to be wondered at that their alarming frequency tends to lessen, in the minds of those who are nearest to them as spectators — the newspaper men — respect for societies whose leading upholders are so often found wanting in honesty and purity. The fact cannot be ignored that a certain amount of obloquy is brought upon any institution which is found to be upheld by a considerable number of persons who prove to be possessed of immoral characters — one of the worst traits of which is hypocrisy.

Among other things at which I have frequently heard skeptical journalists express disgust, and which, while it is no logical argument against the correctness of religious theories, may have strengthened their doubts, is the whining piety of murderers who so often swing from the scaffold with the avowed conviction that they have "made their peace with God," and that they are going straight to heaven, to "dwell with him and his angels," and to be "blessed for ever;" while the victim, probably not a bad sort of person, is —

> Cut off even in the blossom of (his) sin,
> Unhousel'd, disappointed, unanel'd;
> No reckoning made, but sent to (his) account
> With all (his) imperfections on (his) head!

Before me lies a newspaper, in which the following paragraph, by mere chance, thus opportunely catches my eye:

UDDERZOOK'S EXECUTION. — Udderzook is to be hung at West Chester on Thursday. During the past few days he has undergone a marked change. He looks now as though hope was fast fading from his bosom, and his expression denotes his having awakened to the consciousness of his awful situation. He expresses a hope to share in the all-forgiving power of God.

This is an example of a class of cases to which journalists often allude in severe terms, not only in private conversation, but also, as is well known, in their editorial writings.

The Boston daily *Herald*, a paper of large circulation and of liberal and independent views, gives a certain amount of space in its columns to all, without discrimination, who wish to express their sentiments or opinions on questions of general interest, only making it a condition that the communications be courteous in tone and of no unreasonable length. A few years ago, when the proposition of adding a religious amendment to the Constitution of the United States, and of so taking the first step toward destroying religious liberty — a very cornerstone in the foundation of our nationality — was agitated, some one wrote to the Boston *Herald* to advocate the measure, arguing that a constitutional recognition of Christianity would increase its strength and influence, and that with the enhancement of religion, crime would naturally abate. A day or two afterward some one else wrote to the *Herald*, in reply, as follows:

Editor of the Herald: In writing to you on a question of religion, a correspondent has recently maintained that a belief in Christianity is necessary as a check upon such as are disposed to commit crime. I claim that this is no argument as to the correctness of Christian theories; and I also claim that religion does not restrain men from committing crime. Nor do I wish to beg the question. In support of my assertion I cite the fact that there never was a murderer hanged in this country who did not go to the gallows a believer in religion; and all, with but one or two exceptions, have died with prayers on their lips and in the full hope of everlasting happiness. I believe I am safe in asserting that not one of the class styled "Infidels" has ever been hanged, or even convicted of a heinous crime in this country. Let me mention a significant fact, supported by statistics: the Auburn Penitentiary contains about fifteen hundred convicts — all believers in Christianity; and what is still more striking is, that among the inmates of this prison the ministry is more largely represented than any other profession or trade — the number of clergymen being twenty-five! I ask if those facts support the theory that a belief in the divinity of Jesus Christ prevents men from committing crime?

Thus journalists are continually handling this subject of religion, either for themselves or others, and thus are they constantly brought face to face with statistics, for and against; and whether those who have become skeptics are on the right road or not, I believe it would be only reasonable to concede that, together with their orthodox brothers, they have aimed at impartiality in their researches and reasonings.

I have noticed a great similarity in the experience of dissenting journalists with whom I have conversed on the subject of religious skepticism. Nearly all — I do not remember any exception — were born of Christian parents, and brought up "in the nurture and admonition of the Lord;" they began to think and reason independently at about the age of manhood; began to lose confidence in the reliability of the Scriptures; to doubt the divinity of Jesus Christ; the existence of a devil and hell; of the New Jerusalem, with golden streets and walls of precious stones; finally, (many of them,) of a Supreme Being. Some never got so far as this; some halted at Unitarianism, Universalism, Deism, etc., as before intimated. In all cases, however, about the first article of the orthodox faith to be abandoned was the burning hell. It would therefore seem that a fitting injunction to those who wish to remain believers in the Christian religion would be: "Don't take the first step; don't give up eternal punishment."

I do not wish to obtrude my own views on religion, but I think I should fail to be entirely ingenuous, if I did not, while on this subject, state that, like many other journalists, I have long entertained religious views of the widest liberality. Nor have my conclusions been hasty. They have only been reached through many gradations of deliberate thought. I have never given up an old theory before its untenability was presented to my mind as entirely unequivocal.

But I do not believe that a person's opinions on this or any other subject will ever involve his moral character. The most honorable of men may be found among Skeptics, just as some very dishonorable persons are to be found among those professing religion. A rascal will be a rascal, even though he be arrayed in a bishop's robes; an honest man will be an honest man, even though he be branded as an "Infidel!"

In conclusion, let me say that it was impossible to make this work complete, to make it what its title purports, without alluding briefly to this subject — "The Religion of Editors;" and having taken it up, I could entertain no thought of dealing with it in any other way than frankly and truthfully. And I believe it is due to the large number of skeptical journalists, whose power for good or evil is ever great, to say that in abandoning the forms of religion they have not abandoned truth and integrity. If they have let go the shadow, they have clung still closer to the substance. If I have observed with reasonable penetration and judgment, I believe they have a code of ethics — no written code — that is noble, and good, and worthy of any being, mortal or immortal, a code that says: "Be just, for the sake of justice; be truthful, for the sake of truth; be honorable, for the sake of honor; be nothing and do nothing either from fear of punishment or hope of reward; do right always, and only *because* it is right."

CHAPTER XV.

THE PAY OF NEWSPAPER MEN.

ON the subject of the remuneration of employed newspaper men, I find an article in *Harper's Monthly*, from which, as the views of the writer are entirely correct, I make the following extract:

> The suppression of half our daily papers would greatly advance the art of journalism in the United States. Five, six, seven daily papers in a city of less than a hundred thousand inhabitants! Some of these have a corps consisting of one individual; and where there are three persons employed, the paper feels itself entitled to some rank in the world of journalism. One consequence is that two-thirds of all the working journalists in the country receive less than the wages of good mechanics; and another consequence is that the daily press, published in the midst of an intelligent people, is sometimes a daily miracle of calumnious inanity. Falsehood and folly in daily papers are not so much an evidence of depravity as of poverty. Intelligence and character are costly; frivolity and recklessness are cheap. The incessant abuse of individuals is one of the few resources of an empty mind. It cannot discuss principles; it cannot communicate knowledge; it cannot enliven by wit and good humor; nothing remains to it but to assail character. And even where the decorums of the press are strictly observed, we find in the columns of newspapers which are struggling for life amazing exhibitions of helpless ignorance. The nauseating trail of fifteen dollars a week is seen all over them, a sign of that agonizing contest for existence which goes wherever ten are trying to subsist upon means insufficient for five.

Many persons somehow or other drift into journalism who were never fitted, either by habit or education, for that calling. The result is, they never rise above positions of mere "drudgery," but remain "hewers of wood and drawers of water" in the Sanctum all their lives. Never attaining advanced positions, they seldom receive salaries much above fifteen dollars a week, and so they go through a life with the idea that they are journalists, when the truth is that they are less than good entry-clerks, and the fruits of their great minds' labors are incomparably smaller than those of the hands of a skillful mechanic. If I had to decide whether to be a good mechanic or a poor journalist, I would not be a second in deciding to be the former.

On the other hand, many of the brightest journalists in the United States have passed through those gloomy stages of "moderate pay," and risen to positions the salaries of which place them far above petty financial troubles. Some of the most brilliant men in newspaper history have worked for from five to ten dollars a week; and — must I tell this "secret," too? — have more than once suffered from an insufficiency of food, more than once "gone hungry." But such men, in whom there was something of depth, and greatness, and firmness of purpose, did not remain long in the realms of "Bohemianism;" and many who once found themselves obliged to live, somehow, on five dollars a week, now feel that they are too poorly paid at five thousand dollars a year.

One of the few comparatively wealthy editors I happen to know once told me that when he first settled in a certain large Western city he "made himself generally useful" in the editorial department of a daily, a whole summer, for five, and, later, six dollars a week. In the autumn another paper engaged him at twenty, which was soon advanced to thirty dollars a week.

He "stuck to it," became one of the proprietors, finally the senior proprietor; the paper prospered, owing to his judicious management; and, although he has ever been prodigal in his expenditures, he is worth half a million dollars. "Good luck" aided him in a considerable degree, but his success was largely due to natural genius, industry and perseverance.

I believe the majority of us have passed through the "hard-up" days, the days of "dead-brokenness." What is the use of denying it? I have worked for five dollars a week, and slept on a pile of exchanges. I have seen the time that "circumstances over which I had no control" dictated to me the necessity — not merely the propriety — of eating plainer food than I would have liked — plainer food than the kind I needed — and of not even wasting any of that. I have seen the time — why should I conceal the truth? — when a person I know very intimately has gone without food for days at a time, and that when in excellent bodily health and blessed (?) with an unusual appetite. I have seen the days of threadbare clothes, of dilapidated shoes, and a "shocking bad hat," and I remember that I have blushed at the thought of belonging to the "Shabby Genteel," and when it brought the hot blood to my face to hear careless, and happy, and well-fed, and well-clothed people merrily singing this chorus of a well-known song:

"Too proud to beg, too honest to steal,
We know what it is to be wanting a meal;
Our tatters and rags we try to conceal;
We belong to the 'Shabby Genteel!'"

Cases of actual destitution, however, are by no means frequent in journalistic life. They are episodes, usually in the earlier part of the editor's professional career. I never saw one who had the foolish pride, among his brother journalists, not to acknowledge such little former embarrassments and laugh at them, years afterward; yet all had such an amount of pride at the time that they would have starved and died rather than acknowledge that they were hungry. It is a strange pride, but its existence is quite common. I know of nothing that it would be harder for a truly proud-spirited man to do than to go to any one and say, "I'm hungry," when he is really suffering from a want of food.

I know a certain newspaper man who told me a rather amusing story of going without victuals awhile in St. Louis, and I made the following sketch of it for *Saturday Night*, the publishers of which paper have given me their cordial permission to reproduce it here:

HUNGRY.

"Hungry?" said Mose. "I should say I was once; and — Lord, pity the poor! — I had never thought it was so hard before. I never told you about it? No? Well, I thought I had. To tell the truth about it, though, I was a little sore on the subject for a year."

"How was it, Mose?"

"I'll tell you, for I can laugh at it now. In the summer of 'sixty-six I was on a tour through the Mississippi Valley, as correspondent for a well-known paper. I reached St. Louis one Friday evening, expecting to find a remittance awaiting me at the post-office. It had not arrived yet, but I would have taken my oath, before a notary public, that it would come on Saturday. The truth is, I had met with such genial company on the steamer from Memphis up that I had not kept back any fair reserve fund; so I looked upon that expected remittance with a good deal of veneration.

"Intending to stay in St. Louis two or three weeks, I took a furnished room not far from the Planters' Hotel, paying one week's rent in advance. Next thing to be looked after was meals. I took supper at a restaurant, and had a dollar left. On Saturday morning I took breakfast, and then went to the post-office to get my letter; but — confound it — there was none for me. I could have murdered that clerk when he drawled out, 'N-n-o!' in answer to my inquiry. Well, I went to the post-office twice more that day. I saw a different clerk the last time — a more generous-looking one — and my heart beat with hope; but he could n't lie — there was no letter for me, and much as he may have felt pained about it, he had to tell me so.

"Evening finally overtook me with five cents in my pocket — and no letter. In despair I purchased a glass of beer — for it was warm weather — and prepared to stare a very quiet Sunday in the face. I — but wait a minute, and I'll get you my diary; then you can read for yourself."

Mose went up-stairs, and soon returned with a well-worn diary.

"There," said he, opening to the place. "Begin there."

He lighted a cigar, and sat with his feet on the mantel, while I read his almost illegible pencil-tracks.

Saturday Night, bedtime.—No remittance to-day. Last cent gone. To-morrow is Sunday, and Heaven knows how I am to live through it. No meals provided for, and I don't know a soul in St. Louis. Must I go till Monday morning without — eating? It cannot be! Some unexpected accident will throw a meal in my way— I feel it.

Sunday Morning.—I have slept late this morning. I seldom have any appetite to speak of in the morning; but it just happens this time, with no prospect of nourishment, that my stomach is howling. What am I to do? Well, I must walk out. Perhaps a little exercise will do instead of break-fast — though exercise, simply as an article of diet, is not recommended by physicians.

Sunday Noon.—I feel actually hungry. Drank a great deal of water, this forenoon, to sort o' fill up. Tried to read. Walked out twice, but only returned each time feeling more and more — hungry.

Sunday Evening.—Twenty-four hours since food has entered my stomach. Experience a sense of faintness and prostration at the lower end of the breast-bone. Knees weak. Feel no tendency to vigorous physical exer-tion. I am hungry — very hungry. Could eat nails.

Sunday Evening, nine o'clock.—Rather early, but I shall retire. Will try slumber as a substitute for food. Providence has thrown nothing in my way. I did walk a couple of miles, thinking I might find some money, but in vain. Have drunk water ravenously all the evening. What if no remit-tance comes to-morrow? I must not think of it, or I shall go mad!

Monday Morning.—Passed a rather restless night. Got up eight or nine times, and drank water with a freedom new to me. Think I must have been slightly delirious. Dreamed repeatedly of meals. Dreamed once of a whole roast ox. Awoke. Smell of beefsteak coming fiendishly up from below, where landlady is preparing breakfast — peaceful, happy breakfast — for family; but not for Mose! Bewildered with appetite. Glance at uppers of my boots. They look good. Think of starving sailors.

Monday, eleven A. M.—Joy! Remittance arrived. Ordered beef-steak and mutton-chops both at restaurant. Felt as though I could eat all on the table, including napkins, and a leg or two of the table itself. Hungry? Whew! Singular, though, could n't eat much, after all. Very little satisfied me for the time. Could n't eat half a meal. Wondered how it was. Concluded that stomach got out of practice. But I feel very happy, as I clutch a little handful of greenbacks. Think now that I was a fool to go hungry all day yesterday. Should have explained matters to the benevolent-looking landlady, and got something to eat. Would n't pass another such day. Would beg first. I wonder how it feels to starve? Must now write a letter to the ——— Journal, on the manufacturing interests of St. Louis. How I do pity the poor!

Not every newspaper man has been in actual want, but there are times when, through various adverse circumstances, the best of journalists, may be thrown "out of a job" for awhile, and being improvident to the extent of having "nothing ahead," their minds being generally occupied by nobler thoughts than those relating to the accumulation of money, they find these exigencies very awkward, to say the least. On one occasion, while connected with the press in a large city of the Atlantic Coast, I met an old friend who had for some time been managing the editorial department of a well-known Western daily paper, but had been obliged to give it up and leave the locality on account of becoming a victim of the ague. He had a family and but little means, and I told him I would look around and try to find an opening for him. I soon learned that an assistant was wanted on a paper which I knew very little about, and which, as I afterward learned, was struggling for existence. Having met one of the proprietors, I called on him and mentioned my friend, whose abilities I knew to be such that he could have creditably occupied the position of Managing Editor of the biggest paper in the country. On the strength of my recommendation, the proprietors at once consented to engage him, and requested me to "bring him round." I did so; introduced him and left him to make an agreement with them. I met him in the street a few days afterward, and asked:

"Well, did you arrive at an understanding?"

"Yes," he replied; "but I have to start in on a very small salary. How much do you suppose?"

"Eighteen dollars?" I guessed.

"Only thirteen," said he.

"Rather small, for *you*," I said.

"Yes; but they tell me they have every reason to believe that they are going to make a great success of the paper; that the position of Managing Editor will be vacant within a year, and that I can thus work myself into a fine position, with a handsome salary. I'll, of course, do all I can to build it up."

"Ah? That sounds better. Then you'll try it for the present?"

"Yes; I'm at work already."

We parted, neither having two minutes to spare.

A week later I saw him in the street, leaning against a druggist's sign, with his hands in his overcoat pockets, and gazing thoughtfully at passing vehicles. There was an unmistakable air of leisure about him, and I said:

"Ah! how's this?"

"I've left," he replied.

"What's the matter?"

"Well, Saturday afternoon came round and they began to pay off. They said they were a little short—had n't got fairly under way yet—could n't well pay me *quite* all my week's salary just then, and offered me *three dollars* on account."

"Then you left?"

"Just as soon as I could get my hat on."

"I should have done so, too," I said. "I'm sorry I did n't know they were in such a fix as that, or I should not have advised you to go there."

He soon after took a position on a more substantial paper, with which I believe he is still connected, and on which he made himself so useful that his services were considered worth twenty-eight hundred dollars a year, which is certainly a trifle better than thirteen dollars a week, and only three dollars of that amount "down."

In another city I once had a bit of similar experience, and more of it, as I worked three weeks on a newly-established daily and never got a cent of my salary, which had been fixed at twenty dollars a week, to be speedily advanced to twenty-five, with a still further increase in the perspective. The paper went up, and the proprietor is dead, and — good-by! He might as well have honored me by promising me five hundred dollars a week, as he could have paid that amount just as easily as the stipulated twenty.

Some persons have big ideas of the prices paid for manuscripts by publishers of weekly story papers. The regular writers for such papers are paid an amount, sometimes by the column, that prevents their coming to want, but seldom such an amount as to give promise of the accumulation of riches. I think it would be well enough for a person who contemplates writing for a weekly paper not to count on getting over ten or fifteen dollars per column for his manuscripts — if they are accepted at all; and if he *should* get more than that, the surprise will be on the sunny side. "Blessed are they that expect little" — for obvious reasons.

I once had a position on a literary weekly in which it was a part of my duty to examine manuscripts offered for publication and decide whether they were worthy of acceptation, or entitled to be "respectfully declined." During this period of my life, I was one evening thrown in the company of a gentleman who was introduced to me as Col. Minks.

"The colonel," said the person who introduced us, "is a literary man, like yourself."

This was highly gratifying, to be sure, and I deemed myself in the presence of some eminent historian. In the course of our conversation the colonel informed me that he was "writing a novel," of which he told me the projected title, and for which he said he expected to receive the sum of ten thousand dollars.

I thought this a trifle above the average price paid for novels in this country, and ventured to suggest that he would be very fortunate should he succeed in getting his price, stating that a New York publishing-house had recently offered Dickens himself but twenty-five thousand dollars for his next story.

"Oh, I'm certain of getting my price," he said, confidently; "and I know I'll take no less."

I was, of course, glad to hear it; and no more was said on the subject—I not happening to mention that I was connected with the literary paper alluded to above.

A few weeks later the proprietor of that paper handed me a large mass of manuscript, saying:

"Here is a serial offered by a new contributor. If you have time this week, please let me know what you think of it."

"What does he ask for it?" I inquired, taking up the first sheet or two.

"Five hundred dollars."

Glancing at the title, I was a trifle surprised to discover that it was the production of no less a person than Col. Minks, the ten-thousand-dollar man! Well, there is such a thing as "blowing," you know.

I read the story with the same care and impartiality I should have exercised if I had never met its sagacious author; then did what my duty to the publisher and a conscientious regard for truth compelled me to do — rejected it.

The stories of fabulous sums paid by the publishers of weekly papers to ordinary story-writers ought to be compiled in a convenient form and made an appendix to that piece of history relative to "Aladdin and his Wonderful Lamp."

CHAPTER XVI.

DEAD-HEADING.

IT need scarcely be explained that a "Dead-Head" is one who, for some reason or other, usually on account of his influential position, is privileged to attend theaters and other places of amusement, or to ride in public conveyances, free of charge; or one who may receive free copies of a newspaper, or other publication, or, in fact, any other article of a commercial value, returning no equivalent therefor. The term is indigenous to the United States, where I think the practice of "Dead-Heading" prevails to an extent not yet reached in any other country. I do not know the exact origin of the term "Dead-Head," or how it first came to be applied to a person who receives favors for which others have to pay, for generally the "head" of such a person is, in common with his whole body, in a living condition. Probably a Dead-Head is so styled for about the same reason that one whose business it is to bury the dead is called an undertaker — because he is.

Editors constitute a large class of the Dead-Heads of this country, although in the matter of public conveyances they have a host of companions in the shape of Governors, Congressmen, Mayors of cities, members of Legislatures, City Councilmen, and officers and directors of railroads. While I have to deprecate the practice of Dead-Heading, I am obliged to confess that I myself have never yet felt so high-minded as to decline a pass on a railroad and pay my fare as a matter of preference. It is "the custom of the country," and while it is so I have a delicacy about setting myself up as an example of an unusual degree of conscience — particularly where such a course would be found expensive. Still, I would like to see Dead-Heading, as an "institution," abolished. It seems to me that there must be something that lacks a mere trifle of being precisely right in a system that gives something to certain privileged classes without an equivalent return; and I think the dignity of journalism will be largely enhanced when the practice of Dead-Heading becomes obsolete, so far, at least, as newspaper men are concerned. To that end, I am willing, for one, to do my share and to pay like other people for my enjoyment at places of amusement and for the conveniences of public conveyances, and on the other hand to be paid like other people for my work, so that the incubus of "free-puffing" may also be numbered with the things of the past.

It is true that in the case of theaters there is a tacit understanding that the critic receives his free passes in return for the criticisms he writes; but it seems to me that even in this case the journalist had better pay the usual price of admission, in order that his mind will be left the more free to criticise the play with exclusive reference to its deserts. Besides, it is not only the critic himself that goes to see the play without paying. Free tickets or passes by the dozen are furnished to a newspaper establishment for the mere asking — often without even the asking; and the book-reviewer, the editorial-writer, the telegraph-editor, the general news-editor and the city-editor all go and take their wives, and a friend or two each, without writing a line. It looks almost as if the manager of the theater were saying to the editors: "Come to my theater, and view my expensive scenery and the acting of my well-paid performers, without money and without price; but in return, be kind enough to lie a little for me, occasionally, and tell the public that the entertainment is admirable when you know it is execrable." I say it has this look, although any editor would repel with indignation and scorn any such direct proposition.

In the matter of public conveyances, I think there is still less excuse for Dead-Heading, and the practice has a still worse aspect than in the case of the theater. Railroads, let us note, are usually conducted by powerful corporations; they are intrusted with the lives of millions of people every day, and when in their management there is the slightest departure from rigid care and surveillance, the newspaper editor ought to feel perfectly free to call public attention to it and demand that the dangerous evil be corrected. Then imagine an editor who has just received his annual pass from the superintendent of a railroad on which he frequently travels, sitting down and writing the following paragraph touching that railroad and that superintendent:

The accident which occurred on the New York and Liverpool Railroad last week is shown, by the results of the coroner's investigations, to have been the fruits of an imperfect system of signals introduced by the present superintendent, Mr. —— (naming the gentleman who has kindly sent the pass). Mr. —— is probably a very excellent gentleman in social life, but it seems to us that he is out of his place in the responsible position of superintendent of this extensive steam thoroughfare. It is clear, according to the evidence, that his defective system of signals is wholly responsible for the catastrophe which was so fruitful in suffering and death; and we warn the directors of the New York and Liverpool Railroad that they cannot afford so to trifle with the lives of passengers as to retain in so important a position as that of superintendent one who is clearly deficient in the good judgment requisite to enable him to perform its duties with perfect safety to the traveling public.

Under the supposed circumstances, are there many editors living who could write the supposed paragraph of censure? If not, then does it not look as if, under this system of Dead-Heading, the superintendent and directors were saying to the editor, with the inspiration of the theater manager: "Ride free on our road; take any train you please, as often as you please; go as far as you please; get off where you please; come back when you please; and pay nothing; but—if you see any defect in our road, a public mention of which might injure our business, however much the public ought to know it, keep mum?"

I know that there are many well-meaning and conscientious journalists who will differ with me on this point, possibly expressing opposite views in vigorous language; but I think I speak without any mental reservation whatever when I say that, in urging the abolition of the practice of Dead-Heading, I am prompted only by the most sincere and unselfish wishes for the further elevation of journalism.

I have known Dead-Heading to be carried on, in exceptional instances, to a degree little less than disgraceful; have seen it take such ramifications as to involve whole families, the heads of such families being editors of newspapers. One of the meanest Dead-Heads I ever knew, and the only thoroughly mean man I ever met among practical journalists, not content with riding free year after year over a certain railroad, passing members of his family over it free, time after time, and occasionally a mere friend, who was no relative at all, on concluding once to change his residence, moved his household goods over the whole length of the railroad,— a hundred and twenty miles, — and when the freight-bills came to hand, this person had the "cheek" to take them to the superintendent and ask him to cancel them! This the too-obliging official did; and thus not only did the Dead-Head, his family and a small circle of friends travel over the road at the expense of the corporation that owned it, but his chairs, tables, bedsteads and old stoves and crockery also enjoyed the stately privilege of "going dead-head" — and all because they were the property of a person who was the editor of a weekly paper! In justice to the profession — and I certainly should be the last to do it injustice — I must say that I never knew of more than this one instance of that peculiar kind of Dead-Heading, and that, I am sure, it would be universally denounced, by journalists who deserve the name, as "little and mean." It does seem to me that the amount of assurance displayed on that occasion is only rivaled in history by that of the unfortunate murderer, who, having killed his own father and mother, asked the court to deal mercifully with him, on the ground that he was an orphan!

When I was in San Francisco, I one day met a casual acquaintance who was "running" a weekly paper. He was an enterprising and thrifty young man and a writer of some ability; but he was, as he no doubt believed he had a right to be, an inveterate Dead-Head. He had a valise in his hand, and I asked him if he had "been traveling"?

"I have been up at Grass Valley a week," he said, — Grass Valley being a considerable mining town far up in the mountains.

"Who attended to your paper?"

"Oh, I put it in such a shape before leaving that it would nearly run itself, and left Charlie Stuart in charge."

"How did you find things at Grass Valley?"

"Pretty good. Most of the mines are doing a fair business. I wrote up one or two for our next issue. I of course got some advertisements by promising to do so. I also got over a hundred subscribers to my paper, at four dollars each."

"Very fair week's work. Expenses heavy?"

"Not mine. I traveled free on the California Pacific, and at Sacramento I called on Mr. C—— and got a pass over the Central Pacific to Reno and back. Then I traveled free from Reno to Grass Valley (twelve miles) and back on the stage. (Mighty good stage-line; must give it a puff.) And—would you believe it?—when I got ready to leave and offered to settle my hotel bill, the proprietor said: 'Never mind. That's all right. We don't charge editors anything here. Always glad to see them come and take a look at our place and the mines.' Pretty square fellow, that; but he'll lose nothing by it. He shall have a puff. So, the whole trip cost me only sixty-five cents, and that was for 'incidentals.'"

That is what I call a piece of pure and successful Dead-Heading. Between four and five hundred miles of traveling over two different railroads and a stage-line, and a week's board at a first-class hotel, with an expenditure of sixty-five cents!

CHAPTER XVII.

THE BOHEMIAN.

THE people of Bohemia are proverbially of a roving disposition, probably because adverse wars have sent nearly whole nations of them into exile, and on that account the term "Bohemian" is applied to a class of writers for the press who, lacking fixedness of purpose, and generally lacking the means or faculties necessary for carrying out any very great purpose, wander from Sanctum to Sanctum, from city to city, picking up odd jobs of reporting, compiling, proof-reading, sketch-writing or verse-writing. The majority of them are only in a normal condition when they are "dead-broke," under which circumstances they are disposed to regard the world with the eye of cynicism; but they become happy and contented on receiving from three to five dollars for a bit of work occupying a day or two, with which amount they immediately proceed to pay room-rent and buy some victuals "and things."

The actual "Bohemian" is a queer character, often, but not always, without very great journalistic ability, sometimes well educated and not infrequently possessing a genius for writing poetry. I once employed a Bohemian occasionally, when there was some extra reporting to be done, who was a finished scholar, and could speak and write Latin, Greek, Spanish, French and German, as well as the finest English; yet this singular man was always glad to get a stray job of reporting a railroad meeting or a cattle-show, and considered himself in a position of comparative opulence when he received two or three dollars for the task. How he lived I never exactly knew, but think I was competent to make a pretty fair guess. Certainly he could not have enjoyed many of the good things of this world, as he probably, from one paper and another, seldom received an aggregate of over five or six dollars a week. I occasionally gave him half an hour's proof-reading to do, when I could as well have done it myself, the paper being a weekly, that I might have a pretext for handing him half a dollar or so when I felt pretty sure he sorely needed it, and he was generally delighted to receive that amount for his work. The poor fellow was proud, and I would not have thought of offering him a sum of money as a gift. He never suspected my motive in giving him little jobs of that kind, as I usually contrived on such occasions to seem fairly "driven to death" by a press of business. If he had, I believe he would have declined the work, even if hungry; but as it was, he always went away cheerful and contented, with the full sense that he had earned his money by "helping me out" at a busy time.

There are many men classed among the "Bohemians" who are not by any means to be despised — many who possess brilliant minds; some are poets, of grand and pathetic conception; some could write a history with Macaulay; but untoward circumstances, sometimes domestic troubles and disappointments, have disgusted them with life itself, and set them adrift in the newspaper world, without an aim, without a guide, with little to live for, blasted hopes to look back upon, an empty future to look forward to, and in the midst of the days of which they can say, "We have no pleasure in them." They are all poor — they live poorly — many of them have narrow and gloomy apartments in the upper stories of tall buildings, where, with the meanest surroundings, they live and write, often in hunger, and from which they daily issue in the threadbare clothes which they have carefully brushed to make them look as decent as possible.

N. G. Shepherd, a New York writer for the press, died in that city a few years ago, and I remember that some of the newspapers in mentioning his decease spoke of him as a "Bohemian," stating that irregular habits were the immediate cause of his death. He died but a day or two after writing his last poem, which was based on the fact that a few days before, "at the Morgue in New York, the attire of a drowned woman alone remained for identification." Poor Shepherd sold the poem to *Appleton's Journal*, in which it was promptly published, afterward going the rounds of the press. I here reproduce it, with the remark that, "Bohemian" or not, "irregular habits" or not, it was no little mind that conceived these touching lines:

ONLY THE CLOTHES THAT SHE WORE.

There is the hat
With the blue vail thrown round it, just as they found it,
Spotted and soiled, stained and all spoiled —
Do you recognize that?

The gloves, too, lie there,
And in them still lingers the shape of her fingers,
That some one has pressed, perhaps, and caressed,
So slender and fair.

There are the shoes,
With their long silken laces still bearing traces
To the toe's dainty tip of the mud of the slip,
The slime and the ooze.

There is the dress,
Like the blue vail, all dabbled, discolored and drabbled —
This you should know, without doubt, and, if so,
All else you may guess!

There is the shawl,
With the striped border, hung next in order,
Soiled hardly less than the light muslin dress,
And — that is all.

Ah, here 's a ring
We were forgetting, with a pearl setting;
There was only this one — name or date? — none!
A frail, pretty thing;

A keepsake, maybe,
The gift of another, perhaps a brother
Or lover, who knows? him her heart chose,
Or, was she heart-free?

Does the hat there,
With the blue vail around it, just as they found it,
Summon up a fair face with just a trace
Of gold in her hair?

Or does the shawl,
Mutely appealing to some hidden feeling,
A form, young and slight, to your mind's sight
Clearly recall?

A month now has passed,
And the sad history remains yet a mystery,
But these we keep still, and shall keep them until
Hope dies at last.

Was she the prey
Of some deep sorrow clouding the morrow,
Hiding from view the sky's happy blue?
Or was there foul play?

Alas! who may tell?
Some one or other, perhaps a fond mother,
May recognize these, when her child's clothes she sees;
Then — will it be well?

Mr. George Manson, an experienced reporter, contributed a series of sketches on "Bohemianism" to a New York publication a few years ago, and as they are very true to the life, the reader need not feel sorry if I here quote from them:

There have probably been more Bohemians in literature than in real life. Henri Murger, a famous French author, was the first to immortalize the Bohemians by writing about them. He wrote an interesting novel, entitled, "Scenes de la Vie de Bohéme," in which he created the wanderers, as it were, into a nation. His work was eagerly read, especially by those young persons who believed that they possessed a Bohemian nature, or, if they did not, desired to. The original of the word "Bohemian" is found in Sir Walter Scott's "Quentin Durward." In that book there is mention made of a certain gipsy, who is termed "the Bohemian." But the literary Bohemian has little in common with the Bohemian of gipsy life. Like the latter, he is unconventional, ignores some of the laws of religion (sometimes morality), and has no prejudices; but there the resemblance ends.

Thackeray has given us one or two pictures of "Bohemians" in the characters of "Fred. Bayham" and "Col. Altamont," the latter a fair specimen of the more disreputable class. Thackeray himself, while in Rome, lived in the realms of Bohemia, and haunted the Greco and Lepri.

Dickens, above all other writers, knew Bohemia well. He has given us many characters who possessed the true Bohemian sentiment, mingled with a good deal of evil and dishonesty not necessarily belonging to Bohemianism. Every one remembers, for instance, the character of "Harold Skimpole" in "Bleak House." His philosophy was essentially Bohemian. Skimpole's friends obtained situations for him, but somehow or other he never succeeded, because he "had no idea of time or money." In consequence of this slight defect of character, he never kept an appointment, never knew the value of anything, and of course could not be expected to transact business properly and with profit. "So," says Dickens, "he had got on in life, and here he was! He was very fond of reading the papers, very fond of making fancy sketches with a pencil, very fond of nature, very fond of art. All he asked of society was to let him live. *That* was n't much. His wants were few. Give him the papers, conversation, music, mutton and coffee, landscape, fruit in season, a few sheets of Bristol-board, and a little claret — and he asked no more. He was a mere child in the world. 'Go your several ways in peace. Wear your red coats, blue coats, lawn sleeves, put pens behind your ears, wear aprons, go after glory, holiness, commerce, trade, any object you prefer; only let Harold Skimpole live.'"

Skimpole was lazy. He had the greatest sympathy with the work of the world, although not industrious himself. "I can dream of them," says he, speaking of the negro slaves; "I can lie down on the grass in fine weather, and float along an African river, embracing all the natives I meet, as sensible of the deep silence, and sketching the dense overhanging tropical growth as accurately as if I were there. I don't know that it is any direct use — my doing so — but it is all I can do, and I do it thoroughly." Another of his peculiarities was that he did not feel any vulgar gratitude toward any one. He almost felt as if they ought to be grateful to him for giving them the opportunity of enjoying the luxury of generosity. He was very remiss in the matter of paying his bills, and yet his philosophy on the subject of debt, though probably not shared by his creditors, is, to say the least, very entertaining. He owed his physician. "If he had those bits of metal or thin paper to which mankind attach so much value, to put them in the doctor's hand, he would put them in the doctor's hand; but not having them, he substituted the will for the deed. If he really meant it, if his will was genuine and real, which it was, it appeared to him the same as coin, and canceled the obligation."

When he owed his rent, he thought there was something grotesque in his landlord's seizing his furniture (which, by the way, he had not paid for); "thus making," said he, "my chair and table merchant pay my landlord my rent. Why," argued he, "should my landlord quarrel with him? If I have a pimple on my nose that is disagreeable to my landlord's peculiar ideas of beauty, my landlord has no business to scratch my chair and table merchant's nose, which has no pimple on it. His reasoning seems defective." A butcher, to whom he owed a considerable amount, remonstrated with him for eating his meat. Says he, "Sir, why did you eat spring lamb at eighteen pence per pound?" "'Why did I eat spring lamb at eighteen pence per pound, my honest friend?' said I, naturally amazed by the question; 'I like spring lamb.' This was so far convincing. 'Well, sir,' said he, 'I wish I had meant the lamb as you meant the money.' 'My good fellow,' said I, 'pray, let us reason like intellectual beings. How could that be? It was impossible. You had the lamb, and I have not the money. You could not really mean the lamb, without sending it in, whereas I can and really do mean the money without paying it.'"

Alfred Jingle was another pretty good specimen of the Bohemian; but the very best specimen we have in the works of Dickens is the famous "Wilkins Micawber." He, like many of the lower class of Bohemians of all large cities, was very generally in debt. The only visitors, in fact, that were ever seen at his house were creditors, who came at all hours of the day and night, some of whom were quite ferocious. Sometimes he would become low-spirited in consequence of these obligations. He called himself, on divers occasions, "a foundered bark," "a fallen tower," "a beggared outcast," "a shattered fragment in the Temple of Fame," "a straw on the surface of the deep," and accused the "serpents" of having "poisoned his life-blood." But he soon recovered from these fits of despondence. In the morning he has been known to make motions at his throat with a razor, and an hour later to polish his boots and go down the street humming a tune. On one sad occasion he said, "the God of day had gone down upon him," but before noon of the same day he played a lively game of "skittles." His rule for obtaining happiness was very sensible, and many in our day would be much happier if they were strictly guided by it. "He observed that if a man had twenty pounds a year as his income, and spent nineteen pounds, nineteen shillings and sixpence, he would be happy; but if he spent twenty pounds, one shilling, he would be miserable." After waiting some time "for something to turn up," he said it was necessary for him to make a leap—a spring—but it only ended in his "throwing down the gauntlet" to society, saying: "Here I am. I can do such and such things, and I want to earn so much. Now, take me, or I will not be responsible."

Micawber's manner of paying his debts was a very striking and original one. He borrowed a shilling of David Copperfield and gave him an order on Mrs. Micawber for the amount, and she, it is needless to say, had no money to reimburse him. Poor innocent Traddles, who had lent Micawber over forty pounds, felt happy when Mr. Micawber, just before leaving London, began to say to him, in the presence of others: "To leave this metropolis and my friend, Mr. Thomas Traddles, without acquitting myself of the pecuniary part of the obligation I owe him, would weigh upon my mind to an insupportable extent. I have therefore prepared for my friend, Mr. Thomas Traddles, and I now hold in my hand, a document which accomplishes the desired object. I beg to hand to my friend, Mr. Thomas Traddles, my I O U for forty-one, ten, eleven-and-a-half, and I am happy to recover my moral dignity, and to know that I can once more walk erect before my fellow-men."

In London there is a large class of Bohemians called "penny-a-liners." They go about in quest of accidents, misfortunes and various items of news. They go to the Bow Street office, the various courts of justice, and they are paid a penny a printed line (whence the name) for the matter they write

They often sell the same paragraph to several papers, and in that way make a decent living. Sometimes the City Editor "cuts down" their articles, thus depriving them of "tuppence," or "thrippence," at a clip, which, it is needless to say, is missed. But these writers belong to the lower walks of literature. The London Bohemia, Thackeray says, "is a pleasant land, a land where men call each other by their Christian names, where most are poor, and where, if a few oldsters do enter, it is because they have preserved more tenderly than other folks their youthful spirits and the delightful capacity of being idle."

The American Bohemian is not, strictly speaking, a Bohemian. He does not so readily mount to the philosophical height of the "poor devil author," and abandon all ambition to get on in life. It happens often that the Bohemian reporter has an eye to an editorship; the Bohemian writer of stories for the weekly paper has thoughts of a contribution to the *North American Review;* that the North American Reviewer, in turn, is thinking of writing a book; and the American book-writer will not be satisfied until he has written something which shall make his name truly immortal, and at the same time "fill his pockets." Still, there are persons in the "literary" line, in New York, for example, who may well be styled Bohemians. But they are not to be pitied as we have reason to pity the French Bohemian. The newspaper writer in this country is paid a fair price for his work, and has been known, besides living comfortably, to save money out of his income.

After all, the question recurs, What is a Bohemian? What is Bohemianism? Is there any bright side to it? can one be a Bohemian without drinking too much intoxicating drink; or forever smoking a clay pipe; or idling away precious time; or dressing in the oldest of clothes, and out of taste at that; or disbelieving in the grandness of anything, or, in fact, possessing the many and varied attributes which characterize the persons whom some papers call Bohemians? It seems to us that the proper answer is in the affirmative. If the Bohemian in olden times, when the name first came to be used, was nothing more than a lover of art, and a worker at it, should it not mean the same to-day? And those who, possessing unfortunate and never-to-be-denied traits of character, may call themselves, and succeed in being called, Bohemians, may we not say of them, as truly "good society" says to would-be apostles and "shoddyites" — "Calling yourselves after us does not make you one of us; you cannot have entrance to the Inner Temple."

We would say in conclusion that the true Bohemian is unconventional where he thinks it is wise to be so; is liberal, thus being true to the spirit of the age; and lives by the way, and not for the future, carrying out in life what George Arnold, the Bohemian poet, has so sweetly said in poetry:

Oh, I was made for the present time!
I sing my song or weave my rhyme,
From fear of future troubles free —
For they are naught to me!

I will not mourn for the silent past,
Though pleasures fine it brought to me;
The present moments cannot last
But if they leave no vacancy,
The past is naught to me.

And thus I find in the present time,
That life is fresh and sweet to me;
I still will sit and weave my rhyme;
The future soon will present be,
And bring new joys to me.

CHAPTER XVIII.

THE PRINTERS.

THE "Printer," as he is called by the outside world, is styled a "Compositor" in all printing-offices. He is the man who takes from the "case" the pieces of metal (called "types") with an "h," an "a" and a "t" molded on one end of each, respectively, and places them together in the proper order when the word "hat" is to be spelled. It does not take him long to do it, either. Then he follows this word by a space — a piece of metal like a type would be if shortened by having the letter cut squarely off the end — then another word follows, another space, and so on till a line is formed, and so on till another is formed on top of that, and so on till his "stick" (the little iron frame in which the types are set) is full and ready to be emptied on the "imposing-stone," or on a "galley," as the case may be.

There are perhaps few reading persons who have not some general idea of the manner in which types are put together, and of the simple process of stamping the inked letters, by whole columns or whole pages, upon the white paper, by means of the printing-press. But the general public has little knowledge of the daily and nightly scenes in the composing-room of a great daily newspaper, or of the hundreds of details of the printer's work. To give a vivid idea of the interior of the composing-room, I cannot do better, as the scenes are the same in all large offices, than to reproduce a picture of the composing-room of the New York *Tribune*, and to this end must again make a draft on one of Mr. Cummings's sketches before alluded to as having been published a few years ago in *Packard's Monthly*:

Come into the composition-room at five minutes of seven in the evening. The desk near the door is littered with copy. Fifty printers are lounging about the office in their shirt-sleeves and aprons, smoking, distributing type, correcting proofs, swearing over the poor quality of the gas, and asking what number jumped out first in the evening drawing of the Kentucky or Delaware lottery. One man is employed solely in cutting the copy into sections or "takes," and marking directions for the type in which the captions and sub-captions of articles are to appear. Every strip of copy is dotted with guide-posts and sign-boards, so that the compositor cannot go astray. Here are twenty men carrying off twenty pieces or "takes" of one article. We will suppose it to be an editorial of Mr. Greeley's. The copy-cutter slashes it into twenty pieces of about twenty lines each. The first piece he marks with a blue crayon "1 G," the second piece "2 G," the third "3 G," and so on up to "20 G." The compositors take these pieces from the hook as fast as they are out of copy, and as soon as each piece is put in type the matter is placed on a brass galley (similar to a board with a light strip of wood on each side), and a small square piece of white paper, marked "6 G," or whatever number designates the piece just finished by the compositor, is deposited at its side. You may find "2" and "3 G" hugging each other on the galley, followed by "5," "6" and "7 G," with a space left for "4 G" when finished. By the arrangement described, a dozen or twenty articles may be in process of composition at the same time. One manuscript will be numbered "1 XX," and so on. The commercial review generally goes out marked "Com.," the markets "Ma.," the Washington special "Wa.," Young's editorial "1 Y," etc., and Hassard's spicy criticisms "Has.," etc.

The *Tribune* compositors, with the exception of a half dozen men who work exclusively by daylight, reach the office about one P. M. Three or four hours are then consumed in distributing the type for the night's work. From five to six they drop off to supper, returning about ten minutes of seven. As the hour of seven approaches they swarm around the copy-hooks like bees about a sugar-cask. At five minutes of seven the Chairman of the office shouts:

"Well, it's time — sail in. Who's first out?"

This "first out" is an important matter. It takes in the "fattest" slice of copy in the office, and this frequently turns out a five- or an eight-dollar job in one, two, or three hours. The "first out" goes from one number to another on each succeeding night.

"Eighteen 's first out! Number Eighteen, come up to the bull-ring!" shouts the Chairman.

Eighteen delicately slips his "take" from the hook and drifts to his case, amid the ironical oh's and ah's of his companions, who kindly offer him fabulous sums of money for his luck.

"Number Nineteen!" cries the Chairman. Nineteen "snakes" his take from the hook.

"Number Twenty!" and Twenty follows suit, and thus they go until every man is supplied with copy. The men lay their copy on their cases, and stand, stick in hand, but not a type is picked up until at precisely seven o'clock, when the Chairman cries:

"Time! S-l-i-n-g 'em!"

The type rattle in fifty-five sticks at once, and for ten minutes hardly anything is heard but the steady "click, click" of the metal letters within the steel sticks.

The proof-room bell rings, and the bell-boy runs up the tin box, and draws therefrom a proof-sheet.

"Proof for Number —!" yells the boy.

Some droll typo remarks: "Oh, no, that can't be — must be some mistake somewhere!"

As No. — happens to be a notoriously incorrect compositor, a general laugh follows. No.— retorts with an intimation that the droll typo is suffering from an attack of the jim-jams, and a steady stream of jokes and sarcastic allusions follow, until some witty genius says, in a grave voice:

"Now we 'll have the opening chorus!" accompanying it with a song, usually chanted by a brother typo when on a spree, and another round of laughter follows.

"Who 's got 9 G!" shouts a wiry little fellow, adding, *sotto voce*, "Hang the copy! I believe three weeks at a writing-school would n't hurt Greeley!"

"Hang your copy on the hook if you can't read it!" shouts an unsympathizing companion.

"Oh, he can read it well enough!" chimes in another. "There 's a fat 'take' on the agate hook, and he 's a layin' for it — that 's what 's the matter!"

Here Captain Holmes, a veteran one-legged typo, opens the door, ten minutes late, as usual, and sails for his case like a weather-beaten frigate. The rattle and clatter of fifty-five sticks beating a tattoo on the cases salute him. The captain growls like a boatswain on a man-of-war, then tosses one crutch under his cases, takes off his coat, and propped on his remaining crutch, rolls up his shirt-sleeves with the majesty of an Ajax *en dèshabillè*. He shakes up the few type remaining in his case, gets his copy, and immediately wants to know if "any gentleman has any lower case agate p's to give out?"

"Come here, captain," shouts a comrade, and the captain stumps off, and returns with a fist full of letters, which he dumps in his p box. Then the captain begins composition. In ten minutes a row breaks out. The captain discovers a nest of b's in his p box, and shouts out:

"Ah, Number Twenty, what did you give me when I went to your case?"

"Gave you what you asked for, of course — lower case agate b's."

"Yu-*bee* dam! I asked for p's-for-putty, and you gave me b's-for-butter!"

As the captain is known as an inveterate borrower, a roar of laughter breaks from the whole room, and the captain subsides into a low, lion-like growl.

Here a comrade enters the room, and says that he knows nothing about the row, but he will bet five dollars that the captain is right, for he never knew him to be wrong in his life. Derisive cheers follow, and the captain's indignation again flames forth, and gradually subsides into the stereotyped growl.

A long silence, dotted with the "click, click" of the type, follows. At ten o'clock Clement comes up-stairs, and designates the articles to go in on the first side of the paper. Sam Walter, the old and trusty night foreman, whose Chesterfieldian qualities have endeared him to every printer who has stuck a type in the *Tribune* office for the last eighteen years, dumps the type in the form, amid much tribulation over the work of some "infernal blacksmith," who has corrected nonpareil type with minion, and the pages slide off to the stereotyper's room.

At midnight the copy gives out. Clement is sent for and asked for copy. He has none.

"Shall I let off a couple of phalanxes?" inquires Kimball.

"No, sir," is the reply; "I expect a four-column telegraphic report of Stanton's speech at Cleveland."

"Bogus is in order. Put your names down on the slate as fast as you're out of copy," cries Kimball, and down go a dozen names. When copy gives out the compositors are put to work on matter never used in the paper. This is termed "bogus matter." The office allows the men this privilege, because it would be unjust to require them to hang around the office waiting for copy, in the dead hours of night, without appropriate remuneration. By two A. M. Stanton's speech is all in. The men are divided into seven phalanxes, which are let off, phalanx after phalanx, as their services are no longer needed.

"Have you got 'good-night' from Washington yet, Clem?" asks Kimball.

"Yes; Jim Young* shut up an hour ago, but the Associated Press is telegraphing its usual mess of stuff about the Land Office and the Statistical Bureau. Let off four phalanxes!"

Kimball shouts, "First, third, fifth, and seventh phalanxes close up and slope!"

* The Washington correspondent.

The wearied typos drop their sticks, and totter down the iron stairs. At 2.30 A. M. Dr. Wood comes up from the editorial room, and tosses a blue tissue sheet of paper on the table, with the words "Good Night" thereon.

"No more copy! Here 's a proof for the Correcting Phalanx!" comes from Sam Walter, and the work of the typo is done.

The type is pitched into the pages, which must be in the stereotype room by three A. M., for the paper to catch the mails, and after a hard half-hour's sweating, fretting, swearing and tearing, the newspaper ship is launched for the day, and by four A. M. a dull rumbling in the lower regions announces that the presses are masticating paper, thoughts and ideas that will be scattered throughout the Union before the morning hour again rolls around.

The *Tribune* compositors earn from $20 to $35 per week. During the war bills frequently ran up to $50 and even $70 per week. The printers who formerly stuck type at the side of Horace Greeley have died out of the office. Horace, himself, though a practical printer, rarely visits the composing-room. The last time the writer saw him at work in the composition-room was at three o'clock in the morning following President Lincoln's election, when he ran his eye over the type of the New York election table on the editorial page, and suddenly cried out:

"Here, Sam, bring me a bodkin; some infernal fool has spelled Pittsburg with an 'h!'"

And though the pressmen were impatiently clanging the bells for the forms, Horace deliberately drew a jack-knife from his pocket and dug the h's out before he would allow the form to go down.

Mr. Parton visited the *Tribune* office one morning before daylight. He gives a graphic description of it as it then was:

We are in the *Tribune's* press-room. It is a large, low, cellar-like apartment, unceiled, white-washed, inky and unclean, with a vast folding-table in the middle, tall heaps of dampened paper all about, a quietly-running steam-engine of nine-horse power on one side, twenty-five inky men and boys variously employed, and the whole brilliantly lighted up by jets of gas, numerous and flaring. On one side is a kind of desk or pulpit, with a table before it, and the whole separated from the rest of the apartment by a rail. In the pulpit, the night clerk stands, counts and serves out the papers, with a nonchalant and graceful rapidity, that must be seen to be appreciated. The regular carriers were all served an hour ago; they have folded their papers and gone their several ways; and early risers, two miles off, have already read the news of the day. The later newsboys, now, keep dropping in, singly, or in squads of three or four, each with his money ready in his hand. Usually, no word passes between them and the clerk; he either knows how many papers they have come for, or they show him by exhibiting their money; and in three seconds after his eye lights upon a newly-arrived dirty face, he has counted the requisite number of papers, counted the money for them, and thrown the papers in a heap into the boy's arms, who slings them over his shoulder and hurries off for his supply of the *Times* and *Herald.*

In his "Life and Times of Horace Greeley," Mr. Ingersoll remarks:

Instead of the vast folding-table seen twenty years ago by Mr. Parton, we should now find a number of folding-machines, "fed" by boys, very much as the press is "fed" by men. Into one of these machines a *Tribune* enters in one large sheet, and out it presently drops, folded ready for the carrier or for mailing. The immense editions of the *Tribune* are thus folded in an incredibly short time. Observing the wonderfully rapid, the almost miraculously delicate, exact movements of press and folding-machines, one can hardly help being impressed with the idea that they are living beings, possessed of minds.

The same writer says again:

A fact which will strike any one upon a visit to the *Tribune* office is what I will call its democratic management. Here is a copy of a notice in the composition-room: "Gentlemen desiring to wash and soak their distributing matter will please use hereafter the metal galleys I had cast for the purpose, as it is ruinous to galleys having wooden sides to keep wet type in them locked up. THOS. N. ROOKER."

Mr. Parton alludes to this in his "Life of Horace Greeley," and thinks it must have taken the world many thousands of years to arrive at that word, "gentlemen."

There is no higher class of skilled laborers than printers. If compositors may be rated as mechanics—although their calling almost arises to the dignity of art, and is even styled the "art preservative of all arts"—they are, as a numerous class, beyond all question the most intelligent. From the nature of their calling, accustomed to familiar contact, although in a fragmentary way, with the fresh thoughts of writers; among the first to gain a knowledge of passing events; they become more or less familiar with the great questions of the day, discuss them, and form opinions of their own, often no more circumscribed than those of the editorial writers themselves. Indeed, many of the most brilliant writers of this generation—journalists, novelists, historians, humorists and poets—have risen from the "case," have been practical printers. Franklin, Greeley, Bennett, Forney, Prentice, "Artemus Ward," and a host of others eminent in the world of letters, once stood at the case, coats off, arms bared to the elbows, with a stick in one blackened hand, while the other flew back and forth on its countless errands snatching up the "w's," the "h's," the capital "P's," the lower case "i's," and the quads and spaces.

No class of persons have a finer sense of humor than the compositors in a city printing-office, and the complete history of any single composing-room would have a good deal of the "spicy" in it. They have their leisure moments, when they give way to a spirit of fun and punning, sometimes of the most horrible kind, and the chaffing, and rallying, and bantering, take the most active shape—the sharp sally and keen retort being exchanged with great rapidity. The blundering of a green or awkward hand is a source of much merriment; and when one of that kind happens to make such a ridiculous blunder as to "divide" the word "healthy," or the word "horses,"—both of which cases, and many others as ludicrous, I have witnessed in the course of my experience, — he "never hears the last of it," unless he has the good sense to take it good-humoredly, in which case the rallying is soon dropped.

Occasionally, the exuberant spirit takes the form of practical joking, which is sometimes characterized by an amount of recklessness and "deviltry" scarcely to be commended — a recklessness not surpassed by that of such mischievous people as the students of large colleges. For example:

It was a good many years ago that I was engaged in proof-reading in a job office in New York. The sole proprietor was a staid old gentleman, very strict, very systematic, very economical, very thrifty, very religious. He did not believe in sport of any kind, nor under any circumstances, and regarded it, of course, with detestation and loathing when it took the form of injury to or waste of property. The wanton destruction of one cent would have vexed him as much as the irrevocable loss of a human soul.

One day I sat in the dingy fourth-story back room we used as an office, looking over some work with this stern, spectacled old man, when the door opened and a person came in. The person, in whose face I fancied I saw an ordinary twelve-mo volume, was a well-dressed man, evidently a business man.

"You 're Mr. S——?" he said, in a voice that quivered slightly, as if from the exertion of ascending three flights of stairs with no time to waste.

"Yes," replied Mr. S——, laying a proof down and looking up inquiringly over his spectacles.

"Well," returned the stranger, "I run a hoop-skirt factory, No. 13 C—— Street."

"Yes?" rejoined Mr. S——, who, like myself, evidently wondered what that could have to do with a job printing-office.

But for the man's excited manner, I might have surmised that he wanted to get some cards or circulars printed.

"You — you do, eh?" said Mr. S——, for the reason that he did not know what else to say.

"Yes, sir, I do," responded the visitor; "and I employ sixteen girls."

"Ah? Sixteen?"

"Yes, and the rear of my establishment comes to this alley."

He pointed toward the window, which looked out upon a narrow alley, with a great row of buildings opposite; and I now thought I could begin to see a small ray of light in the direction of printers' mischief.

"O, right opposite?" said Mr. S——, on whom the ray of light had not yet dawned.

"Yes, right across the alley. These girls sit at work near the windows — the fifth-story windows — just across, and on a level with the windows where your printers are at work."

"One story above this?"

"Yes."

He paused for breath.

"How — how do they get along this hot weather?" asked Mr. S——, still at a loss for any pertinent remark.

Our excited visitor did not reply to this question, but deliberately thrust his right hand in his trowsers-pocket, and "fumbled" as if feeling for a pistol. Thinking he might be a maniac, possibly a dangerous one, I watched his movements narrowly. But he did not draw a deadly weapon. When he once more drew forth his hand into the light of day, he held in the palm thereof about twenty-three pica lower-case w's, three or four two-em quads, a couple of two-em dashes, bright and new, jingled them under Mr. S——'s nose, and said:

"Is them worth anything, sir?"

Mr. S—— stared at the man, not so much on account of this extraordinary piece of syntax as apparently to make out which he was — an agent for a type-foundry, or a person of unsound mind. Failing to fathom the mystery, he said:

"I don't quite understand you. Have you type to sell? If so —"

"No, sir," interrupted the stranger, again jingling the bright new types; "I have 'em to *give away*. But what are they worth, anyhow?"

"Well, when we buy type we pay about a cent apiece for such as that. We got a font of just that kind last week."

"Worth a cent apiece, eh?" rejoined the visitor. "Well, all I have to say is, it won't take long to make you a bankrupt if your devilish printers keep on throwing them across at my girls, and keeping them from their work, as they have done the last two or three days."

"What!" exclaimed Mr. S——. "Are they mine?"

His economical soul was in arms.

"Yes," replied the manufacturer of hoop-skirts, as he emptied the types into Mr. S——'s hand, which the latter extended excitedly to receive them. "Those are merely what were thrown in at my girls this forenoon. I suppose ten times as many were swept out this morning, from yesterday's work. One this morning struck one of my girls on the jaw, and hurt her so much that she cried. Now, I have come to ask you if you can stop such doings. They waste your property in doing so, — for I understand that a good many of them types strikes the wall and falls down into the alley, — and at the same time they keep my girls from doing their work, — for they have to keep watching the printers all the time for fear of getting hit in the eye, — and I pay them by the week —"

"Good heavens!" exclaimed Mr. S——, forgetting for the

moment that he was a pious man, and springing from his seat. "Come up-stairs with me, and we'll see about such carryings-on!—And they complaining of being scarce of sorts!"

The two left the office, with rapid and excited strides, to go up-stairs, and I proceeded with my work, losing sight of the case for the time being; but the scene that took place in the composing-room was afterward described to me, by one of the "prints.," as one of more than ordinary richness. Mr. S—— used powerful language in his denunciation of "such work;" made vigorous but fruitless inquiries as to which of the wicked compositors had done it, and threatened to dismiss the whole force unless he should find it out; but was finally pacified by the Foreman, who told him he would do two things: (1) make every effort to discover who the guilty party was, and if successful at once discharge him; (2) exercise an amount of surveillance in the future that would effectually prevent a recurrence of the offense. He also stated to Mr. S—— that there were a number of jobs in hand that ought to be completed for customers as soon as possible, and this largely influenced him to revoke his determination to dismiss the "whole force." The culprit was never detected (outside of the composing-room), but as the specific practical joke of throwing pica lower-case w's "and sich" at the hoop-skirt girls was deemed to be about exhausted, it was peremptorily discontinued.

In the Printer's Art there is of course a system of nomenclature not entirely familiar to the whole people; yet it seems to me that any one ought to be able to understand the plain English used in the following description of a scene I once witnessed in our composing-room, when I had stepped in to give some instructions concerning a dead ad., of a column in length, and to say that it need not be kept standing:

As I entered the composing-room, two of the compositors,

known as "little" Billie Crawford and John Reddy, were having a bit of a wrangle, merely in fun, I at first thought, when Billie remarked, with some sarcasm:

"O, yes; you might get through with a good deal of real work in the course of the day, if you did n't spend half your time running around and trying to pick up fat."

"Exactly," retorted Reddy; "but I don't set up in the regular business of stealing sorts, as every man in the office knows you do!"

"Say that again, and I'll make dead matter of you!" said Billie, angrily.

"You!" said Reddy, with a sneer. "Why, you're as contemptible as an agate hair-space!"

"And you," retorted Billie, "are as mean as a bottle-shaped comma!"

"Pooh! You're as trifling as a diamond period!" said Reddy.

"Boys," said I, wishing to pacify them, "I beg that you will not—"

"It 's his own ill-temper," Billie interrupted; "and I despise him as I do a dirty proof in nonpareil or agate!"

John Reddy was now in a thorough passion, and thinking that such language could not be justified so easily as a line of pica, wide measure, laid down his stick, containing three or four lines of leaded brevier that he had just set, walked around the stand that was between them, and gave Billie a hanging indention on the margin of the ear. Billie was engaged in distributing a dead sheriff's notice, and was so surprised at the attack that he unfortunately pied nearly a stickful of solid agate.

At the stand next to Billie's, Charlie Meagher was setting up a leader in bourgeois, leaded, with full-face head, and he rushed to the spot, stick in hand, to separate the angry boys, dropping his rule on the way. But Billie's blood was up, and he seized a handful of lower-case m's, and threw them at Reddy, one or two of them striking Meagher in the face.

This enraged Charlie himself, as he was rather quick-tempered, and he seized a column-rule, to strike Billie with it; but Reddy had got over his anger, and was magnanimous enough to interfere to prevent his being hurt by Charlie, and he did so by flourishing an old side-stick that he picked up from the floor, and telling Charlie to keep back.

At this point, Charlie Brittain, a heavy-browed, spectacled, big-whiskered old "print.," and a fine workman, looked up from his work — he was engaged, by the way, in over-running a paragraph of nonpareil in which there was an out — and seeing what the matter was, came over from his case at the opposite side of the room to pacify and correct his younger comrades. Unfortunately, at the time he approached, Billie seized about a line of long primer quads, and threw them at Charlie Meagher, and one of them struck Brittain fairly on the nose. The good-hearted old compositor was also very quick-tempered, and he sailed in, not caring much whom he should hurt, only determined to hurt somebody; and being near the imposing-stone at the time of being struck by the quad, he seized a foot-stick and began striking out at random among the three excited compositors.

The scene was one of great confusion, and at this important crisis, John Craig, the Foreman, came in with some new rules. He was in a great hurry to lock up a form that lay on the imposing-stone, and one which ought to go to press soon, and he rushed up and seized his mallet and shooting-stick before he noticed anything wrong. Even then, his attention was first attracted by a shock to the imposing-stone, caused by Billie Crawford and Charlie Meagher, who had got clinched and were engaged in a regular struggle, reeling against it. Billie stumbled, and his elbow knocked down a planer, some leads and a number of quoins, reglets, and other furniture.

Such lean matter John Craig thought it simply impossible to justify, and he registered an oath that if they did not at once bring out he would make even. There was some dead matter on a galley stowed away on a rack, and this also was pied by the two struggling printers, as they went staggering over to the wall. Craig became very angry at this, and seizing a bodkin he threatened to run in and make solid matter of them if they did not at once desist. But by this time both were so enraged, and so intent on indenting one another, that you could not have inserted a brilliant hair-space between them. They had now clinched, in a desperate struggle, and went rolling and tumbling over like turned S's; and, rising again, went swaying across the room toward some unoccupied cases, just touching the corner of a stand where Ol. Reynolds was throwing in letter, and knocking down a pile of six-to-pica leads that lay on his case.

The uproar was now so great that the Assistant Foreman, Joe Hunter, who had just finished making-up, and was planing down a form, came running over, with mallet and planer in his hands, and in his excitement came in contact with a rack, knocked down a galley and pied seven sticks of live matter, mostly special notices in solid nonpareil. Several others who were throwing in letter — among them two compositors named John Boot and George Williams, and another named Nichols, who had just got a fat take from the hook — left their cases and rushed to the scene to assist in quelling the disturbance.

The culmination of this unfortunate affair was, that in the general struggle and confusion participated in by the contestants and those who endeavored to separate them, an imposing-stone was knocked over, a chase broken, and a whole form pied. Billie, who was lying on the floor at the time, received a cut on the cheek, which cut had fallen from the imposing-stone, and was intended for an "ad." marked "m2deod3m." An unoccupied chase which was also lying upon the imposing-stone fell on the pi, and of course the result was much battered type; and this, in accordance with the Foreman's instructions, was gathered up by the devil and thrown in the hell-box.

It almost seems that this chapter on "The Printers" would be incomplete, if it did not embrace the following graceful verses, by Mr. Thomas MacKellar, which I find in his work entitled, "The American Printer."

SONG OF THE PRINTER.

Pick and click
Goes the type in the stick,
As the printer stands at his case;
His eyes glance quick, and his fingers pick
The type at a rapid pace;
And one by one, as the letters go,
Words are piled up steady and slow —
Steady and slow,
But still they grow,
And words of fire they soon will glow;
Wonderful words that, without a sound,
Traverse the earth to its utmost bound;
Words that shall make
The tyrant quake,
And the fetters of the oppress'd shall break;
Words that can crumble an army's might,
Or treble its strength in a righteous fight;
Yet the type they look but leaden and dumb,
As he puts them in place with finger and thumb;
But the printer smiles,
And his work beguiles,
By chanting a song as the letters he piles,
With pick and click,
Like the world's chronometer, tick! tick! tick!

O, where is the man with such simple tools
Can govern the world as I?
With a printing-press, an iron stick,
And a little leaden die,
With paper of white, and ink of black,
I support the Right, and the Wrong attack.

Say, where is he, or who may he be,
That can rival the printer's power?
To no monarchs that live the wall doth he give,—
Their sway lasts only an hour;
While the printer still grows, and God only knows
When his might shall cease to tower.

CHAPTER XIX.

PROOF.

IF you knew nothing whatever of surgery or anatomy, and a surgeon should tell you that one of his patients had sustained a comminuted fracture of the body of *os humeri*, you might surmise that it was something very dreadful, but would not be prepared to interpret his statement as meaning that the afflicted person had got the bone of an arm smashed, about half-way between the shoulder and elbow. Yet this is just what the surgeon's statement would mean. So, entirely unfamiliar with "the press," you wonder what a printer or editor means when he says "Proof." I suppose it is part of the mission of this volume to explain what "Proof" means; and, as an assurance of the entire truthfulness of this work, I may state that it has not been allowed to go to press until proof of every statement made in it has been obtained.

To make a specific illustration, when a newspaper column (or galley) of type has been set, it is just a trifle more than probable that the compositor, or the several compositors, who placed the ten thousand separate pieces of metal in a certain uniform order, made a few mistakes. They would not be imperfect beings if they did not, in some cases, do so. But, as we wish our paper to be as nearly correct as possible, typographically as well as in other respects, this column of type is laid, with the letters facing the ceiling, upon a table and covered with printing-ink; then a strip of white paper about twice as wide as the column is laid nicely over it, and a pressure applied sufficient to "print" the letters on the paper.

This paper — which has been dampened in order that it might receive the ink more readily — is a "Proof," or "Proof-sheet," and it is handed to the Proof-reader (or to the Foreman or writer, or both, when there is no exclusive Proof-reader employed), and he reads it — writing in the margin, with pen or pencil, words, letters and characters to indicate what corrections are to be made. He sees an "a" where an "r" ought to be, and he draws a stroke vertically over the face of the former and writes the latter in the margin opposite, and makes a leaning stroke on the right of it. He sees the word "lunch" where the word "link" ought to be, and he crosses out the former and writes "link" in the margin. He finds an "i" where an "l" ought to be, and marks the mistake in like manner. He finds a turned letter — a letter that has been put in upside-down — and he makes a short straight mark under it, and draws attention by making in the margin a character similar to the printed figure 9. He finds a word repeated, as "and the the arrest was made," (a mistake called a "doublet,") and he draws a line over the superfluous word, and in the margin makes a character nearly like a bow-knot. He finds a square black spot of ink between two words, where the paper ought to be left white, caused by a space sticking up even with the faces of the letters, and he draws a line under and over it, and makes a cross (×) in the margin. He finds an "out"—that is, he finds that a word or a number of words have been omitted, and he makes a caret (∧) with its apex between the two words where the missing word or words belong, and writes them in the margin. His course is the same when it is a letter or comma or period that is omitted. He finds a letter or word preceding a letter or word which it ought to follow instead, and drawing a line over one, then down between them and under the other, he writes in the margin "*tr.*," which means "transpose." He finds a letter of a different size from the others, and marking this he writes "*w. f.*" in the margin, which means "wrong font." These are but a few illustrations. There are probably from fifty to a hundred—I never stopped to count them—different kinds of typographic errors, to mark each of which the Proof-reader has a uniform and conventional character, and with these various characters he is fully as familiar as any one is with the letters A, B, C, or the figures 1, 2, 3.

Almost every one who reads newspapers occasionally sees typographic errors of the simplest kind, which have either escaped the eye of the Proof-reader, or, having been marked by him, been overlooked by the person doing the correcting. In the hurry of newspaper work, a few mistakes will creep in every day. When the newspaper reader sees the word "then" spelled with two "n's," he thinks, perhaps, that any one ought to be able to see typographic errors at a glance, and that Proof-reading cannot require any great care. But he is mistaken. It is one of the hardest jobs in newspaper work, and is as much a business as type-setting. Indeed, I believe that good Proof-readers are proportionally scarcer than good editors.

Authors and editors of books are often indebted to the Proof-reader for the correction of errors which they have overlooked. I care not how careful a writer is, or how much time he has spent in the preparation of his book, the Proof-reader is certain to discover some errors. Indeed, the author himself, when he sees the proofs of his book, often finds in them the grossest errors, which he has failed to discover in his manuscript. When one's language goes into print it seems to take on a new life, and to lose in some measure the personality it formerly enjoyed, when, as manuscript, it was nearer to its author, and when he was somewhat blind to its faults, as a man is often blind to the faults of his child. When the Proof-reader discovers what he considers an incorrect word or expression, he calls the author's attention to it by drawing a line under it in the proof, making a note of interrogation (?) in the margin, and writing what he thinks would be the proper word. Should the author differ with the Proof-reader, he erases the corrections, and the matter stands as set according to his manuscript; but should he, as is often the case, perceive that the Proof-reader is right, he simply erases the note of interrogation, and the correction is made at his expense or at the expense of the publishers. Correcting in the proofs what were faults of the manuscript is expensive, especially where whole paragraphs are stricken out or added, involving often the overrunning and rearranging of many pages. Authors ought to understand this fully; but many do not, and are sometimes shocked at the expense occasioned by correcting in the proof errors that are too often the result of careless preparation of copy.

To give a clear idea of proof-reading, I here reproduce from Mr. MacKellar's "American Printer" two pages showing what a proof-sheet looks like after the reader has marked the errors on it, and how it appears after the corrections have been made:

AN EXAMPLE OF PROOF-SHEET,

SHOWING THE MANNER IN WHICH ERRORS OF THE PRESS ARE MARKED FOR CORRECTION.

1 a/ Though severel differing opinions exist as to
the individual by whom the art of printing was 2
first discovered; yet all authorities concur in
admitting Peter Schoeffer to be the person 3 Caps
who invented *cast metal types*, having learned
the art ~~of~~ of *cutting* the letters from the Gut-
5 :/ tembergs/ he is also supposed to have been
6 # the first whoengraved on copper plates. The 7 /-/
following testimony is preseved in the family, 8 r/
9 by Jo. Fred. Faustus, of Ascheffenburg: <# 6
10 □ >'Peter Schoeffer, of Gernsheim, perceiving 3 S. Caps.
11 ✓ his master Fausts design, and being himself
12 tr. desirous ardently to improve the art, found
out (by the good providence of God) the
method of cutting (*incidendi*) the characters 13 stet.
in a *matrix*, that the letters might easily be
5 ,/ singly *cast*/ instead of bieng *cut*. He pri- 12 ei/
14 ⊥ vately *cut matrices* for the whole alphabet: 15
Faust was so pleased with the contrivance,
/that he promised Peter to give him his only 17 wf.
16 /daughter Christina in marriage a promise 3 Ital.
/which he soon after performed.
19 as/ But there were many difficulties at first 18 no ¶
with these *letters*, as there had been before 3 Rom.
20 + with wooden ones, the metal being too soft 3 Ital.
to support the force of the im pression: but 9
this defect was soon remedied, by mixing
a substance with the metal which sufficiently tr. 12
5 ⊙ hardened it/

and when he showed his master the letters cast from these matrices,

PROOF-SHEET AS CORRECTED.

Explanations		Explanations
1 Wrong letter.	THOUGH several differing opinions exist as to	
	the individual by whom the art of printing was	2 Upside-down.
	first discovered; yet all authorities concur in	
	admitting PETER SCHOEFFER to be the	3 Capitals.
	person who invented *cast metal types*, having	
4 Doublet; take out.	learned the art of *cutting* the letters from the	
5 Colon instead of period.	Guttenbergs: he is also supposed to have been	
6 Space between words.	the first who engraved on copper-plates. The	7 Hyphen wanted.
	following testimony is preserved in the family,	8 Letter missing.
9 Bad spacing.	by Jo. Fred. Faustus, of Aschaffenburg:	6 More space between lines.
10 New paragraph.	'PETER SCHOEFFER, of Gernsheim, perceiv-	3 Small capitals.
11 Apostrophe wanted.	ing his master Faust's design, and being him-	
12 Words to change places.	self ardently desirous to improve the art, found	
	out (by the good providence of God) the	
	method of cutting (*incidendi*) the characters in	13 A change of mind. "Let it stand."
	a *matrix*, that the letters might easily be singly	
5 Comma instead of colon.	*cast*, instead of being *cut*. He privately *cut*	12 Letters transposed.
14 Space sticking up.	*matrices* for the whole alphabet: and when he	15 An "out."
	showed his master the letters cast from these	
	matrices, Faust was so pleased with the con-	
	trivance, that he promised Peter to give him	17 Type of wrong size.
16 Type out of line.	his only daughter *Christina* in marriage, a	3 Italic instead of Roman.
	promise which he soon after performed. But	18 "Run in." Not a new paragraph.
19 Word left out.	there were as many difficulties at first with	
20 Damaged letter.	these letters, as there had been before with	3 Roman instead of italic.
	wooden ones, the metal being too soft to sup-	3 Italic instead of Roman.
	port the force of the impression: but this defect	9 Close up.
	was soon remedied, by mixing the metal with a	12 Words to change places.
5 Period instead of comma	substance which sufficiently hardened it.'	

In his sketches showing "How a Newspaper is Made," published in *Packard's Monthly*, Mr. Cummings thus alludes to John C. Robinson, one of the *Tribune's* famous Proof-readers:

> Robinson is, without doubt, the fastest proof-reader in the world. He marks his corrections on the side of the proof-sheet without ceasing his reading. A quick-eyed copy-holder is required to follow Robinson's tongue, even on reprint copy. Robinson himself has an eye like a hawk, and, in reading a proof-sheet, his eyes are generally at least five lines beyond his tongue. I have known him distinctly to enunciate a column of fine agate type, *Tribune* measure, in nine minutes. In October, 1863, he was timed by Benjamin L. Glesby and S. T. Selleck, two of the best compositors ever employed on the *Tribune*, when he read and marked the proof-sheet corrections of fourteen columns of solid nonpareil in an hour and twenty minutes. This was done on a wager for seven dollars. The sheets were afterward carefully read by an experienced proof-reader, and but two typographical blunders (both turned s's) discovered.

It is almost superfluous to say that the man who is a competent Proof-reader must have an excellent memory, a sharp eye, a quick mind, good judgment, some knowledge of the various languages, and a thorough knowledge of past and passing events.

CHAPTER XX.

TYPOGRAPHIC ERRORS.

WHEN a man writes anything to appear "in print," if there is anything he does *not* want to see in it, it is a typographic error — a wrong letter instead of a right one, or a wrong word where a right one ought to be, especially when it distorts the sense, as it often does in the latter case, transforming a well-formed and high-sounding sentence into a superior article of bosh. Some typographic errors are highly amusing, except to those immediately concerned, and to them they are a source of much tribulation. When one writes a lofty editorial, and it passes through the hands of some careless compositor and proof-reader with the word "tooth" for "truth," "eggs" for "ages," "maternal" for "material," and "infernal" for "imperial," he may well be pardoned for wishing that several people would drop dead.

I once wrote a serial for a weekly paper, in one chapter of which the word "malingerer" (a soldier who "plays sick" to shirk duty) occurred. Conscious of the great probability that it would appear as "maligner" in the eyes of the compositor, I took the trouble to write a note to the proof-reader, calling his attention to the word, and particularly requesting him to be careful not to allow the wrong word to appear; nevertheless, despite all my pains, he did overlook it, and the readers of my romance learned for the first time that a soldier who feigns sickness for the sake of exemption from duty is a "maligner," no matter whether he has "lied on" anybody or not.

Here is a copy of an advertisement which once appeared in a San Francisco paper with which I was connected; and although I felt somewhat annoyed when the person most interested came in and called my attention to it, I could not help laughing when I took the second look at the last line and noted its very droll appearance:

Phil. J. Gerhardy,

STALL 112, NEW ADDITION TO

California Market,

Entrance on Pine Street, ... San Francisco.

American Beef, Veal, Mutton, Lamb, Pork, etc.,

Of the B Questality, always on hand.

M

The "B Questality" does not seem to mean much of any thing in the English language. Any one will see that "Best Quality" was what was intended, while those not familiar with the printer's art may wonder how such a mistake could have occurred. Easily enough. A "wrong letter" or two had been marked in the proof, and to replace it the printer had lifted out several types, and the space, probably, at the beginning of the word "Quality," and without his observing it, the letters "est" got shifted over and joined the "ality" of the word "Quality." So, when he put the "Qu" and space in, he, with vigilance relaxed, it must be confessed, put them in immediately following the "B," and the paper went to press with a lonesome-looking capital letter, and a word of four syllables not to be found in our vocabulary. In a Boston paper I find a ridiculous error that must have occurred substantially in the same way. It is that paper's custom to place over its regular press dispatches, in small caps: [To THE ASSOCIATED PRESS;] but on the occasion referred to, owing to some such accident as described above, the line appeared thus: THE ASS [TO OCIATED PRESS].

As one of the most amusing cases of typographic errors which have really happened, it may be mentioned that a California compositor made an editor say about a contemporary that it stood "in the front rank of inferior journals." Of course, "interior" was the word intended. No less amusing was a slight error in a Pittsburg paper a few years ago, which paper, in a summary of legislative proceedings, said that "the bill was pasted over the Governor's head." An intruding "t" in the place of a missing "s" made "passed" "pasted." In a well-known book-printing establishment in Philadelphia the slightly vexatious typographic errors of "canary Scotchman" for "canny Scotchman," and "storm-blown fly" for "storm-blown lily," are known to have occurred.

I once knew a gentleman who published a newspaper of whose typographic correctness he was very proud, and he did not scruple to say so; and I remember of his telling me once that he had a mind to offer a large reward for any typographic error found in his paper. This was hyperbole, of course, as it would be very hard indeed to find a *perfectly* "clean" newspaper. Indeed, a newspaper entirely free from typographic errors would be little less than a prodigy. It must be remembered that in a newspaper of the average size there are about two hundred thousand separate and distinct pieces of metal; and it will be agreed that to put all these exactly in their proper places, without so much as *one* slight mistake, and that, too, chiefly in a single day or night, would require the services of beings who have arrived at perfection itself, not one of which class I have yet been able to find.

On one occasion the gentleman alluded to published a few very unfavorable comments on one of my works, which fact, taken alone, was not calculated to disturb me in the slightest degree. On the contrary, after what I have said on the subject of Book-Reviewing in another chapter, it might be surmised that I was rather pleased than otherwise. I suppose, really, (for it was many years ago,) the book was fully as defective as he pronounced it; but I happened to know that his unfavorable allusion to it (an allusion he had gone quite out of his way to make at all) was dictated by a bit of personal ill-feeling that existed between us only for a short time, and the paragraph contained within itself some material which afforded me a beautiful opportunity for revenge. I observed that it was not entirely free from typographic errors, and on going over it as a proof-reader I found *nineteen* typographic errors, and all within a paragraph of less than two stickfuls! Remembering how he had boasted to me that his paper was a marvel of typographic correctness, I clipped the paragraph, pasted it on a sheet of copy-paper, marked all the errors in the usual proof-reader's style, and sent it to the editor with my compliments. I met him a day or two afterward in the street, and extending a friendly hand he said:

"By Jove! That was pretty good; but I'll take my oath it went in accidentally without the proof being read at all."

While accepting his friendly hand, I pleasantly suggested that he might, with great good judgment, relate that romance to members of a certain armed body connected with the navy; adding, hyperbolically:

"Why, my dear fellow, that 's nothing. It 's clean compared with some other matter I noticed in the same number of your paper!"

"Spare me!" he said.

We were friends ever afterward, and I even subsequently contributed many a column to his paper, which columns, I am bound to say, were generally printed with a more careful regard to typographic correctness.

There are extant some verses bearing on the subject of typographic errors, which have been going the rounds of the press for years. I do not know who their author was, but I think them so nearly true to nature as to be worth quoting here in full:

REFLECTIONS

UPON RECEIVING A COPY OF MY FIRST POEM PUBLISHED IN A NEWSPAPER.

Ah! here it is! I'm famous now—
  An author and a poet!
It really is in print! ye gods!
  How proud I'll be to show it!

And gentle Anna! — what a thrill
  Will animate her breast,
To read these ardent lines and know
  To whom they are addressed.

Why, bless my soul! here 's something strange!
  What can the paper mean
By talking of the "graceful brooks
  That gander o'er the green?"
And here's a T instead of R,
  Which makes it "tippling rill;"
"We'll seek the shad" instead of "shade,"
  And "hell" instead of "hill."

"They look so"—what! I recollect
  'T was "sweet" and then 't was "kind;"
And, now to think, the stupid fool
  For "bland" has printed "blind."
Was ever such provoking work?—
  'T is curious, by the by,
How anything is rendered blind
  By giving it an eye.

"Hast thou no tears"—the T's left out;
  "Hast thou no ears" instead.
"I hope that thou art dear" is put
  "I hope that thou art dead."
Who ever saw in such a space
  So many blunders crammed?
"Those gentle eyes bedimmed" is spelt
  "Those gentle eyes bedamned."

"The color of the rose" is "nose,"
  "Affection" is "affliction;"
I wonder if the likeness holds
  In fact as well as fiction?
"Thou art a friend" — the R is gone;
  Who ever would have weened

That such a trifling thing could change
  A "friend" into a "fiend."

"Thou art the same" is rendered "lame,"
  It really is too bad;
And here because an I is out
  My "lovely maid" is "mad;"
They drove her blind by poking in
  An eye — a process new;
And now they 've gouged it out again,
  And made her crazy, too.

"Where are the muses fed that thou
  Shouldst live so long unsung?"
Thus read my version — here it is —
  "Shouldst live so long unhung;"
"The fate of woman's love is thine,"
  An H commences "fate;"
How small a circumstance will turn
  A woman's love to hate.

I 'll read no more! What shall I do?
  I 'll never dare to send it!
The paper 's scattered far and wide —
  'T is now too late to mend it!
Oh, Fame! thou cheat of human bliss!
  Why did I ever write?
I wish my poem had been burnt
  Before it saw the light.

Let 's stop and recapitulate;
  I've d——d her eyes, that 's plain;
I 've told her she 's a lunatic,
  And blind, and deaf, and lame.
Was ever such a horrid hash
  In poetry or prose?
I 've said she was a fiend, and praised
  The color of her nose.

I wish I had that editor
  About a half a minute,
I 'd *bang* him to his heart's content,
  And with an H begin it;
I 'd *jam* his body, eyes and nose,
  And spell it with a D,
And send him to that *hill* of his;
  He spells it with an E.

CHAPTER XXI

PUNCTUATION.

THE great importance of punctuation, and correct punctuation, at that, is not generally appreciated, insomuch that many very intelligent though not professionally literary persons write their letters, or other documents, without ever thinking of such a thing as punctuating them. The difficulty of teaching punctuation cannot easily be over-estimated. It is about as hard to teach punctuation as to teach journalism itself, for the same reasons; namely, there are so few rules which can be safely offered as guides. The general ignorance of the subject is so vast as to amount to a kind of specific darkness of understanding. Every journalist or practical printer sees defective punctuation, or no attempt at punctuation at all, in nineteen of every twenty letters he receives; he will see defective or incomplete punctuation in deeds, wills, mortgages, and other legal instruments; he will see bad punctuation, if any, in every communication or advertisement sent in by an "outsider" to be set up; he will see much miserable and often ridiculous punctuation in costly business signs. On the punctuation of sign-painters, I find an article in the Philadelphia *Sunday Transcript,* from which I make the following brief extract:

The art of punctuation is not thoroughly understood by any portion of mankind, except a certain class of sign-painters that infest this city. One could not learn a better lesson in punctuation than by taking a walk of about one hundred squares through the business quarters of the city, and surveying the numerous signs that adorn the doors, windows and walls of buildings in which goods are sold, or in which professional men "hang out." A few examples which we shall give, may prove eminently useful to such as desire to gain knowledge on the subject present.

Not more than five hundred squares from the State House, there may be seen a gilt sign over a modest shop-door, staring boldly at the passer-by, the purport of which is as follows, to wit:

JOHN, ANDERSON SADDLERY: & HARNESS!

It will be perceived that the learned artist, with that strict adherence to the correct principles of punctuation for which sign-painters are proverbial, has placed a comma after the word "John." This, besides being both correct and elegant, is calculated to give the reader of the sign a little time to breathe after pronouncing "John," before he tackles "Anderson." With his accustomed sagacity and foresight, the artist has left a perfectly blank space between "Anderson" and "Saddlery," presuming, no doubt, that the reader would catch enough breath at the comma after "John" to enable him to utter two words in succession without resting. After this, however, repose seems to be needed; and the obliging artist has tenderly placed a colon (:) after the word "Saddlery," which will give every reasonable man all the breathing-time he could ask before completing his perusal of the sign. Then come the "& Harness," topped out with an elaborate note of admiration (!). This suggests that the reader, having perused all the words of the sign, occupies a little more leisure time in *admiring* it. And who could help it?

The writer of the above, while on the subject of sign-painters, might have added that many of them are not troubled with any very delicate sense of the proprieties of orthography. I have seen in Philadelphia a gilt sign probably costing a hundred dollars that read thus: "Steam Dying Establishment." Dying is seldom pleasant to contemplate, but I think I could never reconcile myself to dying by steam. Such a form of death — always with the exception of being talked to death — would appear to me to be about the most horrible that could well be devised. In these days of collisions and explosions, I could scarcely have wondered if I had seen the sign at the depot of a railroad, or the main wharf of a steamboat line, but I confess to some surprise at seeing it in a fashionable street, with a millinery store on one side and on the other an establishment for the sale of hosiery "and things." Possibly "dyeing" was the word meant by the sagacious sign-painter. If so, that puts a new color on the matter; and I venture to suggest that a more liberal knowledge of orthography would have enabled him in this case to do his work with more "e's".

Defective punctuation — often accidental — is sometimes very amusing. I read in a daily not long ago that "a bycicle race of a hundred and six miles was won in five-and-a-half seconds, less than eight hours." To travel a hundred and six miles in five-and-a-half seconds was a marvelous feat, to be sure; but not half so strange as the fact that the editor thought it necessary to state that that amount of time was "less than eight hours." Why, who ever thought that five-and-a-half seconds were more than eight hours, or even so much? But then drop the intruding comma after "seconds," and we find, what was meant to be said, that the race was won in "five-and-a-half seconds less than eight hours." Of course, every one has heard how a minister of the Gospel was shocked when he found that a paragraph in his sermon on the horrors of intemperance was thus reported and printed in a country newspaper: "Why, only last Sabbath, in this holy house, a woman fell from one of those seats while I was preaching the Gospel in a state of beastly intoxication." A couple of commas would have charged the woman, and not the minister himself, with "beastly intoxication."

I will not be accused of over-estimating the importance of correct punctuation, when I state the well-authenticated fact that not long since the erroneous substitution of a comma for a hyphen involved a loss to the United States Treasury of two million dollars. The case was this: A bill was passed by Congress, and became a law, to admit free of duty "tropic fruit-plants, trees and seeds." The engrossing clerk, thinking he knew just a trifle more than the statesman who had framed the bill (who, by the way, *may have* omitted the hyphen), placed a very distinct comma after the word "fruit," and a law was placed upon the statute-book admitting tropic fruit, as well as "plants, trees and seeds," free of duty,—which ought to have had the effect of reducing the prices of oranges, bananas and lemons,—and before the mistake was discovered and rectified, it caused the loss in revenue of the sum mentioned. When a comma is considered worth two million dollars, what would be the commercial value of a couple of two-em dashes (—— ——), or, say, three consecutive notes of admiration (! ! !)?

CHAPTER XXII.

OUR ORTHOGRAPHY.

IT need scarcely be said that every printer, as well as every writer for the press, ought to be a "good speller;" and in order to become thoroughly versed in orthography, much research and an excellent memory are necessary. Much is to be learned that has not been learned at school. There are a vast number of words in common use in the English language that are spelled in two or more different ways, each way being "correct" according to some authority or other. There are many words as to the orthography of which our two leading lexicographers, Webster and Worcester, do not agree. It therefore becomes necessary for a printing-office to adopt the uniform style of one or the other with regard to certain words and certain classes of words of equivocal orthography, and "stick to it" — "follow Webster," or "follow Worcester," as the case may be. Thus, every editor and every printer ought to be familiar with the distinguishing features of both Dictionaries, each of which, I believe, contains over a hundred thousand words.

Probably, no great harm is done, yet some confusion is caused by having various modes of spelling the same word, and the proof-reader makes many a mark with his pen or pencil that would be unnecessary if we had one universal form of spelling each word in our language, as we certainly ought to have.

In the course of my own literary and journalistic work, I have seen fit to "follow" Webster; not on account of the slightest prejudice in favor of Noah Webster himself or his lexicon, now, like Worcester's, so greatly amplified, but because his system of spelling many words of mooted orthography is at least one little step in the direction of a system of phonetic spelling, which I long to see adopted. And some such radical system *will* be adopted, though possibly not during the existence of this generation. We are always moving in the direction of improvement, and I confidently claim that our orthography will be improved by simplifying it — that our language will be strengthened by being made plainer and more easily written.

The phonetic system will eventually prevail, and our present clumsy orthography, with its many useless letters, will be repudiated. Ay, the time will come — nor is it anything like so distant as the Age of Man from the Azoic Age — when men will look back on the literature of the present day, and laugh at the idea of spelling the word "through" with seven letters, when two (of the enlarged alphabet) will be found sufficient; and of spelling "phthisis" with eight letters, when five at most will do the office; or "sleigh" with six letters, when only two, or at most three, will be necessary. Reform in this matter must originate in the United States, for our English cousins are so very conservative, and to the last minute will stick to their "honour," their "colour," their "waggon" with two "g's," and their "traveller" with two "(h)l's." One of the arguments against the proposed phonetic system of spelling is that it would soon destroy all traces of the dead languages, from which probably a vast majority of our words are derived. Suppose it does? Of what use are the dead languages? Though even your dearest friend die, why should you keep the corpse in the house forever? We must bid good-by to Latin and Greek some day, and the sooner we do so the sooner we shall improve our own language.

I know it will be said that many terms in the sciences — astronomy, anatomy, pharmacy, physics — and in the law are familiarly known among nearly all civilized people of various languages, but these may be "Anglicized" or "commonized," cut down or so arranged as to become a part of the English language, or, to start with, a part of a universal diplomatic language, so to speak. I think that all the people of the world will eventually speak one common, plain and simple language (it may be the English), all with the same dialect, same pronunciation, same accent and same (when writing) orthography.

As a prelude to this "consummation devoutly to be wished," it has been suggested that some language be adopted as a universal language, for each person in the world to learn and master, in addition to his own local tongue. On this subject I quote from an article written for a well-known journal by a gentleman known to be a careful, penetrating thinker on, and investigator of, philology and kindred subjects:

It has been suggested that the people of the whole world will one day speak the same language — that eventually all living languages save one will be abandoned, and that this favored one will be adopted by the whole world, and become the common tongue of all mankind. This may be too much to hope for. At least it is not likely to be brought about for hundreds and possibly thousands of years; but there is something that may be accomplished within a generation or two that will answer almost as good a purpose. A common language may be agreed upon by all civilized peoples, which every person shall learn in addition to his own, and which shall be taught every child so soon as it has mastered its mother-tongue. This language might be the English, German, French, Spanish, or any modern language that might be adopted, say, by an international philological convention. Such a system once accomplished, no man need know more than one language besides his own, in order to be able to converse freely with people of all quarters of the civilized world. The principle would then be the same that applies now to medical and surgical nomenclature. A physician's prescription, as every one knows, is written in Latin, which is a "Common Language" for the use of the medical fraternity; and, therefore, the prescription of an American or English physician is read with the same ease by an American or English, French, Russian, German, or Italian apothecary. It is related — and it is a good illustration — that a learned American, traveling in Russia a few years ago, whiled away the long hours of a tedious journey in a stage-coach by conversing in Latin with his only traveling-companion, who happened to be a priest of the Greek Church. Neither knew a word of the mother-tongue of the other, but both were familiar with the Latin (although their pronunciation and accentuation were somewhat different), and thus they conversed for hours in a language which had been dead for many centuries. With a universal colloquial, diplomatic, or commercial language (it matters not what it may be termed) once established, any person, whether thoroughly educated or not, may converse fluently with the natives of all countries through which he may travel; and there will never be any occasion for learning half a dozen languages, as some have found it necessary to do, in order to have clear and satisfactory intercourse with the literary, scientific, or commercial world.

With reference to the subject of phonetics, I quote from an article I contributed some years ago to the *California Teacher*, a small magazine published under the auspices of the State School Department:

I advocate a complete revolution in Orthography, looking to the establishment of a system of spelling at least approaching the phonetic. A literary convention representing all the people who speak the English language would be a means by which much might be speedily accomplished in the way of making important and much-needed improvements in our language. Let our present elaborate dictionaries be taken as a mere foundation for a new and grander orthographic structure. Let a system be adopted, perfect in its simplicity, and let every *silent* letter be expelled from our vocabulary. There are thousands of words in the English language which, as they are now spelled, contain from one to half a dozen superfluous letters that are worse than useless, because they are only calculated to puzzle and confound the pupil. I will cite a few examples, writing the same words opposite, in the new form I propose to give them:

Yacht.	Yot.
Though.	Tho.
Through.	Thru.
Tough.	Tuf.
Freight.	Frat.
Wright.	Rit.
Phthisic.	Tizik.

The present orthography of the last-named word is little less than ludicrous. It has been subjected to ridicule by every school-boy, although the object itself, aside from its clumsy orthographic dress, is entitled to great respect.

It is related of a well-known member of Congress, not particularly noted for his research in literature, that he entered a book-store in Pittsburg, Pa., one day, and asked for a dictionary.

"Are all the words in this?" he asked.

"Yes," replied the clerk, "all that are in common use."

The purchase was made, but on the next day our Congressional friend came stalking into the store, with the valuable collection of words under his arm.

"I thought you told me I could find any word in this," he said to the clerk, laying the book upon the counter.

"So you can," was the reply.

"Where's 'physician'?" asked the statesman, with an air of confident triumph.

The clerk opened the dictionary, traced out the desired word, and pointed to it with an emphatic—

"There!"

The public man gazed upon the word, and, while a whole volume of new light broke out upon his face, exclaimed:

"O—that's it?—I thought you spelt it with an *F*."

Very natural, though, was it not?

When I suggest that our orthography be so simplified that we shall write "tho," instead of "though;" "kof," instead of "cough;" "enuf," instead of "enough;" "sla," instead of "sleigh;" etc., I know that the reader will exclaim: "O, that would look *so* odd! We never could reconcile ourselves to it!"

Now, would not English scholars have uttered the same exclamation two hundred years ago, had any one then proposed to write the language as we write it now? Here, for example, is a specimen of the English language two centuries ago, taken from an account of an earthquake in New England, as given in "Bradford's History:"

"This yeare (1638) about ye 1 or 2 of June, was a great & fearfull earthquake; it was in this place hearde before it was felte. It came with a rumbling noyse, or low murmure, like unto remoate thunder; it came from ye norward and pased southwarde."

Does not this look very droll to us? Yes. Would not our present orthography of these words have looked just as droll to the people of those days? Yes. If we could see a specimen of the improved English language of a century or two hence, with its phonetic spelling, would it not look as droll to us as ours would have seemed to our ancestors? Yes. After the improvements of a century or two, will not the words and sentences which we now regard as quite artistic appear as odd as those of our ancestors now appear to us? Yes. Then do not be unnerved or disarmed by that terrible (?) exclamation, "O, how it would look!" Might as well consult Mrs. Grundy at once. Let us move in this matter, — do the work that *must* and *will* be done within a century, — the work of simplifying our orthography, and rooting out its many incongruities and its many superfluities.

CHAPTER XXIII.

A BAD EDITOR.

TO conduct a weekly paper properly involves much labor, yet this labor, compared with the work on a daily, is a mere round of fun and enjoyment. The editor of the weekly paper need not hurry to his office in the morning, nor need he remain late in the evening. He can work with far more deliberation, and his work is (or ought to be) much more studied and elaborate. But he finds no small amount of labor to do every day, and should he absent himself from his duties one day in the week, he must toil perceptibly and materially harder during the remainder of the week to make up for it. He can "arrange" it so as to take a day off occasionally, without employing a substitute; an editor on a daily cannot. The latter has a day's work to do every day, and one hour's absence during the usual periods for working would often be a very serious loss. Altogether, there is not a prettier business in the world, according to my way of thinking, than conducting a respectable, well-established, paying weekly newspaper, with everything working smoothly. There is labor in it, I know, but it is just enough to be healthy, to keep the mind cheerful, as employment always does, without merging into the drudgery, the heavy, wearying, exhausting toil, that presses like a great weight upon the brain of the daily editor.

During about three years I (together with a man named Cranks) published a large weekly paper in San Francisco, which I shall here style the *Enunciator*. It was devoted to news and literature, with a preponderance in favor of the latter; and gave much editorial attention to passing events, the stage, art and music. I am pretty sure I did all I could to make it an engine for the advancement of the public good, as well as my own, and there was a time when it was a fabric whose foundation walls were deeply rooted. But Cranks! He was an extraordinary man, indeed. I must say much of him, because he was such an odd character. I never saw a man like him; I never will; for there is no other like him in this world. There never was, there never will be another Cranks. He belonged to no distinctive class of men, and it would be presumptuous even to describe him as what naturalists would term a "generalization." He was a living refutation of the theory of Darwin. He stood alone, with no match or like. He was Cranks—simply Cranks.

He had lived forty years. He weighed one hundred and ninety pounds. He was five feet seven and a half inches high. He was thick; he was stout; he was "chuffy." He had a round face, that at a short distance might readily have been mistaken for the head of a flour-barrel; his cheeks were puffy; his nose was short, wide, flattish and stubby; his chin unduly depressed; his teeth as prominent as his plethoric lips; his mouth extended; his mustache dark and heavy, but not long; and his neglected hair grew only from the comparatively vertical portions of his head, and hung to his coat-collar, for upon the summit of his head there was no hair whatever, although that portion of the cranium, as has been aptly observed in a popular song, is highly appropriate for the cultivation of the capillary integument. This defect, however, was only perceptible when Cranks's hat was off; therefore it was rarely seen at all. A few of his most intimate acquaintances — not friends — knew it; the world knew it not. Yet let me not be understood to insinuate that bald heads are a reproach. On the contrary, every time I see a bald head I think that if it were mine I would not part with it for any consideration.

Cranks had a forehead. It was situated just over his round gray eyes and flattened nose, and extended from his right to his left temple; but you could not have discovered where the forehead ended, on each side, and where the temple began, because these portions of his head were so jolly round. If you had cut his head off and set it upside-down on his shoulders — he had no neck — the corpulent chin would have made just as good a forehead, and at a short distance you would not have known the difference. *He* would n't, either. Indeed, the world itself would not have been a loser by the change. I am pained to state, however, that this generally unimportant operation was never performed while I knew him.

Cranks had a mouth which, although of immense size, he worked to its fullest capacity at meal-times, for he eat much victuals; and between meals that mouth was ever engaged in "bulling" the tobacco market. Nevertheless, he was a "bear" himself, and he growled like that horrible wild beast whenever spoken to — especially when writing. Yet he was no fluent writer, and he labored over the work like a man trying to roll a hogshead of molasses up a perpendicular wall. He would sit down and smoke and "chaw" tobacco, and scratch paper with his pen, and grunt and growl one hour and twenty minutes, and the result would be three, four or five little pages of manuscript. Then he would stop and say he was "gone in" with work, and would sit and smoke.

Cranks had an abstracted air, like one who does not belong to this world. I don't believe he did. To speak to him and get an immediate answer, was as rare as the Transit of Venus; to get a pleasant answer, as rare as steamships in north latitude 90°. He never approached anything like an attitude of gentleness, except shortly after having seen a funeral procession in the street, for the fear of Death was ever before his eyes. The sight of a harmless hearse or useful coffin sent a thrill of horror through him. I never saw a man who so much dreaded Death. He was continually thinking about Death, talking about it and dreading it. It was part of his very nature to fear Death. He did n't mind living so much, but he did hate the idea of dying —"of falling into naught, of being dead." One day, shortly after he had seen an undertaker's wagon driving along the street, I really pitied him, and, ignoring his graver faults, tried to comfort him. To that end I repeated to him these beautiful lines by T. W. Parsons:

> O, but death is bliss!
> I feel as certain, looking on the face
> Of a dead sister, smiling from her shroud,
> That our sweet angel hath but changed her place,
> And passed to peace, as when, amid the crowd
> Of the mad city, I feel sure of rest
> Beyond the hills — a few hours further west.

But Cranks was posted on Death, and opening a well-marked copy of Shakespeare he pointed with a shudder to this thrilling passage in "Measure for Measure:"

> Ay, but to die, and go we know not where;
> To lie in cold obstruction and to rot;

This sensible warm motion to become
A kneaded clod; and the delighted spirit
To bathe in fiery floods, or to reside
In thrilling regions of thick-ribbed ice;
To be imprisoned in the viewless winds,
And blown with restless violence round about
The pendent world; or to be worse than worst
Of those, that lawless and incertain thoughts
Imagine howling!—'t is too horrible!
The weariest and most loathed worldly life
That age, ache, penury and imprisonment
Can lay on nature, is a paradise
To what we fear of death!

Indeed, his fear of Death was puerile and cowardly; yet while he dreaded both Death and that—

Something after death,
That undiscovered country, from whose bourn
No traveler returns,

he was not a holy man. He was disingenuous, spiteful, envious, disagreeable, malicious, "with more offenses at (his) beck than (he had) thoughts to put them in, imagination to give them shape, or time to act them in."

Cranks hated me; for what reason I know not, but I suppose it was because I was his partner. Certainly, it could have been for no more heinous offense—and perhaps, after all, that blunder of mine was very reprehensible. Yes, Cranks hated me, and I have no doubt would have been glad at any moment during our acquaintance to see me killed—but for the fact that to witness such a tragedy he would necessarily have had to stand in the awful presence of Death. Cranks hated me; and if I entered the office finding him there, or if he came in finding me there, and I greeted him with a cheerful "good-morning," he only answered me with a churlish grunt, if indeed he answered at all, or simply looked "wicked" at me. This remarkable man seemed to regard it as one of the first rules of copartnership, and as entirely essential to the end aimed at by the formation of such copartnership,— whatever may have been his ideas of what that end ought to be,— that nothing like harmony between partners should be for a moment encouraged. Certainly his actions indicated that he entertained such views.

Many of the queer things he did during the three years I was associated with him seem almost incredible — certainly almost irreconcilable with the proposition that he was a sane man. For example, he would hide my pens, paste-pots, blotters, even my scissors,— which was little short of a crime! — or would throw them away or destroy them, merely that he might have an opportunity, when I began to look for them, to say with a very sneering manner that "some people never knew where to find anything," had no sense of system or order; he would slyly tell friends who called to see me that I was out, when he knew I was in the composing-room, and so send them away without seeing me; he would go out of his way to close a window by my table that I had opened to let in a little fresh air, or to open one I had closed when it grew a little too cool; he would contrive typographic errors, not only to annoy me, but to blame me with them when he had actually manufactured them, and destroy the proofs I had read in order that no reference could be made to them to show where the fault was, or was not; he surreptitiously inserted in the paper scurrilous articles alluding distantly to prominent gentlemen whom he knew to be my personal friends, and would pretend that they were communications; and he annoyed me in a variety of ways that were as childish on his part as they were harassing to me. All this, and much more, I patiently endured nearly three years before I yielded to the impulse to "give him a terrible beating," which course finally became unavoidable. After this scene, which occurred in the office, and which I take no pleasure in recalling, he fled from the establishment, and did not return for a period of three days, at the end of which time I suppose he concluded I had grown sufficiently calm not to make him a subject of Death.

Probably the worst feature of this singular man's disposition — from a business point of view — was his prompt and even violent opposition to every project not conceived by himself. Should I make any proposition for the advancement of our common interests, he would oppose it, and even ridicule it, with offensive language. For example, I would say:

"Mr. Cranks, how would it do to run another column of 'ads.' on the first page, to relieve the third?"

"A man must be a fool who has no better taste than that," would be his courteous reply.

On another occasion, I would humbly say:

"Mr. Cranks, in view of the state of our fonts, how would it do to set some of our extracts and special notices in minion, instead of nonpareil!"

"Well" — with a sneer — "any school-boy ought to have more sense than that."

A more important matter would arise, and I would say:

"Mr. Cranks, I have discovered that James X. Smith (a man employed in our business department, for example) is acting dishonestly with us. I think we had better discharge him and get some one else."

"O, I guess you only imagine it," Cranks would reply. "Even if he does knock down, we might get one who would be no better, or who would even be worse. I hate to make changes. Better hold on to Smith awhile."

This, not because he loved Smith, but because he hated me; and as we were equal partners no important step could be taken in any of our departments without the consent of both. This continual conflict might have been avoided by dividing the departments, and allowing each one to run one or more to suit himself; why was n't this done? O, I did propose it once, but of course, as a proposition coming from me, Cranks repelled it with bitterness and wrath.

"Was this man insane?" will be asked.

No, I am sure he was not; yet I will try to be charitable enough — while it is a stupendous task — to say that perhaps he could not help it. He was one of those churlish men who can never be happy except when everybody around them is miserable; and such men usually have within them the qualities necessary to make people around them miserable. "The writer of this has not seen through the thing clearly," some people will say who know something of business copartnerships. "The case is plain enough. Cranks was trying to freeze him out."

No, he was n't. I once offered to buy him out. His reply:

"There is no amount of money that would buy *my* half of the *Enunciator*."

"I would like to dissolve this business relation by some means," I said. "What will you give me for *my* half?"

His reply:

"I would n't give you four cents,— and, what 's more, I'll do all I can to prevent your selling to any one else."

And he did. A gentleman offered me five thousand dollars for my interest, but Cranks promptly told him he did n't want him for a partner; and so, of course, he did n't buy. He would have been a fool if he had, under such discouraging circumstances.

Cranks's extraordinary deportment paralyzed the growth of

the *Enunciator*, as might well have been expected, and ultimately brought upon it and him and me financial ruin. And I must say that I was never so happy in my life as when the voice of the *Enunciator* — in which I had often felt much pride — was hushed forever, and I walked forth into the world again, penniless, but free from Cranks, that incubus that for three years had been pressing me down!

I have thus briefly described one of the most remarkable men I ever met — not because my private affairs are likely to be of the slightest interest to the general public, but because he was a "character" so entirely singular, and one that would indeed make a study. I have not exaggerated in this outline of the man; indeed my once harsh feelings toward him have been softened by a lapse of years, so that I have, comparatively speaking, rather praised him than otherwise; yet had I read in fiction a description of exactly such a character as Cranks, before I saw him, I should have regarded it as a piece of the wildest caricaturing. Entirely blind to his own interests; preferring discord and consequent ruin to harmony and success; a puerile coward, dreading Death, yet daring to domineer in a manner mortally offensive; hating a convivial word in the sunshine of noon, yet nightly indulging in strange orgies; he was to me a problem and a puzzle, and such will remain so long as I live.

Cranks wrote verses. I did, too. But the trouble was, that anything written by myself was always ridiculed by him. However "trashy" my productions were,— and some of them, I believe, were considerably so, — I knew that his adverse, not to say insolent, criticisms were only prompted by his cynical disposition, without reference to their merits or demerits; and this led me to perpetrate a neat little practical joke on him, which, however, had a *denouement* altogether unanticipated by me. One day, after he had impressed it upon me in unusually coarse terms that I was "no poet,"—and he was certainly correct there, for writing verses, even though they be "clever," is not writing poetry,—I got into a proper frame of mind for writing a short satire in rhyme, and its title was, "The Churl." "And thus awhile the fit did work on me," but I did not hand the "poem" in to the foreman of the *Enunciator*. I was conscious of a device of just twice the commercial value of that. I put it in my pocket, and that evening called on a female friend, of much intelligence, to whom I confided my plans. I then requested her to copy my verses, which she kindly did, in her own neat feminine hand; and next I dictated, and she wrote, the following note:

SAN FRANCISCO, May 14, 18—.

MR. CRANKS:

DEAR SIR:—I frequently write verses for pastime, but have often declared that I would never have any of my effusions published. Nevertheless, I herewith inclose my latest production, which I am vain enough to think might be worthy of seeing the light. If you agree with me, you may publish it in the *Enunciator*, of which I am a regular reader; but please attach no name to it, as I do not wish my friends to know that it is mine, and that I have thus broken my vow not to do what they have often importuned me to do—namely, "appear in print."

Respectfully yours,
MISS TREE.

The note and the "poem" were inclosed in a large envelope, addressed in the same feminine hand to Mr. Cranks, and dropped into the Post-office. On the second morning afterward, Cranks and I being alone in the editorial room of the *Enunciator*, he spoke to me almost pleasantly, which of course astonished me very much. In fact, I began to fear that he was losing his mind. Addressing me familiarly by my last name, without the cold form of "Mr.," he said:

"You did n't drop round last night?"

"No," I replied; "I went to the California Theater. Were you here?"

"Yes, an hour or so," he replied, carelessly. "Being here alone, with everything quiet around me, an idea struck me, and I sat down and wrote a little poem. I never wrote with such ease in my life. In fact, the poem seemed to flow out of its own accord. Ah, it's *in me;* there's no use in talking. That, now, *is* a poem," and he held up several sheets of manuscript, shaking them triumphantly. "Ah," he continued, rather "more in sorrow than in anger," which was of course a very abnormal condition for him to get himself worked into, "if *you* could only write like that!"

Then he handed me his manuscript that I might read it, and so learn what real poetry was. I knew that he had once or twice written some very clever verses, and I prepared myself to give his latest effort at least all the praise it should, in my judgment, merit. Imagine, then, my astonishment,—not to say disgust at his mendacity,—when I glanced at the first page and found it to be my own poem, "The Churl." Impressed with its merits,—shall I say?—and little suspecting its source, he had copied it in order to show it to me in his own handwriting and make me believe he had written it himself. If he had watched me narrowly, he must have seen me start when I looked at the title; but, probably fearing that I might observe a significant expression, that of conscious deceit, in his own face, he turned away, ostensibly to light his pipe. Quickly regaining my composure, I deliberately read the poem to the end, discovering that it was copied word for word, and then pronounced it very fine indeed, remarking to Cranks that I thought he had never written so good a thing before. I don't think yet that I uttered a falsehood in saying so.

"The Churl" was promptly published in the *Enunciator*, and was copied by a few exchanges that happened to need a poem very badly. I intended to leave Cranks "alone in his glory," thinking that, bad as he was, it would be next to cruel to inform him that I was cognizant of his deception; but he referred to "his poem" so frequently, and even compared it with some which I was known to have written, so unfavorably to the latter, that I began to see that it would be impossible permanently to hold my peace. Whenever he took up an exchange and found his (?) poem in it, he would modestly (?) say:

"Ah, here 's 'The Churl' again! It 's going the rounds. I knew it would when I wrote it."

"Cranks," said I, turning from my writing-desk and gazing calmly upon that round face of his, "did it ever occur to you that there might possibly be some *mystery* about *Miss Tree?*"

He was struck dumb.

"Cranks," I continued, "it just happens that *I* wrote 'The Churl,' and a lady friend copied it for me and also, at my dictation, wrote that note signed 'Miss Tree.' I took that course in order that you might criticise it without knowing that it was mine, and so pass an impartial judgment upon it. But I never once expected that you would so ignore the beauties of entire originality as to pass it off for your own."

He was almost paralyzed with chagrin and mortification; for, debasing as it is to tell a lie, it is doubly so to be caught in it. His cold gray eyes opened wide, then nearly closed; his face grew red all over, then turned pale, with a slightly greenish tinge; and his whole countenance was one great round picture of crouching and cowering malevolence. He opened his mouth as if to speak; but changed his mind, turned away with a mere grunt and a half-snappish air, bent over his table and pretended to write. He did n't speak to me again for two or three days, or look straight into my face for as many weeks; and no reference was ever again made to the disagreeable matter either by myself or my wonderful partner.

CHAPTER XXIV.

THE "ENUNCIATOR."

I HAVE some pleasant memories of San Francisco, if it *was* the scene of bitter trials and "hard luck." Some of the best friends of my whole life were found there; and several faces in the "Bay City" have fixed themselves upon my heart—enduring rays of sunshine. The very thought of them is sufficient to cheer me a little when "things go wrong," and I am not in a buoyant mood. I often, too, recall the city and its surroundings, which are before me yet like a beautiful picture. I think of the cooling summer winds that sweep in from the Pacific, just without the Gate; of the sweet air and spring-like skies that alternate with the innocent showers of the "rainy season" — the time of our freezing winters in the same latitude of the Atlantic slope and the Mississippi Valley; of the beautiful harbor, dotted with green islands and fringed with white sails; of Suncelito, blooming with strange wild flowers in December; of Yerba Bueno; of Alcatraz, standing up like a little Gibraltar out of the inland sea; of the serene little city of Oakland, daily visible beyond the bay, with her thousand of spreading trees, her sweet gardens of flowers and vines, her many lovely homes; of the ships gliding in and out through the Golden Gate — the great black steamers floating up to the wharf, with the news from the Orient and a thousand yellow Chinese; of Telegraph Hill, to whose summit I have often climbed and looked down upon the face of the broad harbor, thinking of the bright future of San Francisco, and prophesying how mighty her commerce must sooner or later be; of the thronged streets of the Golden City, often in other days the scene of violence and open murder, but now crowded with busy people who swell the wealth of the State; of the Twin Peaks, over toward the south, that rise up and look down upon the city and bay from a height of six hundred feet; of the smooth road to the Cliff House, beaten by the thundering hoofs of fleet horses, followed by flying wheels; of "Seal Rock," standing up out of the water, barely away from the shore, that great mass of granite upon which the slimy seals glide up to bask in the sunshine and all day long utter their mournful howls; of the smooth beach, beaten by ceaseless breakers that, with fringes of foam, roll in ever and ever from the wide, wide sea; — think of these with that fondness and longing that nearly every one feels for our Pacific shores who has lived upon and left them.

That *Enunciator!* I worked untiringly to build it up, to make it a power in the land; and for awhile, notwithstanding the difficulties that environed me, had a reasonable hope of ultimate success. But the millstone — Cranks — was tied about the neck of our journal, with a knot of more than Gordian intricacy, and the end was inevitable.

Yet Cranks was not the only adverse element in and about the office of the *Enunciator*. The money receipts of a paper are its food and fuel, and it is all-important that its financial affairs should be carefully and correctly attended to. A portion of our business, including the collecting, was intrusted to another eccentric character, named Nathaniel Bumps, to whom we paid forty dollars a week for the exercise of his talents. Mr. Bumps was a clever business man, portly in form, shapely in face and feature, genial in disposition. He would have been a tower of strength in his department, but for one or two little shortcomings, the principal of which was that he did a little too much in the "genial" line. This fault, so far from growing "small by degrees, and beautifully less," as I dared to hope it would, was deep-rooted, and rapidly assumed such healthy proportions as to make Mr. Bumps a reproach, rather than a credit, to the *Enunciator*.

Nathaniel Bumps drank plain Bourbon whisky, in large quantities and at frequent intervals; and such was his memory of things many times viewed, that he could have minutely described the fixtures and informed an anxious inquirer how many glass tumblers there were in each and every drinking-saloon in San Francisco. To say that he could at short notice recommend a friend to the particular saloons at which the best liquors were to be had, would be a work of supererogation.

"Is there any place," the friend he met on the street would ask, looking about with a half-anxious expression of countenance, "any place around here where —"

"O, yes!" Nathaniel Bumps would interrupt, — for "his heart too truly knew the sound full well," — "O, yes! There 's Barry & Patten's, in Montgomery Street, where you get mighty fine whisky, but it 's a two-bit place; and there 's Martin & Horton's, corner of Montgomery and Clay, their Bourbon is fine, and only a bit; and there 's 'Dave's,' 613 Sacramento Street — he sets out a stavin' lunch, and has some fine rye that he got in last Saturday; and then there 's Harris's Sample Rooms, in California Street, just below Montgomery; and there 's the Cosmopolitan, good whisky, either rye or Bourbon; and I like the place because they set out thin glasses!"

One Monday morning I sent him to Vallejo (a thriving little city across the bay, northward from San Francisco, and about thirty or forty miles distant) on business that ought to occupy about a whole day, but I did not expect him to return to the office before the following morning. Before going he said:

"Confound the luck! Last week, when I had most to do and

was most anxious to get through with it, I met a party of fellows that I could n't get away from, and now I 've got behindhand. I must make up for it this week. This thing of running around drinking is played out. I 'm going to quit it, right square; and, by Jove, I 'll insult the first man that asks me to take a drink!"

I did not see him again till Saturday morning, when he came into the office — perfectly sober, it is true, but very nervous, and his face much "sun-burned."

"Ughm!" he said, rubbing his hands together uneasily, as he took a seat at his desk to give me a statement of his business transactions at Vallejo, — for I had the general care of the business department, while I at the same time did most of the editorial work, — "Ughm! Oo-oo-oo-oo!" — with a shudder; — "I don't feel very well this morning — have n't felt well for several days. I think it must have been the *water* at Vallejo."

I was a trifle out of humor because he had remained away so long and neglected his duties in the city, but the implied proposition of Nathaniel Bumps deliberately drinking a glass of *water* struck me as being so exceptionally funny that I had to burst into a fit of laughter. I could n't help it. He looked up at me innocently, smiled a knowing smile, and went on with his work. [I knew myself that the Vallejo whisky was "horrible stuff."]

But for the characteristic obstinacy of my partner — Cranks — who of course promptly opposed the proposition when I made it, I think I should have removed Mr. Bumps to some other sphere of usefulness long before the termination of the *Enunciator's* career. Cranks himself fairly hated Bumps, but would have suffered anything (with the exception of Death) rather than consent to his dismissal, such dismissal being desired by his partner. So, I had to bear with the weaknesses of Nathaniel Bumps, while his sprees grew more and more frequent and extended, and the finances of the *Enunciator* grew more and more precarious. I finally got into the way of enduring all this with calm resignation, and ceased to be surprised, or even annoyed, if I sent Bumps out on Thursday or Friday to begin collecting in order to meet the usual demands of Saturday, — from three hundred to four hundred dollars, — and did n't see him again before the middle of the next week. That got to be an old thing. Any person with a good general idea of conducting a business of any kind will readily perceive how pernicious such a state of things must have been.

In the latter days of the *Enunciator*, we had a general "streak of bad luck." In the language of Hamlet's mother,

> One woe doth tread upon another's heel,
> So fast they follow.

We had correspondents in various parts of the State who occasionally sent us mining or agricultural news, and now and then brief accounts of anything remarkable — sometimes amusing — that might occur in their respective localities. On one occasion a correspondent at Marysville sent us an account of a ridiculous affair that occurred there — and it was published in the *Enunciator*. Briefly, it was to the effect that an Englishman, representing himself as a nobleman, with the title of Sir William Ward, took rooms at an hotel and expressed a desire to spend a few days in gunning. He boasted so much, in so short a time, of his shooting, his wealth, his ancestry, and was in general so "airy," that some of the mischievous young men of the place conspired to make him the victim of a harmless practical joke. There was no such a thing as a wild duck in the neighborhood, but they told him that that species of game abounded in all directions, and arranged to guide him on the following day to a place where he might shoot a bagful or two. Then they spent a part of the night in making a few wooden ducks, which they properly painted, ballasted and placed in a neighboring pond. Next day they led him to the spot and got him to banging away at the wooden images; although it was clear that had he been half the sportsman he pretended to be, he must have detected the trick at a glance. His disgust when he discovered the real state of things, and his prompt departure from Marysville, were humorously described by our correspondent, followed by a statement that "Ward" was discovered to be an impostor,—no nobleman at all;—and when I handed the manuscript to our Foreman there was certainly no shadow of a "monitor" within me to whisper that I was about to commit the "crime" of libel.

I should never have given the subject a thought again, but for the fact that a few days after the publication of the correspondence a respectably-dressed Englishman, whom I had certainly never seen before, came into the office and called my attention to it. He stated that his name was William Ward; that he was the person referred to in the communication; that he was an Englishman by birth, but not a nobleman, and had not so represented himself; that he had come from Australia, where he had lived some years; that he had been in California *nearly five weeks;* and that he felt his reputation so much damaged by the publication of our Marysville correspondence that he must, in justice to himself, demand a pecuniary satisfaction; although, to be sure, no conceivable amount of money could *fully* indemnify him.

Cranks turned pale.

I told "Mr. Ward" that I did not know him; that the article alluded to was sent by a correspondent; that we had understood it to refer merely to some one traveling under a fictitious name and title; and that certainly nothing could have been more distant from our intentions than to libel any actual living human being; and, more for pastime than anything else, I asked him to what extent he believed his reputation to have been damaged by the publication of the correspondence in the *Enunciator*.

He thought that ten thousand dollars, in gold, would make it about right, so far as money considerations went.

Although highly amused, I suggested that there was such a thing as a street in San Francisco, and with an apprehension creditable to him, he took the hint and left.

"Now, we're in a devil of a scrape!" said Cranks, who, feeling that Death might after all be somewhat distant, began to recover from his fright, and at the same time to recover his normal condition of ill-nature. He had never uttered a word in the dreadful presence of "Sir William Ward."

"It will amount to nothing," I replied, resuming my work. "A mere adventurer, I see plainly enough."

On the following day, while I was making a canvass of the drinking-saloons, in search of Nathaniel Bumps, whom I had not seen since the middle of the previous week, when I had sent him out to collect three or four large bills, an officer of one of the courts entered our office and served a "process" on my partner as one of the defendants in a civil suit in which William Ward was the plaintiff; which of course alarmed Cranks very much, for, in his supreme ignorance of the law, how was he to know but that Death might somehow or other be mixed up with the matter?

Yes, (Sir) William Ward had employed a lawyer of the "shyster" school and entered suit for libel against the proprietors of the "*Enunciator*," laying his damages, with great accuracy, at ten thousand dollars. This man, it will be remembered, had been in the country about *five weeks;* yet the publication of a humorous article in a weekly paper, with a circulation of less than four thousand copies, had damaged his reputation to the extent of ten thousand dollars! I shudder to think what "his bill" might have been if he had lived in the United States a couple of years or so at the time the "libel" was published, and been established in a profitable business! In another chapter I shall have something more to say of libel-suits and libel-laws; but here is a simple statement of a case that speaks volumes. Mark the conclusion: After some delay, made necessary by the usual legal formalities,—I having meantime engaged a lawyer to defend the case to the last, giving him a retaining-fee of one hundred dollars,—this (Sir) William Ward intimated a willingness to make a new estimate of the value of his reputation, and thought he might take *fifty dollars* as indemnity for the damage sustained, and "call it square!"

Now the galling part of it was, that during my absence from the office, Cranks, probably thinking that such a course might prevent a sudden termination of his life, and so defer the approach of Death, signed an agreement to pay this amount, thus committing the firm to a compromise with the villainy of blackmailing! In doing this, he was guilty of little less than a crime. It was compounding felony, and I would rather have emptied the already waning treasury of the *Enunciator*, in the way of costs, than to have seen rascality rewarded with even the pitiful sum of fifty dollars. However, we were now committed to it, and the money had to be paid.

About this time a number of petty annoyances and losses were inflicted upon the *Enunciator*, and it seemed as if heaven and earth were conspiring with Cranks to "bust it up." A printers' strike, taken alone, would not have been such a serious matter, but of course it had to come right along with the series of other perplexities. Our compositors were very good workmen, and good fellows, too; but they belonged to the Printers' Union, and had to strike along with the rest. In common with other publishers and employing printers, we declined to yield to their demands, and the result was the greatest difficulty in getting the *Enunciator* out, and even then it involved additional expense. One of "the boys," who little suspected the poor financial condition of the *Enunciator*, dropped in to pay me a friendly visit one day, his hands in his pockets and his Sunday suit on, and said, in the course of some conversation on the subject:

"We all hated to strike, Mr. ——, and would have been willing to work on, so far as this office is concerned; but we belong to the Union, and of course could n't help it."

"Well, George," I replied, "you know very well that I have always been disposed to do full justice to the compositors, but I really do think the Union is asking too much. Have you any idea that your strike will succeed?"

"Yes; the boys all think it will. Don't you think so?"

"No, sir-ree, George," I replied, emphatically; "no use contending against *capital!*"

I put on a very grave look when I said this, and George sat in thoughtful silence, not suspecting that I could scarcely restrain a burst of laughter at the idea of having classed myself with the capitalist, when there was not a printer recently in our employ half so poor as the proprietors of the *Enunciator*.

I think that one of the saddest things in the experience of the printer and newspaper publisher is the "piing" of a form. What printers call a "form" is, for example, the type, properly set up and arranged in final order, from which one whole page (or it might be two) of a newspaper is to be printed. This is "locked up" — if I say "wedged," I will be better understood — in what is called a "chase." The chase is a square iron frame, something like a window-sash with all the glass and cross-pieces removed. The chase lies on a large table, about three and a half or four feet high, whose top is a smooth slab of stone (or iron), called an imposing-stone. Within this chase the columns of type are placed by the foreman, or assistant foreman, which operation is styled "making up." But the form does not quite fill out the chase, and in the crevices at the bottom and one side are placed what are called "side-stick" and "foot-stick," and between these and the iron frame of the chase the foreman, with his mallet and shooting-stick, drives square and slightly tapering sticks of wood a couple of inches in length, and these are called quoins. They are driven in tight, causing a pressure upon the types from all sides calculated to hold them so firmly in their places that the whole mass may be lifted and carried to the press, which is often out of, and whole squares distant from, the building in which the composing-room is situated.

It will be readily understood that it is important to "handle with care" this heavy mass of type, weighing, say two hundred pounds, for the form cannot be so firmly locked but that a sudden shock may start the types from their places and cause the whole mass to crumble into a disorderly heap. Such a calamity, which sometimes occurs, is called "piing a form," and the scattered type is called "pi." So careful was I to prevent such an occurrence, that late on many a Saturday night I have stood by the hand-cart that waited at the door, with a revolver in my pocket, to guard one inside form that had been carried down and placed therein to be conveyed to press, while the strong man made a second journey up-stairs for the other. I thought this precaution necessary because reckless revelers were in the streets all night, and many of them would not have hesitated to "pi" a form — not through ill-will toward the *Enunciator*, but merely "for fun." One Saturday night, or rather Sunday morning, — for it was past two o'clock, — I had the good fortune to prevent this piece of innocent sport. A party of four or five bacchanalians came reeling along, and one of them said, "Hello. Let's upset this old cart." He led the way, and the others gathered around to assist in his laudable undertaking. I did not like, if I could help it, to "commence shootin,'" as Artemus Ward says in his account of desperado life in Nevada, so I merely sung out, with my hand none the less on my revolver:

"O, say — by the way — is that you, Charlie?"

They hesitated. The name of one of them did happen to be Charlie, and of course, thinking I must be some one he knew — I was standing in the shadow of the door-way, and the night was dark — he replied:

"Yes; is that you?"

"Yes. Don't disturb that cart, please; there is something in it that belongs to me."

"O, all right," was the reply; and as they walked away he added: "Won't you go up to the corner and take a drink?"

"No, thank you," I replied. "I'm waiting here for a man."

So, the whole party retired, and I had saved my form without resorting to the taking of human life.

But, in the days of its waning fortunes, the *Enunciator* did not escape the disaster of a "pied form," although in the pride of its strength, when it might have laughed at such a mishap, it had enjoyed a wonderful immunity therefrom. The paper contained thirty-six columns, each thirty inches in length; and it will be seen that the piing of one of its forms, of nine columns, was not calculated to excite much mirth on the part of those, editors and printers, who had labored so carefully to get the matter up.

It was one rainy Saturday night — that is, Sunday morning, after two o'clock, when my weary week's work was done. The strong man had taken the first form (page two, editorial) from the imposing-stone and was beginning slowly and carefully to descend the flight of stairs from the third floor, on which our editorial- and composing-rooms were, and I was sitting on a corner of my writing-table, on the eve of lighting a cigar before following him down to the street to watch it while he should come up for the other inside form, — the two outside pages having been already printed, — and Cranks sat in an armchair, scowling at me (because I was his partner) through a dense cloud of smoke which he drew from a strong pipe, and sent out into the air; when we were startled by a thump — a rumbling sound — a loud crash — a continuous rattle and uproar, accompanied by a perceptible trembling of the floor and quivering of the walls.

An earthquake was of course the first thing to be thought of, as we used to have one of more or less vigor every week or two in San Francisco and its vicinity; and Cranks, thinking that he might be in the immediate presence of Death, shouted, "O, Lord!" dropped his pipe, scattering sparks and ashes in every direction, sprang up and flew wildly out of the room. I expected to hear him tumbling down stairs, as I had heard him several times before when the building was "shaken up" by a harmless earthquake, but I was disappointed this time. I was still waiting for the brimstone to burn off the match with which I was about to light my cigar, when he came back to the door, having merely taken a few steps in the hall, which was well lighted with gas, and said:

"O! — just — come — here!"

I shall never forget how Cranks looked at that moment. His thick form appeared shorter than usual, probably being slightly bent with fright; his hat had fallen off, and in the gas-light the bald top of his head glittered and shone in a wild fantastic way; what hair he had growing around the sides of his head was all disordered, and actually stood out in every direction,

> Like quills upon the fretful porcupine;

and on his distorted face, now about the color of pure hickory-ashes, there was such a look of consternation and despair as really startled me. I began to think that the universe had collapsed, that he had just got the news, and that we were on the eve of

> The wreck of matter and the crush of worlds.

It was "the wreck of *matter*" only; for when I went out into the hall and looked down the stairway, I saw that the form of our editorial page was "pied."

"O, piteous spectacle!" The types, the spaces, the em-quads, the two-em quads, the leads, the rules, the quoins, the reglets, the side-stick, the foot-stick, the furniture, were scattered in awful confusion from stair to stair, from the top to the bottom of the flight; and at the foot of the stairs, to which he had tumbled, the strong man was in the act of struggling to his feet, with the empty chase—which now looked nearly as interesting as a second-hand picture-frame with no picture in it—around his neck, like a horse's collar, though it did not make nearly so neat a fit. There were horror and anguish on the poor fellow's face as he looked up at me and said:

"Why, 'pon my word! I—I—did n't—mean to do it! I slipped!"

Heaven knows that I did not suspect him of having done it purposely, and for the moment I forgot my own misfortune in pity for him, especially as I noticed the blood trickling from his forehead, just over the right eye, and I said:

"O, that's nothing." [Such a lie!] "Did you get hurt, Dennis?"

"Nothin' but a bruise or two," he replied, rubbing his elbow, and nose, and forehead.

"Well, accidents will happen," I said, although I never before so sincerely wished they would n't. "There's two bits,"—and I tossed him a silver quarter,—"go up to George's at the corner, and get a drink of good brandy."

The fact is, I feared he might be injured internally, and, as he had a large family, I should have felt conscience-stricken if he had died in my service at a time when I was unable to give his widow a pension. He picked up the bit of silver, and started for that "corner" that was "open all night," and when he returned, I was glad to note that he looked much better. Meantime, Cranks and I, assisted by a compositor who had not yet gone home, proceeded to gather up the scattered type, for it was worth a hundred dollars or so, and we had no notion of allowing it to assume the attitude of rubbish.

Yes, it was sad. Nine columns—two hundred and seventy inches—twenty-two and a half feet of type, in lines of two and a quarter inches in measure—all wrecked—all our articles gone—my editorial carefully prepared with reference to statistics of the mining and agricultural products of the State—an unusually fine poem—a pathetic appeal to harsh parents—a peculiarly sarcastic hit at some abuses in the city government—all gone, *gone*, GONE. If I had been "given to the melting mood," I never could have found an occasion more fitting.

What was to be done? We could not think of issuing our paper with one page blank. Well, I went and woke up Mr.

P——, one of the proprietors of the daily *Bulletin*, and, telling him what had happened, asked him if he would be kind enough to allow us to use one of the forms of his Saturday evening issue in the place of our pied one. He said "Certainly," although he and I had given each other more than one "rap" in our respective papers. The fact is, there is no finer sense of courtesy anywhere than that existing among members of the newspaper fraternity; and I believe I never yet saw an editor or proprietor of a paper but would lend matter, his press and everything to his worst enemy in the profession in cases of terrible exigency like this. So we took out one small paragraph from the form of our third page, and inserted a few lines in bold letters, explaining what had happened, and so accounting for the "eccentric appearance" of the second page of the *Enunciator* — gladly giving credit to the *Bulletin* for helping us out.

I have mentioned elsewhere in this volume that editors are disposed to be generous, and I have seldom seen any who were otherwise. Horace Greeley, whom I so frequently have occasion to mention in speaking of editors, was noted for his generosity, although he was no doubt often imposed upon. He says, in his "Recollections of a Busy Life," something like this: "I have invested largely in human nature, and I lament my loss of confidence in it more than my loss of money." Indeed, it would be strange if intellectual men did not possess the highest share of noble qualities, among which is pity for the distressed, coupled with an impulse to aid them. I hate to say that I ever did any one a kindness; but if I did, it was through selfishness after all, for, if one takes pleasure in doing an act of any kind, I do not see that he is entitled to a great amount of credit for it. But it is to illustrate how what is called generosity is sometimes — shall I say often? — rewarded, that I introduce the subject here; and it has also a bearing upon the falling fortunes of the *Enunciator*.

A man named Jordan, with but one arm, came into our office, one day, and Cranks, my evil genius, introduced him to me as an old newspaper-carrier. I asked him what he was engaged at now, and he said "Nothing." He had recently been engaged in the Post-office as a letter-carrier, but owing to ill-health had been obliged to give it up a few months previously, and now must wait for his turn to get on the list again. It was very natural for me to ask him "how he was fixed." Could he live comfortably awhile without employment?

No. He had very little money left; doctors' bills, you know, and —

I thought awhile, then said:

"There is a carrier on the *Enunciator* who owns a route and wants to dispose of it. He would sell it for a hundred dollars or so. Probably you have n't the means to buy it?"

"No — not quarter enough."

"Would you like paper-carrying again?"

"O, yes; anything for the sake of employment."

I liked his frank manner and honest appearance, and I pondered a few seconds and said to Cranks:

"Suppose we should buy the route of the carrier and let Mr. Jordan run it?"

To my astonishment, Cranks readily assented to my proposition, a thing he had never done before.

"Very well. Will you take hold of it, Mr. Jordan?"

"O, yes!" he said, joyfully. "But how about paying for my papers?"

"That will be all right. You need not pay us for any papers till the end of the first month, when you do your collecting. That will be giving you a good chance. We usually require security in a case like this, but I won't from *you*, Mr. Jordan. I think I know an honest man when I see one."

So, I bought the route of the other carrier, and, while retaining its ownership, gave it trustingly into the charge of Jordan. He came and got his papers every Sunday morning, bright and cheerful, and for weeks nothing happened, except that he borrowed ten dollars of me — Cranks having assured me that he was perfectly reliable. A month went by, and he did not pay any money, or say anything about it. Six weeks, and I ventured — very gently — to ask him, one day, if he had been collecting yet. No, he had n't. He had been busy canvassing his route, and was going to add a couple of hundred subscribers to his list. He would collect in another week. Two or three weeks went by, and he deliberately abandoned his route and absconded, owing us three hundred dollars. Before abandoning, he carefully collected every cent due from subscribers on his route. I afterward learned that, instead of having left the Post-office on account of ill-health, he had been discharged therefrom for a very sufficient reason, and, what may seem on the verge of the unfathomable, my partner knew it!

I have been "taken in" as badly as that more than once, — although such experience, I trust, will never make me an abandoned cynic, — and another notable instance occurred while I was one of the proprietors of the *Enunciator*. I subsequently wrote an account of it (in the form of a sketch that might be taken for an imaginary one) for *Saturday Night*, — accurate in every particular, except in the matter of names,— and, with the permission of the proprietors of that paper, to whom the sketch now belongs, I make it the sum and substance of the next chapter.

CHAPTER XXV.

"MY FRIEND GEORGE."

[*From "Saturday Night," April* 26, 1873.]

IN the spring of 18—, I went to California by steamer. A couple of days after sailing, when I had about recovered, I was sitting on the hurricane-deck, looking down into the blue sea. Another passenger sat at my elbow, on the same long seat by the railing, and he said to me:

"I've been trying to think where I've seen you?"

His own face was not unfamiliar.

"I cannot say. Where do you hail from?" I asked.

"Philadelphia."

"I, too, have resided there for some years."

"I thought so. O, yes; now that I come to think, I remember where I saw you. If I mistake not, you were a party in the B—— libel case. I was a witness."

And he informed me what my name was.

"Correct. Let me see—your name is—"

"Miller—George Miller."

I rather liked him.

He was five feet seven inches high, and weighed a hundred and thirty-five pounds. He was not fleshy, but rather muscular. His face, especially, which was characterized by prominent cheek-bones, in marked contrast with a narrow chin, was not burdened by an undue amount of flesh. He had black, curly hair, gray eyes, a nose prominent at the bridge, and a sparse mustache. His age was thirty. He was affable.

During the voyage our acquaintance ripened into a friendly intimacy. He was a good fellow, with a fair sense of humor, and his ways were frank and open—almost boyish. At Aspinwall his pocket was picked of three hundred dollars—all he had. But I assisted him in various ways and made it as comfortable as possible for him. I little thought then that I should ever find it come in my way to employ him as a detective.

George had left his wife in Philadelphia,—she was an estimable little Quakeress, only twenty, as I subsequently ascertained,—and was going to

California to build up his fortunes there, and then send for her. He had been unfortunate in business. He possessed more than ordinary qualifications for a mercantile calling, and on arriving at San Francisco he tried hard to get a situation as book-keeper. But just at that time San Francisco was flooded with persons seeking employment, and it was about as difficult to procure a very desirable and remunerative position as it was to become a member of Congress. So, with willing hands, George did the next best thing—he took a position as conductor on a street-car, and was thus employed, by spells, for a year or two. At times, he even acted as driver.

I saw him often, and occasionally got on his car, at his cordial request, and took a ride with him to the terminus of the line and back. He was always lively and cheerful. I felt pained when I looked at his good-natured, sun-browned face, and meditated that he was fitted for a higher sphere. He told me that he was laying by money, and would send for his little wife some day. But poor George had a weakness—one that has afflicted many an intellectual, high-minded, honorable man.

He drank.

At times he drank to excess, to the end that his employers' interests were prejudiced. He was, therefore, discharged several times; but recovered his position each time, after an interval, because he was a good fellow—and promised to be. But by-and-by he was dismissed for good, on account of drinking an unusual quantity, and failed to get a place on the road again, either as conductor or driver. Then he "straightened up," and remained idle a good while, but ultimately secured a position as driver on a line of horse-cars just established in the pleasant little city of Oakland, over the bay.

He did n't "drink a drop" for some time, and I entertained pleasing hopes for his future. But at last he took to it again, with unusual avidity, and lost his situation in Oakland. He then returned to San Francisco, and sought employment for months.

Meantime I was editing a weekly newspaper, in which I had purchased an interest, and George often called on me at our sanctum—sometimes perfectly sober. I bestowed frequent little favors, and exerted myself to procure employment for him. Poor fellow, I did pity him!

By-and-by I thought I could make room for a clerk in our office, and sought George, but could not find him. A note addressed to him and dropped into the Post-office, did not bring him to light, although he was in the habit of calling regularly at the "general-delivery" window for his letters. He was absent from the city. A few weeks later, when he turned up again, I had occasion to employ him in an entirely different capacity. I will tell how it was:

I had missed several pairs of scissors, — an indispensable article in an editor's office, — and I bought a new and rather costly pair, which I locked up in a drawer of my writing-table. One morning they were gone! I had certainly left them in my drawer, as usual. I asked my associate if he had seen them, also our business man, who was in the same room. They had not. I deemed the occasion a fitting one for profanity. My partner and our business man both laughed at me, and so I laughed, too, and pretended that I was n't much annoyed.

"There has been a thief about," said I, "for I perceive that strange hands have been in my drawer, although I found it locked."

"That 's singular," said my partner.

"Oh, by the way!" said our business man, placing a pen behind his ear, "Mr. Bartlett told me that some things had been stolen from his office. The same thief may have been up here."

Mr. Bartlett was a lawyer, whose offices were on the floor beneath our office and composing-room. To reach our floor it was necessary to ascend two flights of stairs, passing Mr. Bartlett's doors in the corridor of the second floor.

"Where is my Shakespeare?" asked my partner, abruptly.

"I have not seen it."

"Nor I."

He searched everywhere. It was gone!

"I would n't lose that book for fifty dollars! I 've had it twenty years!" he said, vehemently.

Then *he* swore and *I* laughed.

But further discoveries followed. Several other books were missing — Byron, Moore, Burns, and a dictionary of authors.

"Why, the thief has carried off an arm-load!" exclaimed the business man.

The deed had evidently been done during the previous night, and, singularly enough, the intruder had locked the doors after him, and left everything in an orderly condition — except what he had not left at all. A week passed, and our nocturnal friend remembered us again. A "Webster's Unabridged Dictionary," "Homer's Iliad," and several other valuable works disappeared. More articles had also been conveyed from Mr. Bartlett's law-offices. The thief had locked the doors after him, and, to his credit, left everything tidy.

We raved, and called in a detective.

"Have you any suspicions?" he asked.

"Yes; we discharged a carrier, not long ago — a worthless fellow, named Jordan, whom we had found both unreliable and dishonest. We have published a notice warning the public that he no longer transacts any business for us, and now he is evidently having his revenge. These thefts are plainly committed by some one familiar with the building. I consider it next to certain that he is the thief."

This positive opinion I delivered to the detective, who started on the suspected person's track. He found him in his own lodgings, in a disreputable quarter of the city, but no clue. Nevertheless he acted as his shadow for awhile.

Another week and another robbery! More books, some umbrellas and other things went. Mr. Bartlett lost more law-books, a meerschaum pipe, some postage-stamps and stamped envelopes. It was the same neat kind of burglary. It began to look like a mystery.

Half a week, and another visit from the thief. A large volume, entitled "Historical Miscellany," and some other valuable works of reference disappeared. The poets had already been exhausted. A gold pen, some keys, an ebony ruler, and some other useful articles, went the way of the books. All the drawers in the establishment had been unlocked, investigated and locked up again.

A couple of days, then another visit from the thief. We told the detective. He said it was n't Jordan. Still, I thought it must be. He asked who else would come within the range of suspicion. I told him we had implicit confidence in all our employes. He shook his head wisely, and noted their names and residences.

That night our clock was stolen, and — yes, incredible as it may seem — we discovered that the thief had actually made him a bed of old newspapers in a back room we did not use much, and slept! Such audacity was something new and novel in the annals of crime. Clearly he was not averse to a-rest.

Who could it be? We began to suspect all our employes, one by one, from the foreman down to the devil; and I fancied I could see each one in his turn put on a decidedly guilty look. I even went so far as to suspect our exemplary business man; nay, I even wondered if it might not be my partner, suffering from *kleptomania;* and I verily believe he half suspected me.

The thief came oftener and oftener — almost every night — and got into the habit, not only of sleeping regularly in our vacant room, but also of making his toilet there, finding a place for his comb on the window-ledge, and leaving off, in a corner, his soiled collars and worn-out neckties. Once he left a shirt that had been worn since washed, though not worn out, and it would scarcely have surprised me now if his washerwoman had called for it. It was bewildering.

My partner and I took turns sitting up in the corridor whole nights on guard. I sat there many a night in the dampness and gloom, with my revolver in my hand, momentarily expecting to hear the sly footfall of the thief on the stairs.

But he came not.

No sooner did we relax our vigilance, however, than another visit honored our absence; another night's repose was enjoyed in the vacant room; and another invoice of useful articles walked off — among them our business man's meerschaum pipe, which he highly prized. The detective said it must be the Chinese; for they are sly, crafty, and very immoral.

I had told George all about it, and one morning, when I met him on the street, it occurred to me that here was a chance to do him a good turn.

"George," I said, "I am fairly worn out watching for that sneaking thief, and so is my partner. We cannot lose half our night's rest and perform our daily duties besides. You are not doing anything; now, suppose you watch for the rascal a few nights. I will give you two dollars and a half per night."

"All right!" he said, eagerly.

The poor fellow was delighted with the temporary employment, and was duly installed as watchman. I employed him eight nights, and paid him twenty dollars.

But the thief came not.

Then I told him he need not watch any more, as the robber had probably left the city, or been caught up on some other charge. Besides, he had already carried off nearly all our "portable property," and probably would never come again.

But he did come on two different nights after that, took some things, went to bed in the vacant room, rose with the lark, and we saw him not. He was a dark, mocking mystery, — an invisible presence floating in the air,— and I felt a half-superstitious thrill crawling clammily down my spinal column. I had heard of such things as spirits. A feeling of helpless resignation took possession of us, and we began to feel as though everything in our office belonged to that thief, and that we were merely employed there, temporarily, to furnish him with things to carry off. Who should say but that he might eventually turn us out, and run the whole thing himself? He already possessed a controlling interest. But —

"Good-morning!" said Mr. Bartlett, as he bolted into our office one day. "I have a clue!"

"What!"

We sprang to our feet. Was he mortal, after all?

"You know," said Mr. Bartlett, "that I told you some stamped envelopes were stolen from me. Well, on each envelope were printed the words, 'If not called for, return to C. Bartlett, San Francisco.' The thief has been stupid enough to use these envelopes in corresponding with his friends; two of them have not been *called for*, and, thanks to an excellent postal system, duly returned to me. Here are the letters, signed with the full name, without doubt, of the thief himself. A good hand he writes, truly."

"Who — who is it?" I asked, breathlessly.

"Some one whom I do not know. I have brought up the letters to see if you happen to know the writer. Here they are."

I opened one of the letters, while my partner took the other, and my eye quickly sought the signature. Heavens! My brain grew dizzy. Was I dreaming? The neat autograph was that of my friend George! The letter was written in his own faultless hand, and boldly signed, "George Miller." I was fairly stunned.

"Do you know him?" asked Mr. Bartlett.

"I know him well," I replied. "This is his writing — his signature; but he is the last person in the world whom I could have suspected of dishonesty!"

"Where may he be found?"

"I do not know where he lodges at present; but I meet him almost every day."

"He must be arrested."

"But do you consider this conclusive evidence?"

"Unless he can give some plausible explanation as to how he came by these envelopes. I have already found some of the books that were stolen from me. The thief had sold them at a book-stand in Leidesdorff Street. The dealer says he would know the man he bought them of. Besides, if this Miller is the guilty party, it will soon be apparent when he is arrested. Are you willing to assist me?"

"Yes—if it were my brother! I can scarcely dare to think him guilty, but if he is, he is the most heartless ingrate and deceitful rogue that ever lived! Meeting me daily, face to face, with cordial words of greeting, and stealing from me at night. I cannot believe it! He is above such deeds—incapable of such duplicity. Nevertheless, I shall assist you in accomplishing his arrest, then let the truth be unfolded, be it palatable or not."

The evidence, though purely circumstantial, was almost convincing, and during that whole day my troubled thoughts ran on the subject. At times I concluded that it was a plain case; then again drove the thought from me, vowing that it was simply impossible that my friend George could be a thief! In the course of the day it occurred to me that some traces of the thief might be found in the vacant room in which he had slept night after night with such nonchalance. I repaired to that room, and among the disordered newspapers I caught sight of one that was not a copy of our own paper, neither was it one of our exchanges; and its irregular creases indicated that a bundle had been wrapped in it. I seized it eagerly, and on the margin found, plainly written in his own handwriting, the name of George Miller—my friend George!

It must be so; if I were neither dreaming nor insane, my friend was a thief! Yes, and worse than a thief—a dissembling, ungrateful wretch, who had at the midnight hour invaded the premises and pilfered the property of one whose hand had fed him when his prodigal ways had reduced him to penury! And I asked myself: "Was there ever anything like it?"

Next morning I met George on the street. He was smiling and good-natured as ever, and not a shade of deceit or uneasiness crossed his countenance. Then I said to myself: "It is preposterous!" But I remembered the crushing evidence already in my possession, and resolved to keep the promise I had made Mr. Bartlett. I spoke pleasantly as usual to George, though with a painful effort, and asked him if he had any prospect yet. He little imagined that I had in my pocket then a bit of circumstantial evidence that would go a long way toward surrounding him with the dismal walls that sometimes do stand between evil-doers and society. I had to act a deceitful part, and it wrung my heart to do so; but I remembered that, if he indeed were guilty, he was, and had been for a long time, acting a far more deceitful part with me.

"George," said I, "if you have not struck a job yet, call and see me at the office at five o'clock this afternoon. I have a good deal to attend to-day, but shall be at leisure by five. I want to consult you about an important matter; but, remember, I can't promise that it will prove to be of any great advantage to you. Can you come?"

"Certainly! What time — five?"

"Yes — five, sharp."

"All right; I'll be on time."

I knew he would, for he ever evinced a marked fondness for my poor society. I next called at the police-office, saw my detective, and informed him of the astounding discoveries I had made, and of the engagement at five o'clock, and he promised to be punctually on hand.

The hours passed along, and as five o'clock approached, my detective and one of his sagacious colleagues came in. My partner and the business man were present, and Mr. Bartlett also came in, making a party of six. One more was required to make up the magic number. We were all seated; it wanted five minutes of five.

Footsteps were heard ascending the lower flight of stairs.

"How shall we know him? It might be some one else," suggested one of the detectives.

"If it is any one else, I will introduce him; if it is he, I will not. It may be that I have introduced him to too many already."

"If it should be a stranger?"

"You would know that by his actions."

"Yes, of course."

The footsteps were heard on the second flight of stairs; then in the corridor between our office and the vacant room. In another moment the door opened, and my friend George walked in.

He half-hesitated, and cast a curious glance at the strangers.

"Well, George," said I, "you 're in time."

"Yes."

"Take a seat."

I did not introduce him.

An awkward silence ensued — a painful silence, during which I could hear the beating of my own heart. Probably ten seconds had elapsed, when the silence was broken by one of the detectives, who coolly said:

"I believe you are the man we wanted to see. Come and go round to the office with us."

"What! the police-office?" quickly responded George,— no longer My Friend George,— whose guilty soul now looked forth from every feature of his face, as though a mask had suddenly dropped.

He comprehended in an instant that his guilt had been discovered, and without another word arose from his seat and meekly accompanied the detectives, who walked on either side of him. His whole bearing suddenly changed to that of a coward and sneak, and I fancied that I could see his very form and figure shrink materially in dimensions. It would have been an appropriate moment for a yawning chasm to open in the earth, swallow him up and hide him from the sight of men.

Yes, George was the thief, and fancy my pain and mortification as the dreadful truth became too apparent. He whom I had looked upon almost with affection; whom I had regarded as a man of honor and culture, with but barely one little failing; whom I had introduced to scores of my friends, recommending him as a sagacious business man, and a perfectly trustworthy gentleman — he, after all, a petty thief! It touches my sensibilities to this day to think of it.

George was taken to the chief's office, questioned and searched. He doggedly denied his guilt, but made enough conflicting and utterly irreconcilable statements to convict a regiment of thieves. In his pockets were found the key of Mr. Bartlett's desk — which happened to fit my drawer — and a number of other keys, which it was found on investigation would open all the doors and drawers in the building. He had still in his pocket some of Mr. Bartlett's "return" envelopes, and some other little articles stolen from his and our offices. He was also brought face to face with the proprietor of the book-stand, who clearly recognized him as the man who had sold him a number of Mr. Bartlett's law-books. In the face of all this, and other overpowering evidence, he persisted in denying his guilt, piling lie on top of lie, and stupidly contradicting himself, till it would have been a waste of time and an insult to common sense to pursue the investigation further. He was mercifully prosecuted — by Mr. Bartlett only — on a charge of petty larceny, and the judge of the police court, remarking that it was the clearest case in the world, sentenced him to three months' imprisonment.

I should not neglect to say that I visited him twice in the station-house before his trial in the police-court, when he sullenly denied his guilt, lying with a rapid tongue and a shockingly bad memory. I have never seen him since.

I subsequently learned that his invasion of our office was not his first crime. Parties who knew him told me of a score of his misdeeds, equally infamous. He had forged a check in New York before I ever saw him; he had stolen several watches, and borrowed others without returning them; he had obtained money by false pretenses; he had been guilty, time and again, of low tricks and petty subterfuges to cheat the confiding; he had rewarded numerous favors with the basest treachery; and he kindly remembered one man who had sheltered and fed him several weeks by decamping, between two days, from the hospitable roof, and carrying with him his benefactor's watch, money and clothing. To crown all, he had not journeyed to California so much to build up his fortunes as to escape the clutches of the law, which sorely threatened him in Philadelphia for a piece of rare rascality!

Thus abruptly terminated a "friendship" that I had fostered for three years; during which time, with all my fancied sagacity in the matter of peering down into the depths of a human heart, I had failed to discover, or even suspect, the true character of this brazen dissembler.

CHAPTER XXVI.

THE BORE.

IF there is one annoyance more than another to which editors of newspapers are subjected, it is the Bore; if the Bore afflicts one class more than another it is the Editor. Yet, of all men who ought not to be bothered when they are at their work, the Editor stands first. The Editor of a newspaper — particularly of a daily — has much peremptory work to do, and very often cannot afford to spare *one minute* of his time. His work is imperative, and if he neglects it for a period of anything like five minutes, he must work to the verge of intense straining for the next thirty or sixty minutes to make up for the lost time.

You may drop in and talk to a man engaged in manual labor, and not seriously interrupt him; you cannot do so with the Editor. He works with his mind; you take his attention, you occupy his mind, you irritate that mind, you "bore" it, and for the time he is powerless. Suppose you should go into a carriage-maker's shop, find him hurrying to have a certain wheel done by five o'clock, and suppose you should constantly pick up his tools, as he lays them down for a moment at a time, so that when he reaches for them he does not find them, but must drop his work and go to hunting for them —suppose all this: how would he get along? How would he like it? Well, you commit no less a breach of decorum when you go into a sanctum and "bore" the Editor when he is at his hard, hard work. His tools are his brain faculties, and when you occupy them you take his tools, and, as it were, scatter them around over the room. To do this wittingly, even for one minute, during an editor's working-hours, is little less than a crime.

I was once, with a couple of assistants, conducting a small daily, when time and again a really very good-hearted gentleman, little realizing the enormity of his conduct, came in during busy hours, sat down, and talked, and talked, and talked, almost by the hour, and even took up exchanges and read aloud therefrom multitudes of stale paragraphs, often when I was "hurried to death," and when I was "cudgeling" my dizzy brain over a piece of unusually cabalistic manifold copy, or straining my whole intellect in wild endeavors to penetrate the mazes of an "out." This I endured many and many a day because I could not find it in my heart (although many an editor could very soon have succeeded in finding it in his) to hurt the innocent man's feelings by putting a sacred truth in some such shape as this: "I 'd be very much obliged to you if you would n't interrupt me while I am at work." He did not understand the case; he meant well enough, and he would to-day be shocked if he knew how much he used to annoy me.

Bores do afflict every paper, more or less. The highest-toned New York daily is not free from them. Why, many a time the door of the editorial-room of such a paper as the New York *Herald*, *World*, *Tribune*, *Times*, or *Sun* has opened, and a country subscriber has stalked in and sat down to "have a chat" with the Editor. In such newspaper establishments as these, however, measures are generally taken to guard against promiscuous intrusion. But even the most stately newspaper has its Bores. If measures are taken to exclude "Tom, Dick and Harry," the Bore enters in the person of some loftier being—something that towers above "the masses." Influential men—Governors—Members of Congress—Mayors of Cities—"eminent divines"—all come in occasionally when they are not wanted, although it is generally because they don't understand the situation. I have more than once had a

United States Senator, Member of the House of Representatives, Governor of a State, or Mayor of a City "drop in" on me at a busy time, when I would much rather have seen the telegraph messenger, or the devil from the composing-room. To set aside all possibilities of doing any one an injustice, however, even by implication, I must say that I have never yet been "bored" by a President of the United States. I think, however, that every editor who has been on a large and influential daily paper will say that I have not exaggerated with regard to the Honorable Senators and Members of the House.

But it is in the Sanctum of the weekly paper that the Bore shines with his maximum brilliancy, assumes his grandest proportions. It is there that he is "at home;" there that, with a frightful atmosphere of leisure surrounding him like a halo, he leans back in a spare arm-chair, throws his feet up on the Editor's table, and thus sits, and bores, and bores, and bores! It is there he comes, and the Editor thinks he is "never going to leave." The great trouble is, he is often a well-meaning, good-hearted fellow, whom no gentleman would like to insult, if he could help it. I remember that once while publishing a San Francisco paper mentioned in the foregoing pages, a writer used to come in, sit down, and blow, and, incredible as it may appear, deliberately spit tobacco-juice into a disordered pile of exchanges lying upon the floor. I am probably a mild-tempered person, and I never said a word, nor even looked cross, to intimate that such a proceeding was other than highly satisfactory to me; but I do know editors who would have brained him.

Then there was another party, named Pickles, that inflicted himself upon me while I was conducting the same paper. He was a "writer," and once or twice brought in little articles that I deemed "worth publishing," after which there was no getting rid of him. Indeed, I used to miss him when he came in only once a day. There was a sort of delicious void in the atmosphere of that sanctum when Pickles stayed away, for example, a whole afternoon. In such cases my short moments of rest were usually occupied by such mental talk as this: "I do wonder where Pickles can be. Not dead, I — No. I never have been a lucky man." Pickles had not within him any elements of literary greatness, and I learned to dread, as I learned to recognize, the sound of his footsteps on the stairs. But then he was *so* good-natured. Why, he would have been a humorist if he had been "smart" enough.

One day Pickles came in when I was very busy — very busy, indeed. He carried under his arm a great mass of manuscript, and I shuddered as I contemplated what might be in store for me. He laid it down before me on a proof for which the foreman was impatiently waiting, and opened his discourse by paying me the following high compliment:

"Mr. ——, I have great confidence in your good taste and good judgment — more than I have in any other man's in California; and —"

"Yes? Thank you," I replied, almost as much flattered as the smooth-tongued Mr. Chester was flattered by the glaring compliments of Simon Tappertit; and I gently removed the manuscript from my proof.

"The fact is," Pickles proceeded, "the fact is, I've been writing a romance. I thought I'd keep it from you, and treat you to a little surprise."

"Ah — yes — exactly."

This demon imagined that his "literary" work was of such importance that had I known he was "writing a romance" my mind must have dwelt upon it day and night, to the exclusion of interests at the first view slightly nearer to me.

"I intend to publish it in book form."

"Do you?"

I now felt better.

"Yes, although" — I now felt worse — "I would not object to your publishing it first as a serial in your paper."

"No?"

My heart sank within me.

"No — But we 'll talk that over after you 've read it."

"Yes, after — exactly — after I've read it? Well, yes, I see."

"Yes, I'd like you to read it critically and tell me what you think of it."

"Very well. I'll just take charge of it, and — call in again, say, about Saturday."

"All right."

After a couple of hours he left, and strange to say, he did not return before Saturday, thereby missing two whole days, a circumstance entirely unparalleled by any preceding circumstance in the history of my acquaintance with him.

Well, I am impressed with the conviction that I knew enough of Pickles's literary powers to put it in the form of an axiom that he could n't write an acceptable romance; so, I merely glanced at the manuscript and laid it away in a drawer till he should come in again. He "looked in" with a beaming face and a cheerful "Hello," on the ensuing Saturday.

"Well," he said, "did you — did you —"

He hesitated. Perhaps he felt that my decision in reference to his "romance" was too important a matter to be communicated very abruptly; like the old darkey who said: "Massa, one ob your oxes is dead. Todder, too. 'Fraid to tell you ob bofe togedder, fear you could n't bore it."

"Mr. Pickles," I said, calmly, "I have looked over your

manuscript,"—so I had,—"and—of course you want me to be perfectly frank with you?"

"Ye—yes; O, yes," he replied; but his countenance fell. The man evidently had a presentiment of evil.

"Well, then, Mr. Pickles, I must say, in all candor, that I did not find the story to be what I might have wished. To tell the truth about it, which I know you wish me to do—"

"Certainly"—pale, and with dry lips.

"To tell the truth about it, in writing this story you have not done yourself justice—," nor had he; for he ought to have been at work with a hatchet and saw,—"and I advise you not to attempt to get it published. At least, keep it six months or so, like Virgil used to do, and then you can look over it again and view it more calmly than now, when it is so fresh from your mind. I trust you will not blame me for thus being entirely frank with you?"

"O, no; not at all," he said; but I could see that he commended me in the same degree that the bishop commended Gil Blas for kindly notifying him (in accordance with the good man's own instructions) that his powers were beginning to fail.

It is useless to try to conceal the fact that, as "society" is at present "organized," your dearest friend will hate you for pointing out his defects,—such as he cannot himself see,—no matter how pure and unselfish your motives in so doing may be. Shall we get over that some day?

Pickles took his manuscript, took his departure, and—O, joy!—never more came into my sanctum. After all, there are some things that work together for our good, if I may be pardoned for paraphrasing Scripture.

While conducting the *Enunciator* in San Francisco, which paper I think I have alluded to once or twice before, I probably had as fine an opportunity as is afforded anywhere to learn what a newspaper Bore is; and I once published in that paper — files of which I have preserved — a humorous article on the subject, by "O. Job Jones," a writer alluded to in another chapter, and although it may read like hyperbole, it is nearer to the truth than it is to caricature, and I here reproduce it:

THE BORE AND THE SANCTUM.

"Ours" is such a genial nature that we often go mad with pride and joy at the thought of the wide circle of friends who, in their leisure moments, drop in upon us during our business hours, to bore our lives pleasantly away. As they rarely stay longer than three or four hours at a time, we enjoy their visits very much. These visits are certain to occur at times when our duties are most pressing, and hence we are very much stimulated and encouraged by their lively and agreeable conversation — to proceed with our work with great deliberation.

Here is a fair average diary of one of our busiest days:

We arrive at our office feeling that there is a day's work before us, and we go at it with a will. We take off our hat and coat, push back our hair, assume our chair, take up our pen and proceed to put into the shape of an editorial our deep cogitations on a subject in metaphysics that agitates the public mind. We write:

"In the interminable intricacies between subject and object, we cannot help leaning to the opinion that in a concentration of individual identity the empiric theory, derived as it is from ethnologic rather than from psychologic de —"

"Hell-lo!" exclaims a very musical voice at this moment, as the door bursts open and displays the face, all covered with sunshine, of our "friend" Smith.

It is a holiday of his, but in the warmth of his genial nature he never stops to reflect that it is not one of ours.

We cannot help saying, "Good-morning," and trying to appear friendly, as he is n't a bad-hearted fellow. Besides, he may not intend to spend more than half the day with us.

"How are you to-day?" he asks, as he walks forward, leaving the door open, and throws himself into an arm-chair within twelve inches of us, with a perfectly at-home air that makes us feel very happy.

Our ruddy complexion and generally-robust appearance compel us to admit that we are — "O, pretty well."

"At the theater last night?" he asks, in a tone loud enough to go clear across the street and come back fresh as ever.

"Ye — no — yes," we reply, abstractedly, scarcely knowing whether we want to say, "yes," or "no," or whether we really were at the theater or not.

"Which one?"

Beginning to regain our composure, we tell him.

"So was I!" he says. "Was n't that one of the —" and he proceeds to edify us with exhaustive criticisms on the play, we having already "written it up."

"Have you the morning papers?" he asks, at the conclusion of his remarks.

"Yes, there they are," we reply, joyfully.

Now, he will read awhile, and we shall finish our editorial. We once more dip our pen into the ink, and are just contracting our brows preparatory to the elimination of a great idea, and it has barely made a dot on the paper when Smith blurts out:

"O, by thunder! A fellow stabbed last night 'at I knew in St. Louis! Well, I declare! Always thought him a peaceable man. His father —" And he goes on to give us a history of the stabbed man, and the stabbed man's father, and the stabbed man's father's business, and everything pertaining to the stabbed man — in whom and which we feel perhaps as much interest as we feel in the person and affairs of that yellow Chinaman passing along on the opposite side of the street.

There is a pause. We are a little disturbed, but begin to collect ourselves and square around to our work again. That "idea," recently dispersed like the morning dew before the summer sun, is beginning to come back and to concentrate itself again at our earnest bidding. We catch a glimmer of its returning outline. There, we have it. Now, pen, to thy —

Bang! Bump! Thump! It's only Smith's number 13, heavy-soled boots, thrown up on one end of our table, in a free-and-easy way, as he leans back in his chair and places himself in an attitude to squint more complacently upon the morning paper that screens his hideous countenance. The idea vanishes; but the cold perspiration on our brow does not.

We glance boldly at those feet, as if plainly to say that we should feel indebted to their owner if he would kindly remove them; but Smith is intently regarding a paragraph in the newspaper, and sees not our vexation. All is quiet for a minute or two; then, somewhat reconciled to the disagreeable state of things in our sanctum, we begin very slowly to collect our scattered thoughts, and once more to concentrate our great mind upon our subject.

"Oh — ah — say!" Smith exclaims; "did you hear about Wilkins?"

"Who's Wilkins?" we ask, grinding our teeth.

"Oh, I thought you knew him; but — let me see — Oh, no; it was n't you that was with him and me at the Cliff House last summer? No, no — now that I come to think, it was Charlie Brown, of Philadelphia. Well, this Wilkins, he —" And for just twenty-five minutes Smith discourses on Wilkins; but our reeling brain takes no note of the recital, and at the end we cannot record half a dozen words of it.

He reads again; we silently brood over our miseries. We do, at last, manage to add a line to our dissertation. We are beginning to think we shall be able to write two or three stickfuls without interruption, when Smith suddenly draws his tremendous feet from the table and lets them fall upon the floor with a loud crash, flings the morning paper carelessly upon our table, not caring whether it falls upon the manuscript under our nose or not, — and it does, — and says he guesses he'll go, to which we have not the strength to reply.

But he does n't go just yet. He sits uneasily a moment, yawns, drawls out languidly, "O, Lord!" twists himself around in his chair, as though to crush and grind certain fleas that may be biting him, and finally — heavens, what a relief! — gets up and moves toward the door. We are just preparing to say, "Good-morning," as pleasantly as possible, regretting that it might not be "Farewell, eternally," instead, when he stops and stands near the door.

"Why don't you drop round and see a feller?" he asks, with an air of perfect leisure.

"Have n't time," we reply. "We are pressed to death here for time, and cannot get out even to our meals. We are fearfully behind time now." And we dip our pen into the ink with energy and determination.

"Well," he moralizes, "you editors do have a great time of it, I reckon. Worked to death. Well — so long."

We barely answer him, and he passes out, very deliberately closing the door after him, which creaks in a thrilling manner, although it never did so before. We really believe that man Smith carries an evil influence about him. We trust, in all benevolence of spirit, that he may fall down the stairs and break his neck! No such good luck. We hear the clatter of his hoofs on the stairs, slowly — ah, too carefully! — descending to the bottom, and he is safe; safe to come and torment us again, whenever the Evil One puts it into his head.

Now to our work.

"—dition of self-consciousness, as is demonstrated by a re-active principle of —"

"Here we are!" And the door is flung open, to reveal the hateful form of our "friend" Watkins, whose beaming face looks like the Fourth of July.

We make a powerful effort to be civil — barely succeeding.

"Always at work," he sagely remarks, as he takes a seat on one corner of our sacred writing-table, with his feet dangling down, and begins drumming with his fingers. "No rest for the wicked." This he considers wit, and smiles good-naturedly. "Well, what a time of it you Bohemians have!"

Bohemians!

We are silent. We try to speak, but could not utter a sentence for a million dollars a word.

"What's new?" he asks, in a vigorous voice, that sounds as softly musical as the combined manufacture of boilers and the filing of many saws.

"Nothing — nothing," we reply, absently, while our mind dwells in no complimentary terms on "the day he was born."

He thrusts his hands in his trousers-pockets, and changes the position of his body, thus swinging our light table to and fro and threatening to crush it; while we sit champing the end of our pen-holder like an untamed steed chewing a bridle-bit.

Presently Watkins abandons his seat and walks around for awhile, upsetting a chair in his perambulations and making untold racket. Several pictures, hanging upon the walls, bear witness to our refined taste. These become a subject of Mr. Watkins's unasked-for criticism. Then he questions us. Where did we get this one? What is the meaning of that one? Who "did" that other one? When? Where? How long? How much? Which? Who? Color? Shade? Age? Name? These are his queries, boiled down. We convey all the information we can, in the fewest possible words; while Watkins fills up every interstice with voluble criticisms — both of the pictures and our taste.

At last he sits down in an arm-chair and begins a real chat.

Our editorial is gone to the dogs for this time, and we calmly lay down our pen and meditate revenge. We glare upon Watkins, when he is n't looking, with fiendish hate. We could kill him. We could stab, shoot, hang, drown, or brain him. We could! But at last we think of a nobler, purer, sweeter, holier revenge. Watkins has a wife who is a shrew, and who hates one drop of liquor worse than a thousand bushels of rattlesnakes. Watkins dare not drink — unless very much tempted; then when he does, he is certain to go the whole length and as certain of the dreadful consequences. With an outward smile, to conceal our inward malignity, we say:

"Watkins — been hard at work — feel rather dry: let 's go out around the corner and take something."

"Why, I — the fact is —"

"O, nonsense. Come along. Just one won't hurt anybody. You'll wrong me if you refuse to go and take one with me when I so much need it. I *will not* drink alone."

Without another word he allows himself to be led away like a lamb to the sacrifice. We conduct him to a "place" where we know he is certain to meet some old acquaintances.

"Well, what are you going to take?"

He calls for whisky, and we silently hiss between our clenched teeth:

"Now, venom, to thy work!"

We have just drank when several old chums come in, and they sing out:

"Hello, Watkins, old fellow!"

Watkins sees us turning as if to go, and says:

"Hold on. Let 's have another. Here, set 'em up. What are you all going to have, boys?"

"Will be back in one minute, Watkins," we say; "merely want to hail a friend who just passed. Take your drink and wait here."

"All right."

Glasses are set up with joyful clinks, we see the revel begin, and we rejoice as we ponder on what Watkins will catch when he goes home in five or six hours from now; and in a pleasant frame of mind we return to our sanctum, lock our door and complete our editorial.

CHAPTER XXVII.

A NOTED LIBEL SUIT.

IN the year 18— I was connected with a Philadelphia paper pretty well known as the *Sunday Mercury*. Its proprietors were Wm. Meeser and Fred Grayson,—both pretty good fellows,—the former a printer and journalist, the latter a lawyer and journalist. Most of my transactions with the firm were concluded between Mr. Meeser and myself, and it was he who one Monday morning, in autumn, said to me:

"I wish you would write us a good spicy story, like some you have already written,"—for I had contributed four or five serials to the *Mercury*,—"and make it entirely local."

"Very well," I replied, having no engagements that would be likely to prevent me. "Any special features?"

"Yes. Give it strong political bearings. Illustrate in it how Rings are managed; how the public is defrauded by corrupt office-holders; how the people are cajoled and ruled by the manipulators of party organizations; how the masses are led blindly to vote for bad men without knowing it, and often without the moral courage to help it. You see the idea. Of course, picture these things in a romance, in a general way, merely as an illustration. Make no allusion to any distinctive office, or office-holder, and be careful to embody nothing that approaches either a libel or an injustice to any one or any party."

"To be sure. How long a story would you like this time?"

"I don't care. It might run six months if your chain of characters and incidents will hold out that long. As to remuneration, fix your price, and we 'll pay it."

"All right."

This was all — the whole sum and substance of what was said or understood between Mr. Meeser and myself concerning the writing of a fictitious story, the first two chapters of which proved to be the *corpus delicti* on which was based one of the most extraordinary "criminal" prosecutions ever conducted in the city of Philadelphia. I did not again see Mr. Meeser until I had written three hundred manuscript pages of the story, for the reason that I was suddenly called to the country, over four hundred miles from Philadelphia, and it was in the rural region that I did the work. I named my story, "Philadelphia, By Day and By Night," with a sub-title, and sent the first two or three hundred pages by mail to the *Mercury*, and its publication began at once. The first chapter opened with the following picture of a leading "character," true to the life in the abstract, specifically imaginary and fictitious:

The Honorable William Bilman, who held the high position of Tribune of Philadelphia, sat alone in his own office, one summer day, wrapped in a moody reverie, such as he sometimes, in his idle moments, indulged. He was pondering over the many, and curious, and various deeds — none of them good — which he had done from time to time in the course of his political career. Naturally he may not have been a very bad man, but years of planning, and scheming, and contending, and cheating, and defrauding, such as are incident to the career of an unscrupulous politician, had stamped upon his face a look of malignity and cunning. His very eyes indicated that he was used to suspicion and deception, for he never looked squarely at anything or anybody. If he looked at the clock to see what time it was, he, from mere force of habit, first glanced at it out of the corner of his eye, to see if it was looking at him.

As he sat there, with his left hand resting on his writing-table, an annoying fly crawled over the back of it; and he first half-closed his eyes, as if to make it think he was not observing it, and thus render it unwary, that he might take it by surprise; then smack! came the palm of his right hand on the back of his left. But the provoking insect escaped unhurt, for a finger, located between the forefinger and the little finger of Tribune Bilman's right hand, was wanting, and the fly — which otherwise would have been crushed — buzzed off and away through the unoccupied space.

"Curses! Curses! Curses!" pondered William Bilman, glancing furtively, as usual, at the vacant place his lost finger had occupied — it was a finger he had had chewed off in a quiet bar-room fight before he had become so great a man. "Curses on that hound that crippled my hand! I hate him more and more every day! Well, that's foolish, too. Haven't I long since repaid him? He little thought then that I should ever become Tribune of Philadelphia, with power to hunt him down and thrust him into a prison-cell for twenty years! Neither did I nor any one else at that time. Well, he's safe. Twenty years! O, that's a mere trifle. Ha! ha! ha! Where is he now? Working away in his cheerless prison — at this very moment, I'll venture to say — making boots and shoes for his bread and water, with prospects of liberty in about twelve years from now. Ha! ha! ha! Will he live so long? Rather doubtful. Let him ever come out, however, and I'll send him back for forty years! O, *I* can do it! I have the power! I can make out a case of burglary, or larceny, or murder, against him or any man I hate! O, *I* am in a position to glut my vengeance, and put my foot on the necks of my enemies! They called me a *rough* fifteen years ago. Well, suppose I was! I'm not a rough now. No; I'm a great lawyer, and the Tribune of Philadelphia. Suppose I was once concerned in a larceny case; and suppose, even, that was the cause of my first taking a fancy to the law — to learn it, that I might evade it; suppose all this. I've studied the law, learned it, and become a lawyer and Tribune. Haven't I risen, though? Once a *rough*, indulging in bar-room fights, charged with crime, but proved (?) innocent — and now a man of authority, learned in the law, and occupying the proud and potent position of Tribune! Ha, ha, ha!"

Mr. Bilman lay back in his arm-chair, hoisted his feet up on the table, extended his arms and his whole burly form, and took a good laugh. Not a loud, free laugh, such as honest men indulge in when they are amused, but a low, chuckling, strangling, quivering laugh, that was peculiar to the potent Tribune. Then he got up, paced the floor, kicking a chair out of his way, and knocking it over; and presently began talking to himself again.

Now, the gentleman who was at that time the District-Attorney of the county (and city) of Philadelphia seems to have thought, when he read this description of a "character," that it referred to him — not, be it remembered, because he was any such a wretch, or any such a fiendish-looking man as "Mr. Bilman" was represented to be, but because the name sounded so much like his own. This gentleman was Mr. William B. Mann, and his name having been familiar in political circles of Philadelphia for years, he was often styled "Bill Mann," for short. The name "Bilman" — a name I have found in more than one city directory, by the way — sounded so much like the familiar title of "Bill Mann" that he concluded he would be justifiable in instituting proceedings for libel against — not the writer of the story, but one of the owners of the paper in which it was published. This unfortunate gentleman was Mr. Wm. Meeser, who happened to be politically opposed to Mr. Mann, and who had more than once severely criticised his official conduct.

The first installment of the story, embracing the extract already given, and a scene or two in which "William Bilman" figured as a very bad man, was published in the *Mercury* one Sunday morning, and early on Monday morning Mr. Meeser was waited upon by a dreadful constable with a warrant authorizing the latter to take the former's "body." Although appalled at the thought of assuming the attitude of a mere "body," as considered outside of the principles of life and individuality, Mr. Meeser readily accompanied the official, (who informed him that he might as well "go quietly, you know,") and was ushered into the awful presence of an alderman. The District-Attorney was present, and having been duly sworn, he deposed substantially (I write only from memory) that his name was William B. Mann; that he believed himself to have been libeled by Wm. Meeser; that he fully believed that the character of "Bilman" was "meant for him;" that it held him up to ridicule and contempt; that he was not aware of being so bad a man as painted in the "libelous" article; that he had not "studied law to learn how to evade it," but had done so "at the instance of a dear father;" and he prayed that the law might "take its course."

I was not present, nor in the city, at the time, but I think Mr. Meeser waived a hearing, and entered bail; and so the case was brought before the Court of Quarter Sessions with a promptness that did great credit to those whose duty it was to prosecute offenders against the laws of the Commonwealth. The publisher of the "libel" was arraigned as a "criminal," while the writer, enjoying delicious immunity from the law's "meshes," figured only as a witness; which, allowing the story to have been libelous, wears about the same aspect of a fitness of things as would appear in a case where a man is prosecuted for having the misfortune to get robbed and the thief, unmolested, is the principal witness in the case.

With commendable delicacy, Mr. Mann refrained from personally conducting the case for the Commonwealth, as he might have done in his official capacity, and the prosecution was placed in the hands of Hon. Benjamin H. Brewster, at that time Attorney-General of Pennsylvania, and one of the ablest of Philadelphia lawyers, and Hon. Thomas Bradford Dwight, then Assistant District-Attorney. The defense was intrusted by Mr. Meeser to Messrs. I. Newton Brown and John A. Clark, both able lawyers. The judge, who presided over the case with equitable discrimination, was Hon. F. Carroll Brewster.

Poor Bill Meeser! He was brought into the crowded courtroom like a criminal, although graciously allowed the privilege of sitting at a table by the side of his counsel, instead of being placed in the iron-barred dock,—for even the counsel for the prosecution did not deem him so desperate a character as to be likely to attempt to escape, by bounding away over the heads of the dense masses of spectators and jumping out the window,—yes, brought in to be "tried" for a "crime," which, if committed at all, was committed by me!

The trial lasted three or four days, and attracted as much attention as a first-class murder case. The great interest taken in the case by the public was due partly to the prominence of the principal parties, and partly to the fact that it was understood to be largely permeated by the political element; so, the courtroom was daily little less than packed.

After the usual difficulties in securing an impartial jury, success finally attending the efforts to do so, and after the customary presentations of the case, various witnesses were examined, including some "big guns," such as ex-Governor Curtin, who was called to testify with reference to Mr. Mann's commission as colonel of a Pennsylvania regiment which he had led to the field early in the war. Among the witnesses for the prosecution there were probably thirty or forty persons,—some of them well-known lawyers, who swore that they had read the opening chapters of the story in the *Mercury*, and "thought," or "believed," that the character of "Hon. William Bilman" was intended for Mr. Mann. One gentleman of the legal profession went so far as to say, *on oath*, that he was "*certain* of it!" It seemed to me that he was the only person in the court-room besides the writer of the story who was "certain" as to what was in that writer's thoughts when he conceived and portrayed the character of "Hon. William Bilman."

The defense had but few witnesses, as Mr. Meeser and his counsel had from the beginning disclaimed any allusion, in my fictitious story, to Mr. William B. Mann. The principal witness for the defense was the writer of the story (and of this volume). There was some bickering as to how he should be qualified as a witness, the counsel for the prosecution at first insisting on his "taking the book," and he declining to do so, for reasons that I think will be guessed by any intelligent person who has read the chapter of this work entitled "The Religion of Editors." This important witness, having finally qualified by affirmation, stated, with a frankness and candor that ought to have moved even the counsel for the prosecution to tears, that the character of "Hon. William Bilman" was purely fictitious; that it certainly was *not* "meant for Mr. Mann;" that Mr. Meeser had *not* instructed him to libel Mr.

Mann; that there was no collusion between the witness and Mr. Meeser to libel Mr. Mann, or any other man; no hint from Mr. Meeser to the witness, "no ambiguous giving out of note," by which the witness might have understood or suspected that Mr. Meeser desired him to libel Mr. Mann; that at the time of the writing the witness had never even *seen* Mr. Mann, that he was aware of; that the story was written over four hundred miles from Philadelphia, and sent by mail to the *Mercury;* that Mr. Meeser was in the habit of reposing great confidence in the writer, and of publishing his stories without even reading them (so far as the writer knew), or knowing what imaginary characters or scenes were described in them.

The witness was then cross-examined two hours by the Attorney-General, who probably knew how to cross-examine a witness, if any one ever did; but this deep and searching cross-examination, while it developed the fact that several eminent (?) lawyers present did not know the meaning in Roman history, or even the proper pronunciation, of the word "Tribune," left his testimony standing like a rock!

Nevertheless, Attorney-General Brewster, in his summing up, delicately hinted that the writer (I!) might have committed *perjury;* and even the judge himself, in his charge to the jury, alluded very tenderly to the extraordinary testimony of the writer. Worse still, one of the daily papers afterward (unkindly, I think) spoke of the "remarkable statements" of the writer of the story in the *Mercury,* adding: "This gentleman, we believe, belongs in Fayette County, and we advise him to return thither as soon as possible, unless he has the cuticle of a rhinoceros." This merely meant that it looked very much as though the said writer (I!) had sworn to a few lies.

I must confess that I was not blessed with the "cuticle of a rhinoceros," but, nevertheless, my departure from Philadelphia became no early event. I have spent most of my time there since, except when traveling, and expect to remain there most of my time until unavoidable circumstances render it advisable to go and get buried.

I cannot ignore the fact that there were some coincident features of this matter that might well engender a suspicion that the character of "Hon. William Bilman" was at least "drawn from" the then District-Attorney. When I came to see him in the court-room, where I saw his face for the first time in my life, I did think there was a peculiar expression about the eye-brows,—induced, no doubt, by excessive mental application, as in the case of Blackstone,—a sort of perpetual frown, that might reasonably have been compared with the scowl on the face of the mythical "Bilman." But how many people have this same contraction of the brows!

Regarding the name, "Bilman," which many thoughtless people looked upon as *prima facie* evidence that the character was meant for William B. Mann, I have to say that one moment's intelligent consideration ought to show it to be evidence *against* such a theory, rather than in favor of it. Why? There *is* a similarity of sound and of orthography; but scrutinize it more closely. Here we have in the name of the character, first the whole Christian name of "William;" then in the first syllable of the surname we have that name repeated in the familiar abbreviation of "Bil"—with but one "l," mark you; and thus, if meant for Mr. Mann, the tautology would have been as stupid as that in "Peter Pete Smith" or "James Jim Jones," the real names being Peter Smith and James Jones, and would have done little credit to the ingenuity of the writer.

There was another coincidence, striking at first view, but utterly set aside, as evidence, by a careful analysis. "The Hon. William Bilman" was represented as having lost a finger of the right hand, it having been "chewed off in a quiet bar-room fight"—a finger "between the index and little fingers." This was merely a device of the fiction-writer to allow the "annoying fly" to escape, and so to present an example of the petty malevolence of the imaginary character, "Bilman," and at the same time to give him an opportunity to begin his soliloquy. Well, District-Attorney Mann *had* lost a finger of the right hand, by a gunning accident, I think, but it was the index finger itself, and *not* "a finger between the index and little fingers." This fact, it seems to me, while at first suggestive of a mental association, ought to lead any sensible person, after a deliberate analysis, to the conclusion that, of all men living, Mr. Mann was the least likely to have been referred to in the portrayal of the character of "Hon. William Bilman."

I know a gentleman who lost an arm in the recent civil war. There was a time when I did not know him—had never seen him—had never heard of him—when I wrote a novel in which was a character described as having lost an arm in the war. The gentleman having read it years afterward, one day said to me: "If you had known me when you wrote that story, I could have *sworn* that you intended that character for me."

It *was* like him; it described his complexion; the color of his eyes; the color of his hair; the shape of his nose; his size; his gait, which was peculiar; mentioned which arm he lost (the left); and even mentioned a scar over the right eye, exactly such a scar as this real, living one-armed gentleman had over his right eye—the result of an accident in youth; yet he knows, and I know, that I had never seen him or heard of him when I wrote the story. When he made the remark to me, I pondered thus: "How many one-armed men, with just such complexion, just such eyes, just such hair, there may be in the world; and if I had made the character a bad one, how many libel suits I and my publishers might have had on our hands!"

To return to the "Bilman" libel suit: The jury—an unusually "intelligent" one—did not take the same view of the case which I have presented here, and after half-an-hour's deliberation, notwithstanding the very direct and emphatic testimony of the writer (me!) came in with a verdict of—"guilty." A motion for a new trial was made, but, after "due consideration," refused, and the Honorable Court "sentenced" Wm. Meeser,—the penalty fixed upon being a fine of five hundred dollars and nine months' imprisonment in the county prison. In accordance with this sentence, he was "incarcerated" in Moyamensing prison, and remained there for a period of six weeks, when Governor Geary exercised the "executive clemency," to the extent of releasing him and remitting the fine. The affair was not without important results, whether for the public good or not it is not my province here to say. Speedily following it, there arose some feeling against Mr. Mann in his own party, and he failed, at the next county convention, to receive a renomination for the office he had held many years, and at the ensuing general election a talented legal gentleman of the opposite party, Mr. Furman Sheppard, was chosen to succeed him as District-Attorney.

Now, by the conviction of Mr. Meeser, two excellent persons were placed in an unpleasant position; namely, Mr. Meeser himself and the writer of that "libel,"—the latter of whom, unfortunately, had neglected to provide himself with the "cuticle of a rhinoceros." Indeed, I felt it keenly when I found that my testimony was utterly ignored, and when some of my best friends—friends who had reason to know that my testimony was true—rallied me in a good-humored way with such remarks as, "They say you 're a pretty hard swearer." I treated the matter lightly, but I was keenly sensible of the false position in which I had been placed, through no fault of mine;

certainly not through the shadow of a deviation from "the truth, the whole truth, and nothing but the truth."

I had testified that I did not know the District-Attorney. But people would say: "Incredible. Everybody knows Bill Mann." That is, people who did not know *me*. Those who did, knew that at that time I had not lived long in Philadelphia, and that my knowledge of local politics and local politicians was very circumscribed. Why, it transpired in the course of Mr. Mann's own testimony that he and Mr. Meeser were personally unknown to each other, and that he "would not have known him if he had met him in the street!" Yet both had lived many years in Philadelphia.

The finger business I have already disposed of in a way that must be very clear to any intellectual mind; and now let me say, with all the sincerity that is in my nature, that the proposition that the fictitious character of "Hon. William Bilman" could have been intended to "mean William B. Mann," or any other particular person, living or dead, appears to me silly and ridiculous! If the "character" had been like him; if the writer had known him well, and had actually drawn the character with William B. Mann in his mind's eye; if he had described him accurately, I am impressed with the belief that it still would not have been a libel, provided that the writer did not mention the name or position of the then District-Attorney, and did not mean to be understood as intending the "character" for Mr. Mann, or implying that he actually did the disreputable acts which the "character" was represented as doing. I believe that all writers of fiction will see this so clearly at the first glance as to pronounce an opposite theory worthy of being sincerely entertained by no one of keen perceptions.

One of Dickens's most famous characters is "Micawber,"

the man who "waited for something to turn up." It is said that the great novelist "drew the character from his own father," who was precisely such a character, who was just such an improvident man as the shrimp-eating "Micawber." The very name would favor this theory, because "Micawber," unless very distinctly spoken, sounds much like "my father;" yet imagine Mr. John Dickens preferring a charge of libel against his distinguished son Charles, or against the publishers of "David Copperfield!" Imagine any one with an intellect so infinitesimally little above that of the African gorilla that he could believe that, in describing the eccentric feats of "Micawber," Dickens meant, or ever dreamed of being understood as meaning, that his father, the improvident John, did just those things!

One more important point in this case should not be overlooked. It is said that "everything is fair in war," and looking upon a suit in court as a species of war, the conduct of the Assistant District-Attorney was undoubtedly fair in this case, as viewed in the light of that adage. In libel suits the alleged libelous article is read in open court, and it therefore became the province of Mr. Dwight to stand up with a copy of the *Mercury* in his hand and read aloud the two opening chapters of my story — much, I trust, to the edification of the judge and jury. The name of this fictitious character, "Mr. Bilman," frequently occurred in these chapters, and Mr. Dwight, instead of pronouncing the name as it was written and printed, pronounced it in every case, very distinctly, "Mr. Bill Mann." Is it to be wondered at that a powerful impression was thus made on the minds of the "intelligent" jury, who only heard the "libelous" article read, and did not see it "in print"? Witnesses were then introduced who swore, and very truthfully, that Mr. Mann was generally known as "Bill

Mann;" and here to the jury seemed to be a "plain case," in which the complainant's name was undisguisedly mentioned. If the counsel for the prosecution believed they had a clear and just case against Mr. Meeser, does it seem probable that they would have thought it necessary to resort to such an artifice for making an impression on the minds of the jury? This is one of those questions sometimes asked never to be satisfactorily answered.

No one knows better than I do that William Meeser was not guilty of a crime. If any one was, it was myself. His conviction, which I regard as an unfortunate mistake, was due partly to the fact that fiction-writing (I trust this will not be regarded as such) was imperfectly understood by the jury, which caused them to look upon the writer's testimony as "extraordinary statements," partly to the unjust laws relating to libels. In another chapter, I have shown how a journalist may be annoyed and even blackmailed by unprincipled adventurers, who may at any time take advantage of too-rigorous libel laws to rob an editor; but it does seem to me a great wrong that the act of libel should be legally rated as a crime,—that the owner of a newspaper may be arrested, tried in the criminal courts and sent to prison along with thieves, and forgers, and murderers, because an employé, however inadvertently, has written and published in his paper an incorrect statement affecting the reputation of some obscure individual.

I would not be understood as saying that journalists ought to be allowed to say what they please about any and every body, whether true or false. A wholesome check is necessary; but it ought not to extend beyond pecuniary responsibility. The publisher of a paper should be liable to damages, if he should allow his paper to injure any one; and any editor or publisher who owns a paper of sufficient circulation and influence to be able seriously to damage any one's reputation will always be found possessing the means necessary for indemnity. It is no more right to imprison the owner of a paper because one of his employed editors writes and publishes an untruth about somebody than it would be right to imprison the proprietor of a grocery-store because the man he employs to drive his wagon runs over and injures some one in the street. He might properly be called upon to pay damages because of the carelessness of his employé, but certainly he would be no criminal. So, while I repeat that the libel laws were too rigorous, and that the jury probably had not so clear a conception of the case against Mr. Meeser as almost any person will have after having perused this chapter, I must say that it is not for me, nor has it been my purpose, to question the sincerity and fairness of the judge or jury, or even the purity of the motives of the able legal gentleman who saw fit to make the complaint leading to the prosecution of Mr. Meeser.

CHAPTER XXVIII.

THE GALLOWS.

IT is a prerogative of the journalist to see almost every phase of human life, and to witness many strange things from which the general public is shut out. Among these things are executions on the gallows. It has happened in the course of my own experience that I have seen but one man hanged, and on that occasion I did so as a duty, and not through "morbid curiosity." The hanging of a murderer is no very pleasing sight, nor is it a sight for the reporter to shrink from. Indeed, I look upon it with the same indifference I should feel if my duties took me to a slaughter-house, and I should have to observe and write up the manner of killing a bullock or hog.

There are well-meaning philanthropists who believe in the abolishment of capital punishment, and I agree with them that it ought to be abolished — provided capital crime is abolished first. I think that just as soon as the crime of murder becomes obsolete we ought to — and will — stop hanging murderers. The well-meaning philanthropists alluded to seem to expend all their sympathy on the poor unfortunate murderer, seldom wasting a thought on the victim who is struck down in the street, or butchered in his bed, or on the widow and orphans upon whom the assassin has heaped at once an oppressing weight of grief and destitution. But notwithstanding all that good men have said against capital punishment, and after giving the matter careful thought, I have been forced to the conclusion that we ought to continue killing murderers as long as they continue to kill innocent people. I don't care how — whether by hanging, decapitating or shooting; but let us kill them, and kill them as soon as possible, after they have been proved, beyond all doubt, guilty. This, not in any spirit of vengeance ("vengeance is mine; I will repay," saith the Lord), but simply as a measure of self-protection — just as we kill the rattlesnake. We do not kill that reptile in any spirit of vindictiveness; we do not "hate" it, as we have no reason to do so; but we know that it has been "created" with poisonous fangs, and with a disposition to use them, and (grant that it cannot resist the temptation to bite) considerations of the safety of the communities in which the venomous creature is found demand its destruction whenever possible. The object is, not to torture even the rattlesnake, but to kill it as quickly and painlessly as possible — to take the most direct measures of effectually destroying its power to do harm.

The person whom I, in the capacity of a reporter, saw hanged, was "a man in years." He had reached the age of sixty, and the peculiar atrocity of the crime of which he paid the penalty — his victim being a girl of thirteen — showed him to be a man of almost incredible depravity. He had steadfastly persisted that he was innocent until within a short time of the day fixed for the execution of his sentence; then, having abandoned all hope of the "executive clemency," he "made his peace with God," although he had prayed continually ever since his conviction, and at the same time made a confession of the crime of which he stood convicted, and a long list of other crimes — including a murder of which he had never been charged — extending over a series of years; crimes he had committed while daily putting on a show of piety, and crimes of which he had never been even suspected. This confession, if there had been any doubt of his guilt in the case of the murder of which he was convicted — but there was not — would have entirely removed such doubt. [In this connection I am reminded that a murderer was hanged in New York not many years ago, after a powerful pressure of money and influence had been brought to bear to save him; and after the execution it transpired that the same person had once before committed a wanton murder and been saved from the just penalty by a near relative, who possessed great wealth and some political influence.]

At the entrance of the State Prison, within whose walls the legal tragedy was to be enacted, I found the Deputy-Warden, whom I knew, and I handed him the pass I had received from the High Sheriff, saying:

"I suppose that is to be given up here?"

"Yes," he replied, "and it would be hard for a stranger to get in without one."

"Have there been many applications for admission?"

"Over two thousand."

"How many will there be admitted?"

"Only about thirty-five, including the Sheriff's jury, regular officials and members of the press."

"How is the old man this morning?"

"Pretty nervous."

"Did he eat any breakfast?"

"Yes, a couple of boiled eggs, a baked potato or two, and some bread and butter, with a cup of coffee. He really eat with some appetite."

"He'll be hanged at the time you mentioned yesterday?"

"Yes; eleven o'clock, or very soon after."

It was now half-past ten. I entered the door, which was closed and secured behind me, and being familiar with the interior of the prison, where my duties had called me more than once before, I ascended a flight of steps, turned to the right and entered a small room in which visitors were received. When I stood in this room the Warden's office was on my right; on my left a door led into the guard-room, a spacious and well-lighted apartment from whose iron-barred windows surveillance could be kept over the prison-yard, and from which every door and window in the workshops could be seen. Several stout attendants were in this room, and a dozen loaded muskets standing in a rack near them, suggested that they were prepared to quell a possible insurrection by rigorous measures.

After merely glancing into the guard-room, I opened the door of the Warden's office, and went in. He was a gray-haired little man, with as kind a heart as ever beat anywhere in the State, and through a period of many years he had managed hundreds of the worst of men, without once finding it necessary to resort to the use of those frowning muskets, or to any other very harsh measure. Firm as he was kind of heart, he "went the right way about it," and every convict under his charge learned to like him simultaneously with learning that he must obey him, do his duty and submit to the rules.

The old Warden was clothed in black, and as I shook hands with him he looked at me through his spectacles with an expression of sadness he might have worn if he had just "dressed up" to attend the funeral of a lamented person. He spoke in a low tone, and there was a general air of "solemn stillness" in the rooms that reminded me of a funeral occasion.

"I left him a few minutes ago," he said, referring to the doomed man, who had been in his charge a long while, "and I could not help feeling pretty bad."

"How so, Warden?"

"Well, he said to me: 'God bless you, Warden. Wicked as I have been, you have always treated me as kindly as you could, and I 'll think of you with gratitude as I drop from the scaffold!' I tell you, Mr. ——, I could n't help feeling bad!"

His low voice quivered slightly as he said this, and his eyes had that peculiar glistening that denotes no dearth of moisture.

"How did he rest last night?" I asked, barely above a whisper.

"Very well. He fell asleep just at midnight, and never woke till half-past five this morning."

"Do you think he has the nerve to die bravely?"

"I have my doubts, although I have done all I can to cheer him up. I spoke to him this morning about it, and told him to try and meet his fate like a man; and he looked up at me, with the tears ready to start from his eyes, and said he: 'I 'll try to; but, Warden, you know it 'll be a pretty hard walk across that guard-room.' I think so, too."

This had reference to the location of the gallows, which had been erected in the corridor of the main building, the platform on a level with the floor of the guard-room. The doomed man was in the hospital awaiting his final hour, having been taken from his cell and placed there in order that its less gloomy surroundings might have as good an influence as possible upon his nerves. The hospital was an apartment adjoining the guard-room at the end opposite to that at which the scaffold was erected.

I looked around me and saw a dozen or fifteen people I knew, among them the Sheriff. Poor fellow, I pitied him, for he had a disagreeable duty to perform. He came over to me, on tiptoe, and with uncovered head, shook hands with me, and the ordinary greetings were exchanged in low tones. He was very pale.

Others — members of the press, Sheriff's jurymen, the prison physician, an official or two — were gliding about as noiselessly as specters in the Warden's office, the reception-room, and the guard-room, now and then exchanging a word or two in whispers. There seemed to be in everything around us, in the rooms, the walls, the very air, some gloomy sense of the awful scene upon which we were soon to look. Death itself seemed hovering over the prison-walls, like a shadow, sending an icy chill through rooms, and stairway and corridor.

I went into the guard-room, and there felt the same cold stillness that seemed to pervade everything, and on the faces of the attendants themselves there was a look of solemnity such as they might have worn if the great Day of Judgment had just dawned. I stood a moment by one of the well-guarded windows, looking out over the prison-yard toward the workshops, through whose long rows of windows I could see the convicts at work; and I noticed that the sky was slightly clouded, and the daylight fell down within the prison walls with a leaden gloom.

The door leading from the guard-room into the hospital

opened, and a man and woman came out, passed through the reception-room and descended the flight of steps leading to the iron door at which I had entered the prison-walls. They were the son and daughter of the doomed man, and had just taken leave of him forever and ever. I scarcely noticed him; but she was dressed in black, and was crying. This was an immeasurably harder sight for me to look upon than the hanging of the murderer. I caught just one faint glimpse of her face through the folds of a thick black vail; then I turned and again gazed out over the dull prison-yard, and at the rows of windows in the walls of the workshops.

When they were gone, and I could hear their quiet footsteps upon the flight of steps leading out of those sad walls, I moved away from the window, with my face turned from that hospital door, from which the miserable wretch must soon be led. Before me was an open door, leading to the corridor. A step or two brought me upon its threshold and immediately before me was that frightful instrument of death — the Gallows. Its platform was a dozen feet above the cold stone floor of the corridor, with its rows of cells, and about seven feet above the platform, supported by heavy upright timbers on either side of the structure was the "beam," from which the horrible noose hung. The rope had been passed over a pulley fixed in a mortise in the beam, and while the end hanging down had been writhed into a "hangman's knot," the other end was made fast to a cleat on the upright timber on the right-hand side, the length having been carefully calculated to allow the proper fall. A wooden railing three or four feet high surrounded the platform, except that an open space was left where the prisoner was to step upon the platform when he should pass from the guard-room door.

In the center, immediately under the noose, was the trap-door. It was of thick plank, like the platform itself, about two feet square, and so supported exactly on a level with the platform that one might scarcely have noticed it unless he had been looking for it. One side was secured to the platform by heavy iron hinges, while the other rested upon the end of an iron bolt, to which was attached a contrivance so connected with the "spring," which projected above the platform, that a pressure thereon would instantly draw the bolt and let the trap fall. Beneath, a cord was attached to a staple driven into the trap near where it was supported by the bolt, and this run over a pulley at the rear of the scaffold — that side toward the guard-room — and a weight attached, so that the door would not swing back and forth after being released from that fearful hatchway. The whole structure was very massive, the timbers being as heavy as would be used in framing an ordinary cottage, and all, including the platform, was freshly painted a bright blue. It was but a step from the guard-room door to the scaffold, there being between them a space of about two feet, occupied by a platform from which ramified stairways and elevated bridges leading to the various tiers of cells and to the stone floor of the corridor.

One by one the remainder of the spectators arrived, and, like their predecessors, glided about as noiselessly as specters, now and then gathering in little groups about the Warden or Sheriff, asking questions in low tones that were replied to in whispers. It was a strange and awful silence that reigned within those gloomy walls.

Eleven o'clock began to draw near, and eyes wandered frequently toward the hospital-door. The Sheriff went in to inform the doomed man that his time was at hand, and that he must make his final preparations for death. He came out pale and nervous, and whispered a few words to the Warden.

Again the door opened, and the Chaplain, a pale, sickly-looking man, came out and whispered to the Warden and Sheriff. He had been praying for the last time with the guilty wretch, and there were tears in his eyes.

The Sheriff made a sign to his jury, and the Warden conducted them to the door at the scaffold, and pointed into the corridor. They then filed out, descended a few steps to the right, and instead of going down a longer flight to the floor, they walked out upon a bridge that was on a level with the floors of the second tier of cells, and took their positions. The members of the press and a few other spectators then filed through the door, descended to the stone floor and ranged themselves along in front of the scaffold. The number being so limited, it was easy for every one to get a "desirable" position.

I stood directly in front of the gallows, and distant from it about fifteen feet. Now that we were at its base, and looked up at it, it appeared more horrid than before. If I had seen it without knowing its purpose, it might not have looked particularly impressive; but, knowing, it seemed to me to loom up like some gigantic thing of life, some destroying monster, whose impulses were fierce and pitiless. The very timbers had a venomous look, and I half fancied them contaminating to the touch; the railing about the platform suggested to my mind the coil of the boa-constrictor, closing upon and crushing its victim; the beam, with the noose hanging from its center, seemed to look down upon the little party of grave spectators with a frown that was almost human.

The silence was intensified. Not a word was breathed by the waiting spectators. There was not so much as the shuffling of a foot upon the cold stone floor. Breathing itself seemed for awhile suspended, and we stood there like a group of statuary.

I looked up and beyond the scaffold; saw two prison-guards standing by the guard-room door; saw the heads and shoulders of the Sheriff and two deputies; saw them all looking toward the hospital-door, which was not quite visible from where we stand; fancied a slight sound somewhere above us and beyond the scaffold; a cold breath of air seemed to stir through the corridor, and I felt the near presence of the tragedy. My eyes were fixed on the guard-room door. Before me yet is that breathless scene; the statue-like spectators; the frowning gallows; the beam, the hideous noose, the guard-room door.

I saw the Sheriff raise his right hand; noticed a slight movement among the group of five at the guard-room door; then, as they stood on either side, there appeared the Warden and Deputy-Warden, and between them — a face.

Such a face I had never before looked upon. I had seen death in almost every form; I had seen the ashen and distorted features of the dead, who had died amid pain and terror; but never a face like that of the man who found himself stepping out upon that frightful scaffold to be hanged by the neck, killed, and so to pass into Eternity!

The face was clean-shaven, according to the prison rules; it was thin and cadaverous; it was wrinkled, and ashy pale; the features worked and writhed into hideous contortions, as the wretched man struggled with his inward horror, and tried to choke down his emotions; the gray eyes had turned almost white; the lids were distended; and the face looked around upon the assembled men on the bridge and on the stone floor below with such a startled, frightened stare, — such a wild expression of terror, and helplessness, and despair, — such a look of shrinking and amazement, especially when his starting eyes took in the beam and noose, — that it required nerve to look on and not be sickened down to the bottom of the heart.

The Warden formally turned over his prisoner to the Sheriff, and the latter walked out upon the scaffold, followed by his two deputies, who led the murderer between them. His wrists, crossing each other, were already bound together, giving him an appearance of utter helplessness, and his knees trembled so violently that I expected to see them give way, his legs double up and himself fall upon the platform, a quivering mass of human terror. But he stood, half supported by the Sheriff's deputies, while the latter placed his feet squarely upon the center of the trap, the noose dangling at his right ear.

Following him came the Chaplain, paler than ever, and, in the goodness of his heart, he whispered a last word of hope in the ear of the quaking wretch, then retired to a corner of the scaffold near the guard-room door. There he placed an elbow upon the railing, and I could see his white lips moving.

The Warden, Deputy-Warden and two attendants stood at the door.

The Sheriff's deputies bound the prisoner firmly at the ankles and knees, and secured his elbows close to his sides by fastening them to a strap which they passed around his back and buckled tightly. Then one of them drew over that face, and shut out from those staring eyes the light of day for ever, the "black cap" — a sack, rather than a cap, as it was half as large as an ordinary pillow-case. The folds of this dropped down to the breast, and hid the face — that picture of horror — from the view of the spectators. Being dressed in a black suit, the figure now presented a somber appearance, indeed.

Then the other Sheriff's deputy adjusted the noose, slightly lifting the pendent folds of the "black cap," so that the cord should press upon the bare neck. At its touch the murderer started, and trembled so violently that I thought he must fall. But he did not, and all was ready. Once more, a deputy gently placed

23

his hand on the prisoner's shoulder, to put him in the exact position desired, then withdrew it; while the other examined the rope to see that all was clear, and that it would run freely over the pulley when the trap should be sprung. Then they stepped aside, one to the right and the other to the left, and he stood alone, confronting Eternity. He had not uttered a word, except to say in a tremulous whisper, while they were pinioning him: "Don't tie me so tight." These were his last words.

I looked at a clock that was fixed upon the wall near the scaffold. It was four minutes past eleven.

The Sheriff, who stood by the front railing, near the spring, drew from his pocket the death-warrant, and broke the silence by reading it in quivering tones that went rolling along with a hollow sound through the stone-bound corridor, and dying away in the distance. Slowly he read, while the poor wretch stood helplessly awaiting his fate; and finally — it was eight minutes past eleven — came the words:

"*And now, I command you, the said ——, to deliver up your body to me, the said High Sheriff of R—— County, that I may execute the sentence of the law.*"

A half-second of death-like silence, and I saw the Sheriff's right foot move. It was pressed upon the iron spring.

There was a sharp crash, as the trap-door swung down against a "rest" toward the rear of the scaffold intended to receive the shock, and I saw a black figure dart down beneath the platform, like the great iron weight of a pile-driver. But it did not descend to the floor. It stopped suddenly in mid-air, with its head just below the platform, swayed to and fro a few inches, as a sack of corn suspended by a rope might have done, then was perfectly motionless.

The knot was at the back of the neck, and the head, covered with the black cap, drooped forward until the chin rested upon the breast. The neck had been broken; not a muscle twitched; and the body of the murderer hung as inanimate and motionless as the sack of corn to which it has been likened. Suspended there above the earth, with that black pall over the distorted features, it was the very personification of death.

There was a hush, and for a few seconds all were as silent as the walls themselves; then the prison physician and an assistant mounted upon chairs upon either side of the pendent figure and noted the pulsations so soon to cease forever. The pulse continued to beat perceptibly, with wild fluctuations, for a period of seventeen minutes, the physician, watch in hand, announcing its condition at the end of each minute: "Forty-eight"—"Forty-five"—"Forty-five"—"A hundred and thirteen"—"A hundred and forty-two"—"Eighty-one"—"Sixty-four"—and so on, down to—"Very feeble"—"Six"—"Three"—"Heart fluttering slightly"—then—

"Dead."

I hurried up the steps, once more passed the platform with its open hatchway, glided through the guard-room, the reception-room, hurried down the entry-stairs, and out into the frosty February air. Crowds of curious people accosted me with, "Is he hung?" "Is he dead?" "How did he act?" and the like. I replied with a word, sprang into a carriage that awaited me and was whirled away with the speed of an express train.

The vehicle stopped in front of the office door, and I jumped out upon the sidewalk and flew up-stairs. I had already written—and it had been put in type—a skeleton description of the hanging, as I expected it to be; I quickly made a few alterations; put in a few additional lines, no one compositor setting more than a line; it was hurried together; the form locked up and thrown upon the press; and in five minutes more the newsboys were screaming in the street:

"Here 's your Extra! All about the execution! All about the confession! Horrible crimes!"

And so our paper, giving an account of the hanging of the murderer, was fluttering in the wind before his body was cold.

CHAPTER XXIX.

"*TRICKS OF THE TRADE.*"

THE power of the press, for good or evil, cannot well be over-rated. The newspapers of the country, as elsewhere remarked, constitute a kind of perpetual school, in which people keep on learning after they have arrived at maturity and passed out of the hands of the schoolmaster; and so they continue to learn, all their lives, for the pupils of the school of the press do not graduate and leave it, as they may leave a college when they have learned all that is within it taught. There then could be no greater public calamity than the degrading of the character of the press, or the destruction or material abridgment of its freedom would be. Its natural tendency is to do good, rather than evil; to advocate truth, rather than error; and it is its province largely to mold and wholly reflect the opinions and sentiments of the populace. So, its mission is one of incalculable importance. Orators may have a temporary influence over excited assemblages, may inflame and mislead them; but it behooves the newspaper to be careful and truthful, and to reach correct conclusions by the most direct routes, for it speaks to its audience in quiet homes and in moments of sober thought.

As I am relating some "Secrets of the Sanctum," while I

wish to avoid anything approaching a violation of confidence, I don't mind giving one or two incidents in my own experience illustrating the power of a newspaper, and showing what an engine it may be made for either good or evil — in these cases for good, I trust, as was certainly intended.

In San Francisco there are tolerated — or were at one time — abuses that would not be tolerated in any other large city in this country or in Europe. When I lived in that city it was not unusual for a man to gallop along on horseback, through the most crowded thoroughfares, at the rate of from fifteen to twenty miles an hour. Of course people were frequently run over and killed, but that did not seem to strike the authorities as at all prejudicial to the public interests.

Another peculiarity of San Francisco was the considerable number of saddle-horses daily to be found standing on the crowded *sidewalks*. They were horses upon which people living a little way out of the city daily rode in for the purpose of transacting business, and were hitched to iron posts that stood at short intervals along the curb-stone. No sooner would the sagacious horse find himself secured to the post than he would begin to think, like the Caucasian race, of "bettering his condition." Taking a calm view of the moist gutter in which he stood, and of the clean, smooth asphaltum sidewalk, he would very readily detect the superiority of the latter as a place to stand, and so would begin slowly to describe an arc of a circle, of which the hitching-post was the center, like a ship swinging round on her anchor at the turning of the tide; and one minute after his master left him would find him standing squarely across the sidewalk, with his nose toward the street, his ears laid back on his mane, and his tail switching around within two or three feet of a plate-glass jewelry window or broker's door. Streams of pedestrians were continually passing, dodging around the said tail, always in peril of getting a stunning kick on the shins from the iron-shod feet of the animal with its ears laid back; and nobody seemed to think that there was anything wrong about it. Occasionally some good-natured pedestrian would give the horse a friendly slap on the rump, say, "Look out, old fellow," and pass on amid the throng; and the animal merely put on a smiling countenance, laid his ears back a little flatter, and looked merely a trifle more in the notion of kicking out among the knees and shins of the pedestrians, just for fun.

These are only examples of the extraordinary practices familiar in the most crowded streets (notably Montgomery and Kearny) of San Francisco, a city of two hundred thousand inhabitants. It was easily accounted for by the fact that the city had grown so rapidly that it had yet scarcely had time to measure itself, to realize its proportions, and to throw off the habits of a Mexican village; but what would be thought of such things in Broadway, New York; Chestnut Street, Philadelphia; Washington Street, Boston; Fourth Street, St. Louis; or Clark Street, Chicago?

Among other nuisances tolerated in the streets of San Francisco, and which seemed rather pleasing to the municipal authorities than otherwise, were Chinamen carrying their baskets on the sidewalks. While I never regarded the Chinese as a desirable element of our population, I think I did not view them with unreasonable prejudice, and I do not believe that a dislike of them was at all accountable for my aversion to their carrying their baskets along the sidewalks. As not every one is familiar with these people and their habits, a few words of explanation will be entirely in place.

The Chinese Mongol does not carry his burden in the manner of the Caucasian. He is never seen with a sack on his shoulder or a basket on his arm, or propelling a load of vegetables along the street in a push-cart or wheel-barrow. Whatever he carries he manages to divide into two nearly equal parts, and places each in a large basket, generally of the capacity of a bushel or a bushel and a half. Each basket has a strong cord attached to it, in the manner of a bucket-bail; and the cords so attached to the two baskets of the Chinaman are slung over opposite ends of a bamboo pole six or eight feet long, which is balanced upon his shoulder, the pole usually at an angle of ten or fifteen degrees from the line of his course; and so the bearer of the burdens rushes along at a monotonous "dog-trot" in the direction of his destination.

It will be readily seen that these large, rough baskets, often with splinters sticking out in all directions, rushing along over the crowded sidewalks, were no trifling annoyance to pedestrians, and it was my opinion that they ought to be banished from the sidewalks and obliged to take the street, like carts and wheel-barrows. So strongly was I impressed with the equity of such a proposition, that I published in the *Enunciator* an article deprecating the nuisance in strong terms, and calling upon the Board of Supervisors to pass an ordinance abating it. This might not have attracted the necessary amount of attention in desirable quarters, but I resolved that the article should go and be seen "where it would do the most good." I therefore sent a copy of the *Enunciator*, with the article marked, to each member of the Board of Supervisors, and also to each of those gentlemen a note something like the following:

SAN FRANCISCO, February 4, 18—.

SIR: — We send you, by this mail, a copy of the *Enunciator* containing an article in reference to the nuisance of Chinese carrying their large baskets along the sidewalks. We believe that, together with that journal, we are justified in demanding their removal to the street; and we earnestly request that you introduce an ordinance at the next meeting of the Board of Supervisors, compelling persons carrying bulky burdens along on poles to take the street, in common with push-carts and wheel-barrows. This is earnestly wished by MANY OF YOUR CONSTITUENTS.

At the next meeting of the Board, an ordinance to this effect was introduced and passed by a unanimous vote. A fine of five dollars was fixed as the penalty for every violation of the ordinance. The measure attracted considerable attention, and was almost universally commended. In a short time a number of Chinese who disregarded the ordinance were arrested and fined; till at last the Mongols, or some party in their interest, engaged a lawyer, made a test-case, and appealed it, on the grounds of unconstitutionality. The case went to a higher court than the municipal court, and finally reached the Supreme Court of the State of California, where, in accordance with what seemed to me the clearest rules of right, the ordinance was sustained. So, ever afterward, the Chinese with their clumsy baskets took the street, where they belonged, in common with push-carts and wheel-barrows.

About the same time there was a company of supposed capitalists (calling themselves the "Lower California Company") attempting to establish a colony at Magdalena Bay, about the only considerable harbor of Lower California, which province belongs to Mexico, by offering great inducements to emigrants, making representations of the extraordinary fertility of the soil, the salubrity of the climate, and promising to "give every man a valuable farm" who should emigrate to Magdalena Bay and settle in that vicinity.

I knew enough of Lower California to feel astonished at these statements, which were advertised broadcast through California, and upon making a careful and pointed investigation I discovered that the "Company" had a selfish end in view; and never was it more clearly exemplified that "corporations have no souls." This "Lower California Company" had received a grant of land at Magdalena Bay from the Mexican Government, but accompanied with the condition that, to make the grant permanent, a colony of at least one thousand settlers must be established there within a given time, and the end of that period of time was by no means distant. Now, the "Company" valued the grant chiefly because a valuable article of commerce — orchilla moss, from which a substance much used in dyeing is extracted — was to be obtained at the Bay in great abundance; and, with a deliberate cruelty rarely equaled, made efforts to induce people to go there and settle, purely to make valid their grant, well knowing that the soil was as sterile as a powder-horn, that the landscape was one vast expanse of sand and cactus, and that to go there and "settle" was to sit down and court starvation. The "Company," I learned upon inquiry, looked deeper still into the future than the mere accumulation of a million dollars or so from their orchilla moss — their wilder ambition being one day to sell out their claim, after getting a firm grip upon it, to the United States Government for an enormous sum, hoping that the latter party would buy it with an eye to eventual annexation. It must be confessed that the "Company's" ambitions in this direction were not unreasonable in the light of such an atmosphere of jobbery as has of late years hovered over the Congress of the United States. Credit Mobilier — Pacific Mail—Well, that 's off the subject.

Learning beyond any reasonable doubt what the state of things was, I deemed it my duty to put a stop to the business, and determined to do so if there was power enough in a single weekly newspaper to do it. To that end, in peril of a libel suit with a "wealthy corporation" as plaintiff, I published in the *Enunciator* a complete exposition of the scheme, complaining particularly of the "Company's" ambition ultimately to sell out its grant to the United States, and descanting upon the great probability that such a consummation would involve the friendly relations of our country and Mexico; and, indeed, I was as earnest then as I am now in my opposition to any scheme having for its object the success of stupendous jobbery under the guise of "acquisition of territory." Copies of the *Enunciator*, with this article carefully marked, I sent by mail to all the leading public men and journalists of Mexico, from President Benito Juarez down, including all the Governors of States, etc., having obtained a list of their names and addresses in Spanish from the Mexican Consul in San Francisco. The result was, that the subject attracted immediate attention, and all Mexico was excited to such a degree that before three months the Government was constrained to revoke its grant of Magdalena Bay, the "colony" was broken up and the "Company" banished from that "fertile" soil. How a proposition looking to the cession of any of their territory to the United States would strike the minds of Mexicans, may be judged from the following extract from an editorial which subsequently appeared in the *Diaro*, an official organ published in the City of Mexico:

> The Mexican people have always regarded with indignation any idea of a cession of a part, even an inch, of their territory, and to-day the public man who should propose such a thing would not even be judged as a criminal, but we should hand him over to the medical fraternity as a case of extreme lunacy. Such is our conviction, and such is the conviction of all Mexicans. This Government has not made, nor will it ever admit, propositions for parting with a single jot of the territory of the nation. All the press of Mexico will unite in declaring the report to the opposite effect, which originated on the Pacific Coast, to be entirely without foundation.

That the statements of the *Enunciator* were perfectly correct was afterward fully verified. Nor did any libel suit result. Indeed, some persons connected with the nefarious scheme were glad to get away with their necks. The remnant of the "colonists" (many having died of starvation) arrived at San Francisco, one day, having come all the way on foot — a distance of six hundred miles; and the stories they told of their sufferings fully confirmed the *exposé* in the *Enunciator*, and exemplified the perfidy of the "Company."

While residing in the suburbs of San Francisco, my neighbors (as well as myself) were at one time greatly pestered by goats, and other domesticated animals, which were continually leaping fences and demolishing the vines, flowers and shrubbery of lawns and gardens. Inspired by this sad state of things, bordering on vandalism, and urged by my neighbors, who thought that the Pound-Keeper ought to look after the matter, I published the following in the *Enunciator:*

LINES TO THE POUND-MAN.

Pound-man! Pound-man!
Why not come around, man?
The dogs and cats are running wild
As ever they were found, man.

Pound-man! Pound-man!
Where may you be found, man?
If you 're within a fortnight's walk
I 'd think you 'd hear the sound, man.

Pound-man! Pound-man!
Hung, or shot, or drowned, man,
Should be a hundred beasts I know
That daily prowl around, man.

Pound-man! Pound-man!
Goats are on my ground, man;
They nip my roses, vines and grass,
Wherever they are found, man.

Pound-man! Pound-man!
Goats do most abound, man;
They jump my gate, they leap my fence,
As easy as a hound, man.

Pound-man! Pound-man!
Cows are bawling round, man;
They break down all my gates and clear
My palings at a bound, man.

Pound-man! Pound-man!
Pigs root up my mound, man;
They wallow in my "tater-vines,"
With ugly, grunting sound, man.

Pound-man! Pound-man!
Cries of cats resound, man;
I shoot at them with deadly aim,
But not one can I wound, man.

Pound-man! Pound-man!
List to what is sound, man;
These creatures drive a fellow mad —
They utterly confound, man.

Pound-man! Pound-man!
If you'd be renowned, man,
Come free the suburbs of this plague,
And you'll be, I'll be bound, man.

Pound-man! Pound-man!
Credit won't redound, man,
To you in your position if
You don't soon come around, man.

As exemplifying the power and influence of a newspaper, I was visited on the next day after the publication of the foregoing doggerel by a stranger, who said his name was Bean, and that he was the City Pound-man. When he said this, I very naturally concluded that he had come in for the purpose of shooting me, and was just making up my mind to sell my life as dearly as possible, when he proceeded to state his case in such a courteous way as made me see at a glance that he was not insensible of the dignity of the press.

"I just came in," he said, "to ask if I can do anything to relieve you. I think my force really is too small, and there are some quarters of the city that we cannot help neglecting at times. Where is it you live, Mr. ——?"

"Sanchez Street, beyond the Mission," I replied.

"Ah, then I see why you are so much annoyed," said he. "That is beyond our bounds. We have no authority to go further south than Sixteenth Street, and I don't wonder that you have been worried. The bounds ought to be extended, and our force increased."

"It does look so," said I.

"Well," he rejoined, "*you* sha' n't be troubled any more, if I can help it. I have steadily read your paper for the last two years, and like it; and as I believe you are doing good with it, I will take the responsibility of extending my territory so far as to see that you are not much annoyed by goats and cows in the future."

I thanked him cordially; and I afterward discerned a pleasing scarcity of goats in the vicinity of my suburban home. The power of the press must have searching ramifications when even the pigs and goats feel and respect it.

While conducting the *Enunciator*, I did all in my power to make it an instrument for the promotion of the public good, as I think it is the duty of every journalist to do with his paper; and I think I succeeded in this more than once, however signally I may have failed to make it an instrument of good to myself. In addition to what is above recounted, and some other little things I have not the space to mention, I think that reckless riding and driving in the streets assumed smaller proportions, and accidents therefrom became less frequent, owing to articles published in the *Enunciator*, calling public attention to these abuses. I know that good was done in this regard, so far as one person was concerned. He was an "eccentric divine," whose sermons I had more than once severely criticised in the *Enunciator*. His church was always crowded,—not, I fear, by people who went there with feelings of solemnity and with wishes to be made better during the coming week than they had been during the preceding week, but who were rather drawn thither by a spirit of curiosity; because it got to be pretty well known that, especially during the Sunday evening sermons, the reverend gentleman was very mirthful in his ways, and that bursts of laughter and the clapping of hands by way of applause were the rule rather than the exception.

One day I was crossing one of the principal streets, and came within about three-quarters of an inch of being run over (and of course killed) by a horse that galloped along at a furious rate. I only escaped serious bodily harm by making a convulsive and very undignified scramble for the nearest curb-stone, losing my hat in the operation, which useful article of attire was promptly run over and crushed by one of Wells, Fargo & Co.'s express wagons; and on looking after the equestrian who constituted the burden of the fleet animal, and who had directed it through the thronged streets at such a reckless pace, I discovered that it was no other than that same "eccentric divine." I knew him and he knew me by sight, and I will be charitable enough to believe that he did not purposely try to gallop over me because of my wicked criticisms of his sermons; but nevertheless I thought that a man of his "cloth" ought not to go galloping along in that way. I never thought "personal journalism" the proper thing; yet there are persons who sometimes thrust themselves upon public notice in such a manner that they make legitimate news items of themselves; and on this occasion I felt that I was justified in referring to the "divine's" habit of fast riding, which had more than once before attracted my notice. This I did in the *Enunciator* in terms little short of "libelous," giving his full name and comparing him unfavorably with a regular horse-jockey, as he deserved; and the result was—not a libel suit, but that the Rev. Mr. S——, who of course read the article, as I afterward learned, felt it so keenly that he never again rode through the busy thoroughfares of San Francisco "faster than a walk," as the bridge notice says. Probably a life was saved by his "change of heart" in this regard, and if so it was the happiness of the *Enunciator* to do some good at least.

In the more prosperous days of that journal's career a vigorous rivalry once sprang up between it and another weekly paper published in the same city. Each paper was always "running" a serial story, and of course every effort was made by each to "beat" the other in securing a "bang-up" good romance. In those days we had scarcely any novelists in California, and had to depend on more distant sources for our stories—sometimes buying them from Eastern authors, sometimes "stealing" them from European papers, as, in the absence of an international copyright law, we had a perfect legal and reciprocal right to do.

On one occasion a remarkable coincidence occurred: both papers began on the same day to publish the same story, which was taken from the London *Journal.* As neither one could make the story better than the other, the only end now aimed at by each, in the spirit of emulation, was to publish more of the story in each installment than its rival. The amount of the story published in each number of the London *Journal* as it came to hand made a fair installment in the *Enunciator* and in its rival; and as neither could publish more each week than the *Journal* itself contained, the two papers kept even for some weeks; and the fact that they contained just the same portions of the story each week began to attract attention, as the rivalry between the two journals was pretty well known to the public.

At last an ill-fated week came, and brought with it a terrible exigence. My London *Journal*, which I had theretofore received regularly by mail, failed to come to hand. It might have been the fault of the mails, or of the person whose duty it was to mail it, or it might have been owing to the carelessness of the boy whom I sent to the Post-office for my papers; but the stern fact remained the same: it had not come; it had missed. Wild with apprehension, I made the rounds of the various newsdealers' establishments, and asked each if he had a copy of the London *Journal* he could spare just as well as not. I asked in a very careless way, of course, although I would gladly have given two hundred and fifty dollars for one. None of them kept it at all. There was probably but one copy in San Francisco, and that was in the hands of the rival editor. It of course could not have been secured, except through the exercise of a bit of petty larceny, and, although I won't say what the temptation of "opportunity" might have induced me to do, I entertained no hope in that direction. To copy the next installment from the rival sheet and publish it one week later would be to send that paper a dozen lengths ahead of the *Enunciator* in the estimation of the hundreds of people who read both papers. What then was to be done?

I went back to the office on the verge of despair. I sat down and meditated. I could not convince myself that suicide was exactly the right thing, but the necessity for my ever having been born in the first place was in my mind very equivocal and indistinct. If some merciful angel in the form of the cholera or small-pox had come around and carried me away to the cemetery in a creditable manner, I could have rejoiced; but there I was, ruddy, robust, strong, with an appetite like an ostrich, and no prospect of a speedy and honorable death; and so something had to be done. Just in my gloomiest pitch of despair a thought struck me. It was suggested by the very desperateness of the situation. I must write an imaginary continuation of the story. But here was a difficulty. Persons who saw both papers would discover a marked difference, as the irreconcilable heads of chapters must immediately strike the eye. The real story might in the very next chapter kill an important character, while I might guess wrong as to what was in store for him and treat the same character to a "streak of good luck," such, for example, as being awarded a contract for street-paving. Besides, it would not only be irreconcilable with the contemporary installment in our rival, but also with the remainder of the story, which probably had not yet been half published. A few minutes' active thought resulted in suggesting a way out of the difficulty. The plan was to write a long chapter that would be such a complete episode that it could not possibly be affected by anything that might come after it.

I consulted the preceding installment, and found that the hero had been left in a gloomy wood, on his way to a lonely house two miles distant, where he expected to rescue the heroine from several desperate characters who had been hired to abduct her by a wealthy but villainous rival, whose object was to frighten her into marrying *him*, instead of the hero. I deemed that it could do no possible injury to the thread of the story to treat him to a ghost on the way, and I accordingly "pitched in," and wrote a chapter of five-and-a-half columns, setting forth the following "facts:" He suddenly saw a light in the deep wood a few hundred yards to the right of the road; thought he heard also a smothered cry; it occurred to him that it might be the custodians of the heroine, who were removing her to some other place of confinement, to prevent her rescue; instantly ran to the spot; found a deserted log-house; entered it; saw frequent gleams of strange, bluish lights; heard rappings on the walls, and wild, weird songs and laughter all around him; house evidently haunted; the door was closed by invisible hands; apparitions issued from the walls and floor, and some flew at him with phantom swords; he finally made his escape, by jumping from a window, after an hour of horror, and proceeded on his mission.

The two papers were, as usual, issued on the following Sunday morning, and the result of my bit of handiwork proved favorable to the *Enunciator*, because a subject of general remark was the "carelessness" of our rival in having overlooked and omitted the most absorbing chapter in the story. Years afterward, the rival editor and I frequently met on the most friendly terms, and, in alluding to our former active emulation, he would say:

"I don't see how I ever missed that ghost-scene. It's the strangest thing in the world. I always cut out the *Journal's* installment myself, and it does not seem possible that I could have clipped a portion of an installment, leaving a whole chapter — so large a chapter as that, too. Yet, I don't see how else it could have happened."

I finally told him the secret, but not until after both papers had ceased to exist.

There is the very essence of competition between newspapers. Nothing delights a paper more than to "beat" its contemporaries—that is, secure a piece of important news which they have failed to obtain. Such piece of news is called an "exclusive." I have known of circumstances under which a paper would gladly have paid ten thousand dollars for *one column* of news that it might publish six hours in advance of any and all other papers in the country. Not that its profits from the increased sales of that single issue would anywhere nearly have approached this figure, but because such an "exclusive" would have been "a big card," an advertisement that would have been certain to pay in the long run.

As an illustration, I once walked complacently about the streets of a certain little city, carrying in my pocket a bit of news, of about two columns, which I was in honor bound not to publish before the noon of the following day, and for which the sum of five thousand dollars was freely offered by agents of papers published in various large cities, over fifty of such agents being there. So keen was the search for the document, that I deemed it advisable, when night came, to carry a revolver in my pocket as a precaution against possible assault — not by a newspaper man, but by some ruffian who might have learned of its value and suspected that I had it in my possession. That night I went to my office at twelve o'clock, when all was quiet, and had the article put in type, between that hour and three A. M., by two compositors *sworn* to secrecy; and so I succeeded in preserving the document from premature publication, and in publishing it sooner and more accurately than any other paper.

If in this chapter I allude to the fact that a man sometimes pays a reporter or editor to suppress a piece of news in which he happens to figure in a discreditable light, I do so only to say that such transactions are not common, and that they are strongly denounced by reputable journals, editors and reporters. I have known of such a thing being done, but in its principle there is such an odor of blackmailing that it seems to me it ought to be classed with "crimes and misdemeanors."

One day, while I was connected with a Boston daily, an elderly man came into the editorial-room, and it may be judged by the brief dialogue which ensued that he was a pretty direct business man:

"Are you the editor?"

"Yes."

"Well, I'm William P. Brown, of Salem."

"Yes?"

"It was I that was before the Police Court there yesterday, and I would n't have my name go into the Boston papers for the world. Will you keep it out?"

Now, we had no regular reporter in Salem, had sent none there, and in any event the little case he mentioned would not probably have been alluded to in our columns. However, to make him feel as comfortable as possible, and being slightly annoyed at the interruption, I told a deliberate fib, saying, excitedly:

"My goodness! You're just in time. It would have been in type in five minutes more and locked in the form."

"And it is n't too late?" he said, nervously.

"No; rely on it, I shall see that it does not go in."

"Ah, thank you!"—putting his hand in his pocket and taking out his pocket-book,—"*How much is it?*"

"O, we make no charge for anything like that."

"Thank you! Thank you!"

And he pocketed his wallet and departed a happier but not wiser man.

CHAPTER XXX.

HUMORS OF JOURNALISM.

A WHOLE volume might readily be written on this subject alone, and in the present chapter I can only give it, comparatively speaking, a passing notice. It would be a mistake to suppose that all journalists are born humorists, although it would be no mistake to assume that, taken collectively, they have fully as fine a sense of humor as any other class of people. I think, too, that as many funny things occur in a newspaper establishment as in any other institution. The very blunders made in newspaper work often have an element of fun in them not to be found, say, for example, in a carriage-manufactory, where the accidental mutilation of a carefully-polished wheel or two, through some one's awkwardness, would not be considered very provocative of mirth. Yes, and when anything particularly good happens in a newspaper establishment it is taken up, and "goes the rounds." An awkward expression of an editor, however inadvertent; a mistake in "emptying" or "making-up;" typographic errors of an unusual nature; these are not allowed to rest, if they once "get out," but are "passed along," with many appended comments.

As regards the proposition of the editor making a deliberate attempt to be funny, such a thing is never done by any who actually do succeed in being funny. An amusing comment appended to a two-line news item is always spontaneous, and the editor never thinks of its being either witty or amusing. For example, here is a paragraph that went the rounds a few years ago, and in which there is certainly no great depth of humor, but which it is difficult to read for the first time without at least smiling:

> A man named Bloat keeps a drinking-saloon in Oakland, California. Comment is unnecessary.

Another is this, which must have been a serious matter to somebody:

> A man in Williamsport, Pa., fell dead the other day while combing his hair. Yet people will engage in this dangerous practice every day.

Here is another:

> Be very careful in handling buckwheat flour. A barrel of the dangerous stuff exploded in Keokuk, Iowa, a few days ago.

Another:

> A well-known character, with the sobriquet of "Reddy Johnson," was fatally stabbed in St. Louis, the other evening, with a heated poker. Of course, Reddy had to have a hot punch.

Comments like these are added to little news paragraphs usually when the editors who make them are actually in a bad humor, as may be guessed by their half reckless cynicism; and certainly the editor has no more thought of saying anything funny than if he were asking his grocery man how much he owed him — a time when no one is likely to assume the attitude of a humorist.

Awkward language occasionally used, *not* by the ignoramus, but by editors of experience and ability, is a fruitful source of mirth. For example, an Auburn (N. Y.) paper stated not long since that there was to be added to one of its institutions of learning a building "to accommodate an increased number of students two hundred feet long." We have all seen tall students, but students with a length of two hundred feet are new to most of us. They remind me of a story that is told of a tall, slim English gentleman who appeared for the first time in society. "Who is that?" a gentleman asked of a lady. "That is Mr. Adolphus Bunks. He is intended for the church." "Ah? I should think him better calculated for the steeple!"

Another example of hurried and awkward language is this, which has been going the rounds for years, and which, even if fictitious, is perfectly natural and not at all incredible:

> A temperance editor, in drawing attention to an article against ardent spirits in his paper, says: "For an example of the effects of intemperance see our inside!"

The Foreman's occasional blunders in making up are also a source of amusement. While publishing the *Enunciator* in San Francisco we had a department of humorous paragraphs, mostly clipped from exchanges. On one occasion the Foreman, in making up, got a few lines of our market reports mixed up with these funny paragraphs, and the effect was little less than ludicrous. Imagine this paragraph "sandwiched in" between a first-class conundrum and a side-splitting joke:

FLOUR.—Demand active. Sales of good to choice family at $6.75 @ $7.00; fine Indiana brands, $7.25 @ $7.40; California, first quality, $7.50 @ $8.00, with large demand and an upward tendency.

A contemporary called attention to this innocent-looking blunder, which at the time of its commission did not occur to me as being very funny, after the following fashion:

The *Enunciator* has every week a column of funny paragraphs, always good, but in this department of its last issue we find something so exceptionally funny that we cannot help quoting it: [Here followed the "flour" paragraph.] The point of this joke will of course be readily seen. The word "flour," to start with, has a droll, good-natured appearance, and strikes the eye as being in an unusually good-humor. Then, "demand active" is very neatly put, suggesting an absence of anything like rheumatism or gout; while "$6.75 @ $7.00" is simply irresistible. "Indiana brands" is a peculiarly happy hit; and certainly no one could have failed to roar with laughter when he read, $7.50 @ $8.00, with large demand." Our neighbor has a happy faculty of picking up all the "good things" that are going.

It occasionally happens that the Editor, who is clipping little paragraphs from exchanges for certain departments of his paper, inadvertently pastes it on his copy-paper, with other items, wrong-side up. I remember that a proof of my humorous department once came to me with this extraordinary paragraph standing out boldly, and from all around it:

This stove is universally pronounced the most durable, the best baker, either of loaves, rolls, or muffins, with the least consumption of fuel, of any stove or range yet introduced.

I saw at a glance that I had evidently pasted a funny paragraph on wrong-side up, and that the wrong side so presented to the compositor contained a paragraph from an advertisement of a patent stove, and of course I marked it "out."

This mistake of getting the wrong side of a paragraph up is illustrated by the following anecdote, of the authenticity of which, however, I am not in possession:

A certain clergyman, reading from the pulpit a number of religious announcements one Sabbath, some of which had been clipped from newspapers and laid on his stand, unluckily read the wrong side of one of the slips, which happened to contain this advertisement of the business establishment of a prominent member of the church:

BOOTS! BOOTS! SHOES! SHOES! — George S. Brown keeps constantly on hand, and will sell cheap for cash, at No. 10 Pine Street, the largest and best assortment of boots and shoes in town. Give him a call before purchasing elsewhere. m6—1m.

The minister, happening to be a recent arrival, supposed that it was customary in that place to read from the pulpit advertisements of the business of members, and innocently added:

"Brother Brown, I understand, is a very worthy member of this church, and I have no doubt will deal fairly with any of the congregation who choose to patronize him."

It may not be improper to state just here that for a paragraph in a newspaper to appear exactly opposite a paragraph of the same dimensions on the reverse side of the sheet is almost as rare as a total eclipse of the sun observable simultaneously in England and New Zealand. In the first place, a sheet ought to "register" as nearly as possible in the process of printing—that is, the forms in their turn should be so accurately placed on the press that the column on the one side and on the other would be exactly opposite each other, and that the heads of columns on either side should be an equal distance from the edge of the paper. His aim often fails; but even if it hits perpetually, the chances are that not once in ten thousand days of the existence of a paper will two paragraphs of just the same size, same number of lines, and, above all, in the same size of type be found precisely opposite each other on the same slip clipped from a newspaper. But that it may occur and has occured is proved by the following two items, the first of which I once clipped from a Boston paper, afterward finding the other side up and scarcely knowing which item I had intended to quote in a column of miscellaneous paragraphs:

WILLS.— We have heard of a will admitted to probate written upon a paper collar, and have heard of one written with chalk on a barn-door; but here is a new story: The will of Phebe Ann Woodward, late of Kennet Square, Penn., recently found written upon a new slate carefully enclosed in a box and locked up in a trunk, and dated May 9, 1863, has been admitted to probate.

......Among the novelties at the late Lyons Exhibition were certain products obtained from the reed mace or cat's tail, a plant which is very abundant in marshy districts, but which has been utilized only to a small extent, for mats, chair-bottoms, baskets, etc. Some idea of the abundance of reed mace may be formed from the fact that France is capable of producing at least 100,000 tons of it yearly.

This subject of the "other side" of a printed page reminds me of a subject to which, if I failed to refer, I might be considered derelict as the writer of this work. I mean the "patent outside" business. I ought to explain it, because it has furnished one of the best jokes in the annals of journalistic humor. The "outside" of a country newspaper (its first and fourth pages) is often made up of selections, stories, verses, paragraphs of general interest, humorous squibs, and so forth; while the "inside" (second and third pages) contains editorials, the freshest accessible news and the freshest advertisements. It seems to have occurred to some enterprising genius that one well-got up "outside" ought to suit equally well a large number of country weekly journals, and a plan was organized, first in Chicago, I think, by which hundreds of establishments, distant from one another, were furnished with sheets on which to print their "inside," the other side (their outside) of which contained well-selected and neatly-printed miscellaneous matter, always, of course, culled with a careful regard to neutrality, and, in fact, without reference to sectarian or political questions. Among the drollest effects, quickly visible to the practical eye, was the extraordinary dissimilarity in the mechanical workmanship,—the "patent outside" being very clean, having been printed in a large city, on a cylinder-press, and the "original" "inside" with many typographic errors, having been printed in a country town on a hand-press. Now, the joke in this connection that went the rounds of the press, without regard to party, in the autumn of 1873, was to the following effect:

Hon. Wm. Allen was running for Governor of Ohio (and was afterward elected) on the Democratic ticket. The Republican nominee was Mr. Hayes, then, I think, Governor of the State. Governor Allen, "Bill" Allen, one of the honest, old-fashioned men of the days of Jackson, was a powerful public speaker, with a voice like a raging thunder-storm. Some of the Republican papers, in the course of the gubernatorial canvass, made sarcastic reference to Mr. Allen's tremendous voice, and one of them even printed this rude paragraph:

> We understood that after Governor Hayes takes some of the wind out of Bill Allen, he will be offered a position on the coast of Rhode Island to act as a fog-horn.

This of course sounded well enough in a Republican paper, Allen being the Democratic candidate, but did n't look very well in a strongly Democratic county paper. Yet, in such paper the paragraph appeared, being embodied in the miscellaneous paragraphs of the "patent outside" (used by the Editor, entirely unknown to his country subscribers), the compiler of the patent outside having forgotten that one of his first duties was to avoid sectarian or partisan allusions. The Editor of the country paper in question had a lively time of it explaining how such a disrespectful allusion to "Bill" Allen happened to be made in his paper.

Sometimes two different reporters of a city daily happen to furnish the same item of news, and if the City Editor overlooks the matter a "duplicate" is the result. This is not a very serious matter, provided the statements in the two articles agree substantially, but when they don't the joke is certainly on the Editor. The following "duplicate" once occurred in a daily of which, I almost shrink from confessing, I was the City Editor at the time, and so morally responsible for the blunder:

BOY SHOT. — Yesterday afternoon Edward Farrigan, twelve years old, residing with his father at No. 633 Oxford Street, while playing with a pistol in an adjacent alley, accidentally discharged the weapon, and the bullet penetrated his left wrist, producing a very bad wound. Amputation of the hand will probably be necessary.

BOY SHOT. — This forenoon, while a boy named Charles Ellsworth, was fooling with an old shot-gun in Amity Place, Oxford Street, the weapon, which was not supposed to be loaded, was discharged, and a number of shot struck the right arm of another boy, named Edward Farrigan, who was passing along the street, making a slight flesh-wound near the elbow. Farrigan is fifteen years old, and resides at No. 633 Oxford Street. He is an errand-boy for Jordan, Marsh & Co. Fortunately the wound is not at all serious, but he had a narrow escape.

The effect of getting portions of two articles, on two very distinct subjects, mixed in the making-up, is sometimes very ludicrous. For example, a country paper once contained an article describing a revival meeting; and it proceeded to depict the burning eloquence of the preacher in this style:

Raising himself in the pulpit, and lifting his hands toward heaven, while his face seemed lighted up with rays of the glory of eternal life, he appealed to all to jump through the window. Having done so, he ran up the street, like a quarter-horse, with his nose scarcely an inch from the ground; bit two hogs and a cow, flew at Mr. Evans, and might have bitten him and inoculated him with the horrible poison, but for the fact that at this moment Mr. Sterling, the constable, appeared on the scene with a gun, and shot the beast through the head. He never kicked afterward.

Here was a case in which the accounts of a revival meeting and the doings and death of a mad dog got "mixed" in the making-up.

It is related of a country editor that in making-up his paper, a duty he performed himself, he got the closing words of an obituary notice interchanged with the last line of a bitter attack on a rival editor, with the following deplorable result:

Leaving behind her a wide circle of mourning friends, she has bidden adieu to this fair world forever, and gone to that—greatest old rascal that ever existed!

The following is from a communication published in the London *Telegraph*, during the autumn of 1874:

Can any one tell me the meaning of the following paragraph, which I have taken from a contemporary, headed "Building Materials"? Mr. A. W. Chase, of the United States Coast Survey, in a letter to Professor Silliman, says he has seen a curious nest built by the so-called California wood-rat, a little dark-brown animal, described as an intermediate between a squirrel and a rat. These creatures live in dome-shaped structures made of twigs, bark, and grass, built either on the ground or in the lower branches of trees, and frequently ten feet high and six feet in diameter. The one seen by Mr. Chase was composed of large iron spikes, of which there were several kegs in the house, the spikes being arranged with their points outward. Interlaced with them were about three dozen knives, forks, and spoons; a carving-knife, fork and steel; the case, glass, and works of a silver watch, separately stored away, and several large augers.

This curiously-constructed paragraph greatly puzzled me when I read it, nor am I sure that I yet quite penetrate it; but I think there must be an "out" somewhere, or that the compiler, in condensing, failed to preserve the whole essence, as it seems to me that a material break in the thread thrusts itself out from the body of the story. Or, it may have been the result of a "mixture," in which case the right story must have broken off and a fragment of the wrong one have stepped in just after the words, "The one seen by Mr. Chase was composed of —," etc.

In the Philadelphia *Ledger*, a daily paper that is conducted pretty carefully, as a rule, I recently found the following paragraph, standing all alone, as it were, among some short miscellaneous paragraphs under the general head of "Varieties:"

> Yet he seems to possess consciousness to some degree. He is sensitive of tickling or sharp tapping, and he exercises some power of resistance to any attempt to bend his limbs. He is, nevertheless, apparently asleep. Quinine applied on his tongue produces grimaces and other signs of disgust, and a loud noise made at the bedside will cause a quiver through his frame. The history of the case, as far as the doctor could ascertain, is that he had been drinking hard for several years, and quit it twelve months ago. He then took to drinking strong tea. Altogether the man has been one hundred days suffering, having been three weeks ailing before admittance to the hospital.

A person knowing little or nothing of the process by which a newspaper is "got up" might "stop and stare" quite a while over such a paragraph. But the practiced eye sees at once how such a mistake may have occurred. It was probably a blunder in "making up." That is, the person who made up the form inadvertently got hold of the last paragraph of an account — probably three or four stickfuls — of a singular case of physical affliction and placed it on the imposing-stone among paragraphs of all sizes, of both an interesting and amusing character. Probably this was after all the most amusing item in the column. But mistakes will happen. Another, but less plausible explanation would be, that the compiler pasted a paragraph on "upside-down;" but as the proof-reader would probably have detected this at once, the preponderance of probabilities is in favor of the former theory.

A paragraph in a Philadelphia paper begins this way:

> A HUMAN MACHINE. — The Paris correspondent of the Baltimore *Gazette* writes: "A curious phenomenon can be witnessed in the Saint Antoine Hospital. A young man, a singer in a café concert, was wounded during the war in the head by a ball, etc."

I had thought I was indifferently familiar with history, but I have to confess that I do not know in what age this "war in the head" occurred; nor have I the most distant notion of what it was about, who the combatants were or how it terminated. A war in a whole country is bad enough in its devastations, but condense a whole war so as to confine it within a human being's skull, and how the "poor head" thus made the battle-ground must hum! I have suffered much, in various ways, but heaven grant that I may never be subjected to this crowning torture, a "war in the head!"

Says a Philadelphia paper:

> A sign of a Market Street restaurant: "Wines liquors and oysters stewed."

Thereupon, a contemporary, in the "commenting" mood, quotes the paragraph, and adds:

> A good brandy stew is very palatable, but at any time give us port-wine cut in thin slices and fried in butter. A gallon of Bourbon whisky nicely roasted with sweet potatoes and carrots, makes a very fine dinner. But we cannot see how people can eat great chunks of baked ale.

For many years the "country editor" has been a fruitful subject of anecdote, and almost as many stories are extant concerning him as there are of "an Irishman." It is of course needless to say that most of these stories are invented by journalists in their mischievous moments, and also to add that many of the most thoughtful, able and upright men of the nation are "country editors." One of the best stories of which the "country editor" is made the victim, and one which has very generally had the run of the press, is related of an editor somewhere down South, who conceived a plan whereby to "beat" a rival editor. In accordance with his scheme, he hired a man to shoot at him,—and miss him, of course,—just before the time the two weeklies were to go to press, and he had an account of the "attempted assassination" already written up, and even partly in type. Unluckily, the hired "assassin" did n't aim badly enough, when he fired from the wood just without the village, and brought the editor down, "severely wounded." The result was, the rival editor *did* publish a brief report of the affair, while the account already so carefully prepared, and which represented him as uninjured, would n't do to go in; and so the paper of the enterprising editor had to go to press without a word about the "attempted assassination."

Another good one is told of a "country editor" out West, who one day discovered a man hanging to a tree, dead, and thinking to make the item of news an "exclusive," took the body down, concealed it and hung it up again just before his paper was to go to press. But unfortunately he was caught at it, and arrested on suspicion of murder. He had nothing to say on the subject in the forthcoming issue of his paper; but the rival editor had, as he delayed his edition a short time to give an account of the affair, so far as then known, to which was appended this editorial remark: "We always did think this man was a murderer at heart; now we have proof of it."

One of the saddest things that ever happened a "country editor" is thus related: A Jersey editor had occasion to mention, in a complimentary way, a popular clergyman, "Rev. James Dougherty." The compositor to whom was intrusted the task of making the corrections marked on the proof-sheet found that, unless a few letters could be omitted somewhere, he would have a good deal of trouble in the way of "overrunning" a long paragraph. He consulted the Editor, who substituted one or two short words for one or two long ones, and still the compositor said it would be difficult to justify the line in which Mr. Dougherty's name occurred.

"Well, abbreviate the first name, then," said the Editor, meaning to make it "Jas." instead of "James."

But the compositor had his own ideas of the abbreviation of the name of James, and the Editor was shocked, when the paper came out, to find that he had, in his complimentary notice of the clergyman, alluded to him as "Rev. Jim Dougherty."

Hoaxes are sometimes perpetrated by newspapers, and about the first day of the fourth month of the year it is just as well to read the newspapers with great calmness. Many citizens of Boston, on one such occasion, walked down to the beach, in very bad weather, to view an immense whale there stranded,—which animal, I need scarcely hint, only existed in the lively imagination of a reporter on one of the morning papers; and not a few, a year later, called at the City Hall of that city to see some wonderful performing mice which had been presented to the Mayor by a foreign prince, and which his Honor, with a fatherly kind of love for the public, had decided to exhibit for a day or two — free of charge, of course.

Sometimes papers commit the blunder — and feel very cheap over it — of publishing a man's obituary notice in advance of the important event calculated to call for any such publication. I was once connected with a paper that met with this misfortune, and the next day the subject of the notice, not only alive, but in unusually good health, came in and said that of course at some time or other he probably would die, and the notice would have to be repeated ; so he would be obliged if we would, just while we thought of it, change the date of his birth to the 22d of June, instead of the 28th of July, as erroneously stated in the published sketch of his life. It was another man of the same name, but not nearly so eminent, who had really died.

In like manner, editors sometimes write notices of theatrical performances without having seen or heard from such performances, merely surmising "about what they were like" from the previously-published advertisements. This works well enough except when there is an entirely unanticipated change of programme, and the Editor compliments several actors in "Our American Cousin" at the So-and-So Theater last evening; whereas, owing to the sudden illness of a leading actor (one of those so highly praised), it was not played at all, a piece of an entirely different character having been substituted. I have known of such sad occurrences more than once, and when they do happen the Editor is so mortified that nearly a week elapses before he feels like asking the Manager for six reserved seats.

CHAPTER XXXI.

PRIMITIVE JOURNALISM.

WHEN a newspaper is started in a country town, no matter how weak its editor may happen to be, no matter how defective its make-up, no matter how crowded with typographic errors its columns, no matter how bungling its press-work, it is still a step in the right direction. It is a step toward the dissemination of news and knowledge, and the interchange of thought; toward inviting and encouraging the discussion of important questions affecting the general welfare; toward spreading enlightenment, and dispelling prejudice, ignorance and superstition. A newspaper is always a step in the right direction; and the man who has built one up where there was none before, is, like him who has caused one blade of grass to grow in a spot where before all was barren, a public benefactor. Nor do I believe that any one ever yet started a newspaper with the deliberate intention of doing public harm with it, even for his own aggrandizement.

Fifty years ago newspapers labored under many difficulties that have since been removed (particularly in large cities) by the invention and adoption of wonderful machinery; but those same difficulties are still encountered by many newspapers in remote quarters of the country, the proprietors thereof possessing limited pecuniary resources. The defects often extend to the editorial, as well as the mechanical, department of the country paper; and indeed it would be unreasonable to expect from the editor of a country weekly the same keenness, foresight, readiness and judgment we find in the editor of a city daily. The "country paper" and the "country editor," therefore, as hinted in another chapter, frequently become the subjects of humorous allusions, but are far from being the subjects of contempt. I see something to admire, something to respect, in the poorest and weakest editor of the smallest and most unpretending "country paper," for I find him laboring to add something to the good of his community, to enhance the knowledge of his neighbors, and to inspire them with sentiments which, in all sincerity, he believes to be in the interests of truth—and he is much oftener right than wrong.

On the Pacific coast, rude in its freshness from the hand of nature, barely abandoned to civilization, by wild beasts and wild men, "Primitive Journalism" has held many a revel within the past quarter of a century; and in the newspaper world of California, Oregon and Nevada, there is a free-and-easy, a jolly, reckless, devil-may-care spirit that must provoke mirth wherever it touches. It is rich in pointed expression, in blunt words whose meaning cannot well be mistaken, in statements entirely ingenuous and unambiguous.

For example, a Nevada paper says:

> The many friends of Bill Thompson will regret to hear that he was hashed up by a catamount the other day on Nixon's Hill, while lying in wait to shoot a Chinaman. This was always a world of disappointment.

Hundreds of such paragraphs go the rounds; and who can help smiling at the bold simplicity with which, in this case, a subject so momentous to Mr. Thompson is treated? Who, too, would fail to gather from the tone of this paragraph that the loss of Bill Thompson (probably a desperado) was not exactly regarded as a public calamity?

There appeared in a San Francisco paper, a few years ago, a burlesque account of the editing a country paper on the Pacific coast, written by a humorist—"O. Job Jones"—who never attained the distinction of an Artemus Ward, a Mark Twain or a Josh Billings; and although it goes into the regions of hyperbole, there is in it an air of naturalness suggesting that its author had "been there," and which also suggests that it would not be out of place in this chapter:

THE WEEKLY THUNDERGUST.

BY O. JOB JONES.

Tired of the restrictions of life in the city, where one is surrounded by courts of justice, magistrates and policemen, We decided to go to an interior town and start a country newspaper. We chose for the scene of Our journalistic labors the rising town of Revolverville, and soon established there a first-class paper, which we styled the *Weekly Thundergust.*

In the same town there was already published a weekly "sheet" of despicable characteristics; it was known as the *Blunderbuss*. It was a political paper; and We, of course, in starting Our own ably-conducted journal, took strong political grounds on the opposite side. We launched out under difficulties, to be sure. We were not cursed with "dead loads" of "collateral," and were obliged to come before the public in a spirit of modesty. We possessed but a little over a quart of type, both upper and lower case, and a small copying-press, which We were able to run without assistance; and with these limited appliances We could only appear before the public with a four-page sheet, quarto size.

We were, of course, sole editor and proprietor; We employed Ourself as foreman and compositor; We were Our own boy; and We did Our own press-work. Besides all this, We canvassed for subscribers, solicited advertisements, collected bills, and attended to the mailing department. The disbursing of the establishment was also one of Our own duties.

Despite all the disadvantages under which We labored at the beginning, Our paper prospered; its circulation swelled to one hundred and thirty-seven in the short space of two months, and We gave Our patrons a treat by enlarging it half a column. To say that "things went on swimmingly," would fall as far short of an adequate expression as it would be trite; so, We won't say it.

However bitterly We and the editor of the *Blunderbuss* hated and reviled each other in a political way, we were socially and fraternally on intimate and friendly terms, ever ready to lend each other a helping hand in the way of getting our papers out. For example, should one run a little short of letter of any particular kind, he had no hesitation about going to the other and borrowing some to help him out of a tight place; and when he got stuck on a word he came to Us in the most brotherly manner and was granted free access to Our Dictionary; while We were always at liberty to visit his establishment and refer to his copy of Smith's Grammar, or the eight exchanges that shed a ray of journalistic light over his sanctum.

But in our editorial columns we uniformly painted each other with the blackness of darkness, charging our pens with the bitterness of gall and the gall of bitterness.

One day, feeling in an unusually happy mood, We penned a scathing rebuke to the *Blunderbuss*, in which We blackened the character of the editor, traced his pedigree, and called his grandmother anything but a gentleman. In our enthusiasm, We made it rather longer than our leaders usually were, so that, when it came to be set up, it about cleaned out Our case of five-line pica,— a commodious size of type which We were in the habit of using in Our editorial columns. In fact, Our letter of this size ran out, and We were obliged either to substitute a few of another size,— and We had nothing nearer than minion,— or go to Our bitter friend, the editor of the *Blunderbuss*, and borrow what We required. We needed the letter "d," to complete the word "black-hearted," having used an unusual number, with dashes between them, in the course of Our allusions to Our contemporary. We also lacked the "r" in "liar," and the "y" in "double-dyed."

So, laying down Our stick, We left Our article in type and went over to the *Blunderbuss* office, across the street — very hastily, too, for it was near Our time of going to press. We readily obtained the letters We wanted, and returning to Our rooms We discovered that some fiend in human form — it may have been the "devil" of the *Blunderbuss* — had actually entered Our sacred composing-room in Our absence and carried off the type in which We had just been setting Our leader, We having left it nearly finished, as stated, on a galley.

Appalled at this startling discovery, We rushed frantically across the street again and communicated the heart-rending intelligence to the editor of the *Blunderbuss*.

"Too bad!" he exclaimed, with a kind-hearted oath. "Do you think you can find the rascal? Here, take my revolver!"

"No, no; not now!" We said. "Next week I will take a holiday, hunt him up and shoot him."

"Well, what can I do for you? I will lend you whatever type I can,— or," said he, as a bright idea seemed to strike him, "I can lend you some excellent matter already in type which has been crowded out of the *Blunderbuss* by a whole column of 'ads.' that came in a little while ago. Just the thing,— several able articles,— take whichever you want. You will have no bother with it. It has already been corrected and is ready for the press."

"Glorious!" We exclaimed, with animation. "An article of two or three stickfuls will do. What are the subjects?"

"Well, there is one poem of eight verses, on 'Friendship.'"

"O, confound the poetry,— and friendship, too; I don't believe in it! What else?"

"An editorial on 'Chinese Immigration as one of the Fine Arts.'"

"That may not be consistent with the tone of the *Thundergust*. Anything else?"

"Yes; a very elaborate article on 'Julius Cæsar,' contrasting him with P. T. Barnum and George Francis Train."

"That's the thing! Where is it?"

The editor went into his composing-room and soon returned with the article in type,—which was just about what We wanted,—and without even looking at it, trusting to the good taste of Our contemporary, We rushed across the street, placed it on Our imposing-stone, with Our other matter, made up Our paper, locked Our forms and went to press.

In another hour Our paper for that week was issued.

Heavens! "Horrors on horror's head accumulate!" What were Our consternation and chagrin at discovering that the borrowed article We had laid before the public was not, as the perfidious editor of the *Blunderbuss* had represented, an essay on J. Cæsar, but a most withering dissection of Ourself—Us, the editor of the irrepressible *Thundergust!*—and this poisonous load of invective against Ourself had appeared before the public in Our own editorial columns! It was sickening to the journalistic soul to think of it!

As an example of the barbarous style of the editor of the *Blunderbuss*, We quote it:

"THE EDITOR OF THE THUNDERGUST—WHO, WHAT, WHERE, AND HOW HE IS.

"This would-be demagogue—this creature (we cannot style it a man)—this concentrated batch of moral corruption—this hideous monster whom it were base flattery to call an alligator, crocodile, terrapin, mock-turtle, frog, toad, scorpion, bumble-bee—that at present scourges this honest and intelligent community, is named o. job jones. Of course, it must have some name. It lacks even the poorest traits of the common cur; a bull-dog is dignified compared with it! It has not the common instincts of a cat; its clothes fail to fit it; it is unable to dance; it is ugly, hateful, abominable—red-faced, red-nosed, red-mouthed, red-eyed—anything but *read* in common decency; it stole cents from its grandmother when a boy (a pity it has not retained them, for it has none now); it swears, lies, cheats, steals, gambles, gets drunk every night, and breaks other commandments too black to mention! Its very dishonesty is the brightest spot on its character! It would murder, did not its cowardly heart restrain it. But we shudder to think that a strict sense of duty has compelled us to pollute these pure columns with its name! Why waste further words on it? However, what better could be expected of the *party* with which this wretch is identified? We pause for a reply."

The discovery of this horrible item in Our own columns came near paralyzing Us. We felt that it would prove Our ruin. Yet We were mistaken. It actually built Us up; for while many who read the article, believing it to be genuine, and accordingly giving Us great credit for truth and candor in speaking of Ourself, others perceived that We had been the innocent victim of a shameless trick; public sympathy was enlisted in Our favor, and in two short weeks Our circulation had swelled to one hundred and ninety-eight, and We had a column and three-quarters of advertisements! We also had seven papers on Our exchange list.

What might have been the end of this prosperous state of things, had it been allowed to go on, it is impossible to say. But, alas! an evil day came, and misfortune overtook Us! One day, about a month later, when local items were scarce, We very injudiciously published a little fictitious story concerning the wife of a prominent citizen, reflecting slightly on her character, and some were foolish enough to get indignant about it. The husband was absent at the time, or he would probably have put Us to the inconvenience of killing him; but the "citizens" waited on us in relation to the matter. Quite a concourse of the bloodthirsty rascals — two of her brothers among them — collected in front of Our office, calling loudly for Our gore, while a delegation of nine, bringing with them a good, substantial rope, entered Our sanctum and urgently invited Us out to deliver a brief address to the mob. Luckily We had seen their approach and taken measures to avoid this honor. We had raised Our back window and seen that the coast was clear in that direction, and We nimbly sprang out, and — the darkness of evening favoring us — made the best time on record in the direction of a thick grove of trees, which We boldly faced — leaving behind Us Our valuable type, Our neat hand-press, Our manuscripts, Our money — $1.35 — and Our hat.

As a matter of course, it would not have been safe for the people of the town had We exhibited Our intelligent countenance in that vicinity again, so We have not been heard of since; but We subsequently succeeded in obtaining a copy of the next week's *Blunderbuss*, in which was a full account of Our exodus and the circumstances attending it, and in which the editor had perpetrated a coarse and cruel jest concerning Us, to the effect that We had become imbued with piety, stopped publishing a wicked political newspaper, and gone to making *tracks*.

CHAPTER XXXII.

OUR DAILIES AND WEEKLIES.

I THINK there is in this country an aspect of newspaper enterprise that amounts to grandeur. Not that we are free from grave defects; not that even our ablest journals might not in some respects improve their style; not but that things are done and allowed in many of our newspaper establishments that ought not to be done and allowed; not, in a word, that we have arrived at perfection, an attribute that does not seem yet to have fastened itself upon any human being, in any sphere or vocation; but because, in our impatient thirst for news and new ideas, we have penetrated the remotest spots of earth and the deepest mazes of science and thought. When a newspaper establishment sends an expedition to the heart of Africa, in search of a scientific explorer whose fate is doubtful, and even succeeds in its object (as in the case of the Stanley expedition, sent out by the New York *Herald* in search of Dr. Livingstone), it does an act worthy of the dignity of a nation.

Many other instances might be mentioned in which immense expenditures of money and talent have been freely made by American newspapers in the interests of science, benevolence, civilization, accounts of which read almost like fiction.

I have already said that the weekly journal may be conducted as a pastime, compared with the daily; yet it is a great work to conduct even a weekly as it ought to be conducted. But it is the daily that is the giant. It is the daily that lifts up its mighty proportions, as it were, the Temple of Thought. It is the daily whose voice, like the waves breaking with endless murmurs upon the sand, is speaking all day long, and through the deep still hours of the night, making and molding public opinion, and almost saying: "I reign." Once I walked through the press-room of the New York *Tribune* with a well-known literary gentleman, who stopped and, with a thoughtful expression upon his poetic face, pointed to an eight-cylinder press that was thundering away and sending the rapidly-printed sheets into the folding-machine, remarking:

"Hercules was a fool to that!"

"It is through much tribulation that we enter into the kingdom of heaven," says one of the apostles; and it might be added that it is through much more tribulation that a man ever reaches either intellectual eminence or financial prosperity in running either a daily or weekly newspaper. The most constant attention and the most careful supervision of details are necessary to lift a paper up to a standard of respectability and to financial success. Eternal vigilance must be exercised to keep its columns pure and to exclude from them such questionable matter as might make it worthy of popular condemnation; and its finances must be managed with the most delicate care. The expenses of a newspaper — especially a large daily — are enormous, amounting in some cases to between twenty-five thousand and thirty thousand dollars a week, and the calculations for a margin of profit must be well made, as an excess of expenditure over receipts would soon destroy the equilibrium of such an institution, and possibly lead to a general crash.

The expenses of a weekly are proportionately smaller, but assiduous work is necessary to success. Among the various trials that editors of papers — particularly weeklies — have to endure, is the work of reading many manuscripts, both "communications" and "voluntary contributions" from persons whose defective style is mainly due to the fact that they are wholly unaccustomed to writing for the press. Sometimes the Editor is seized with a spirit of malice, and publishes an average "contribution" as his only means of being revenged upon its writer for boring him. Here is an example of this kind from the Philadelphia *Sunday Times*, and it shows what kind of "stuff" an editor is daily called upon to read and "do something or other with" in the process of separating the wheat from the chaff:

TO A FRIENDE.

BY J. S.

Do you remember those happy hours
of the by-gone olden time
when side by side we gathered flowers
or murmord some sweet old rhyme
often those hours do haunt me
and in fancy i linger still
where the silvery sun floshed so clear
from the shade of those Lovely hills.

The trouble is, there are too few people who have a proper sense of what the true mission of a newspaper is. Many seem to think that its columns should be given up at random to Tom, Dick and Harry, for the insertion of trash, such as the above "poem," or in the still less pleasing shape of "communications" on subjects personal, and not touching the general welfare. "The true business of a newspaper," says the Worcester *Spy*, "is to publish the news, report what is going on in the world and discuss questions of public interest." This is the case in a nutshell. The Editor does not do his duty to his subscribers if he does not endeavor to give all the news possibly obtainable, with careful and impartial editorial opinions, and to such matter give the precedence over everything approaching the sphere of trash.

In the United States more than in any other country newspapers are read by the masses, and here the papers are more numerous, grow to larger proportions, generally, and have a wider range than newspapers in other countries. "Nothing interests the American more in Europe," a well-known American journalist writes from London, "than the curiosity of the people of all classes in regard to the United States. It must be confessed that there is far more knowledge of the older nations in our country than there is among the Europeans in regard to us. The average American is more fully posted upon matters of government and society abroad than the average Englishman, Frenchman or German, and this results from several palpable influences, of course, the inquisitive spirit of our people, and chiefly to the vigilant attention paid to foreign matters by our newspapers." There is a great difference between American and English newspapers. The latter, while aiming to be truthful, dignified and impersonal, are heavy and dull. The American journals, while going the whole length in news-gathering enterprise, find space for "spice," and nearly all have their little "squibs" in the editorial columns, and departments of light paragraphs, original and selected, with some such head as "Odds and Ends," "All-Sorts," "Chaff," "Frivolities," "Varieties," "Jocosities," or "Fun." Our weeklies especially devote a fair share of space to the "rich" things that are "going the rounds," and many of them give in each issue a column of humorous paragraphs as productive of healthful mirth as a first-class comedy.

I believe the American newspapers do no great harm by making their readers smile; but if it is an offense so to do, it is one of which the English press is seldom guilty. True, the English have their humorous papers, such as *Punch*, *Judy* and *Fun*, which occasionally "get off good things," but, take them one day with another, they are very grave compared with the American humorous papers. If you pay threepence for *Punch*, and if you get your "threepenny 'orth" of fun out of it, you certainly get a dollar's worth of the article out of a ten-cent American humorous paper.

I have been led to make these comparisons because an English gentleman not long since saw fit to inform me that the papers "at 'ome" were incomparably superior to the American papers, adding, in a bantering way:

"Why, in England, we laugh at the American papers!"

Upon the suggestion that probably they did "laugh at our *humorous* papers, which was more than we could do at the English humorous papers," he manifested a lively disposition to change the subject, and exhibited a sudden and wonderful interest in the weather, which he remarked was "bloody 'ot."

I have made these allusions in no spirit of unkindness, for I am certainly without any shadow of prejudice against our English cousins. I have among them many excellent friends, and they are a jolly good set of fellows; but they cannot help giving at least full credit to the excellence of things "at 'ome, you know."

The following, appertaining to the American and English press, and containing much information on the subject, I quote from Mr. Ingersoll's "Life and Times of Horace Greeley:"

When Mr. Greeley arrived in England (in 1851), the discussion of "the taxes on knowledge," which had for some time attracted much attention from the general public, had reached Parliament, where the repeal of such taxation had many friends. A committee, of which the Right Hon. T. Milnor Gibson was chairman, and the celebrated Richard Cobden one of the members, had the subject in charge, and requested Mr. Greeley to appear and give them the results of his experience and observation. He was examined at great length by the committee. The taxes complained of were an impost upon advertisements, and a stamp-tax of one penny per copy on every newspaper. The substantial portions of Mr. Greeley's examination were as follows:

Your duty is the same on the advertisements in a journal with fifty thousand circulation, as in a journal with one thousand, although the *value* of the article is twenty times as much in the one case as in the other. The duty operates precisely as though you were to lay a tax of one shilling a day on every day's labor that a man were to do; to a man whose labor is worth two shillings a day, it would be destructive; while by a man who earns twenty shillings a day, it would be very lightly felt. An advertisement is worth but a certain amount, and the public soon get to know what it is worth; you put a duty on advertisements, and you destroy the value of those coming to new establishments. People who advertise in your well-established journals, could afford to pay a price to include the duty; but in a new paper, the advertisements would not be worth the amount of the duty *alone;* and consequently the new concern would have no chance. Now, the advertisements are one main source of the income of daily papers, and thousands of business men take them mainly for those advertisements. For instance, at the time when our auctioneers were appointed by law (they were, of course, party politicians), one journal, which was high in the confidence of the party in power, obtained not a law, but an *understanding*, that all the auctioneers appointed should advertise in that journal. Now, though the journal referred to has ceased to be of that party, and the auctioneers are no longer appointed by the State, yet that journal has almost the monopoly of the auctioneers' business to this day. Auctioneers *must* advertise in it, because they know that purchasers are looking there; and purchasers must take the paper, because they know that it contains just the advertisements they want to see; and this, without regard to the goodness or the principles of the paper. I know men in this town who take one journal mainly for its advertisements, and they *must* take the *Times*, because everything is advertised in it; for the same reason, advertisers *must* advertise in the *Times*. If we had a duty on advertisements, I will not say it would be impossible to build up a new concern in New York against the competition of the older ones; but I do say, it would be impossible to preserve the weaker papers from being swallowed up by the stronger.

Mr. COBDEN. — Do you then consider the fact, that the *Times* newspaper for the last fifteen years has been increasing so largely in circulation, is to be accounted for mainly by the existence of the advertising duty?

Mr. GREELEY. — Yes; much more than the stamp. By the operation of the advertisement duty, an advertisement is charged ten times as much in one paper as in another. An advertisement in the *Times* may be worth five pounds, while in another paper it is only worth one pound; but the duty is the same.

Mr. COBDEN. — From what you have stated with regard to the circulation of the daily papers of New York, it appears that a very large proportion of the adult population must be customers for them?

Mr. GREELEY. — Yes; I think three-fourths of all the families take a daily paper of some kind.

Mr. COBDEN. — The purchasers of the daily papers must consist of a different class from those in England; mechanics must purchase them?

Mr. GREELEY. — Every mechanic takes a paper, or nearly every one.

Mr. EWART. — Having observed both countries, can you state whether the press has greater influence on public opinion in the United States than in England, or the reverse?

Mr. GREELEY. — I think it has more influence with us. I do not know that any class is despotically governed by the press, but its influence is more universal; every one reads and talks about it with us, and more weight is laid upon intelligence than on editorials; the paper which brings the quickest news is the thing looked to.

Mr. EWART. — The leading article has not so much influence as in England?

Mr. GREELEY. — No; the telegraphic dispatch is the great point.

Mr. COBDEN. — Observing our newspapers and comparing them with the American papers, do you find that we make much less use of the electric telegraph for transmitting news than in America?

Mr. GREELEY. — Not a hundreth part as much as we do.

Mr. COBDEN. — An impression prevails in this country that our newspaper press incurs a great deal more expense to expedite news than you do in New York. Are you of that opinion?

Mr. GREELEY. — I do not know what your expense is. I should say that a hundred thousand dollars a year is paid by our association of the six leading daily papers, besides what each gets separately for itself.

Mr. COBDEN. — Twenty thousand pounds a year is paid by your association, consisting of six papers, for what you get in common?

Mr. GREELEY. — Yes; we telegraph a great deal in the United States.

From this time forth the unpopularity of "the taxes on knowledge" rapidly increased, and they were at length repealed. The people of England are very greatly indebted for having the Cheap Press so soon as they did to the Founder of the New York *Tribune.*

CHAPTER XXXIII.

ONE WORD MORE.

WHILE I have been vain enough, in the course of this work, to praise the calling in which I am myself engaged, to descant upon the difficult and valuable work done by journalists, and to applaud the mission of Journalism, I have not been, and am not, blind to the imperfections of those (myself included) who conduct this great institution — the Press. I am not visionary enough to hope that within this generation we shall reach Utopian perfection, but there are some faults in the newspaper world — as well as within every other sphere — that I trust may soon be corrected. Some of our journals have reached a point of purity, of dignity and greatness at which they stand up like monuments. Such are the journals that ever and always aim to be fair, courteous, truthful, never descending to rude invective, coarse language or personal abuse. I trust that the time will soon come when editorials dictated by personal malice will be numbered with things obsolete.

I want to see the time, even in this generation, when "deadheading" will also be classed among the things that have passed away; when every editor will buy his theater ticket and pay his fare in the railroad car, like other people.

Editorial "puffery" has already been abandoned by most of the advanced journals of the country, but is still an "institution" in the establishments of the several lower strata of newspapers. I would like to see that, too, become entirely obsolete. While the habit is fostered, the editor can no more be truthful and ingenuous than a lawyer pleading the case of a culprit whom he knows in his heart to be guilty. When the merchant, or any other business man, has anything to say in praise of his wares, or his professional qualities, let him put it in the form of an advertisement, over his name, that it may so stand for what it is worth, without the sign and seal of the Editor, who is so often called upon to vouch for things of which he knows as little as the oyster knows of the Nebulous Theory.

I also yearn to see Jenkinsism rooted out of the field of Journalism, where it never properly belonged. It is a vile weed; like Interviewing, it has sprung up in a night; may they both be plucked up and cast out in the light of day!

Bohemianism! I scarcely know what to say, to wish or to hope concerning it. Certainly it is a less objectionable feature of journalism than the two just mentioned. Well, let it rest. It is an episode in journalism, rather than a thing belonging to it, and it may one day disappear along with some other uncomfortable grades of society, as society itself reaches, by many gradations, clearer perceptions of the "fitness of things."

I want to see — might I say, above all?— the time come when the tone of a newspaper may never once be dictated, or prejudiced "in the estimation of a hair," by financial considerations — when every journal will speak just as boldly against abuses practiced by a corporation that advertises extensively as it would if that corporation did not advertise at all.

I long to see the time when "servility" shall have ceased; when no man, or set of men, or party, or power shall dictate the tone of a journal to the end that it shall waver one hair's breadth from sincerity and truthfulness.

It is much to hope for; but I do hope for these things, believing, yes, *knowing*, that my hopes shall ultimately be realized. We are all moving in the direction of light; standing on the hill-tops, intellectual men should be the first to catch its glimmerings; they will be ever; and the time must come, and soon, when the Press of our country will be nearer perfection than now — when nothing vile, or little, or mean will remain to cast even a shadow of reproach upon journalists, the men who walk in the van of Progress and live and move in the domain of Thought.

www.ingramcontent.com/pod-product-compliance
Lightning Source LLC
LaVergne TN
LVHW020235110826
845151LV00003B/927

* 9 7 8 1 4 2 5 5 3 1 5 1 5 *